THE LAW (IN PLAIN ENGLISH)®

for

RESTAURANTS

and Others in the Food Industry

Leonard D. DuBoff
Christy O. King
Attorneys at Law

SPHINX® PUBLISHING
AN IMPRINT OF SOURCEBOOKS, INC.®
NAPERVILLE, ILLINOIS
www.SphinxLegal.com

First Edition: 2006

Published by: **Sphinx® Publishing, An Imprint of Sourcebooks, Inc.®**

<u>Naperville Office</u>
P.O. Box 4410
Naperville, Illinois 60567-4410
630-961-3900
Fax: 630-961-2168
www.sourcebooks.com
www.SphinxLegal.com

This publication is designed to provide accurate and authoritative information in regard to the subject matter covered. It is sold with the understanding that the publisher is not engaged in rendering legal, accounting, or other professional service. If legal advice or other expert assistance is required, the services of a competent professional person should be sought.
From a Declaration of Principles Jointly Adopted by a Committee of the
American Bar Association and a Committee of Publishers and Associations

This product is not a substitute for legal advice.

Disclaimer required by Texas statutes.

Library of Congress Cataloging-in-Publication Data
DuBoff, Leonard D.
  The law (in plain English) for restaurants and others in the food industry
/ by Leonard D. DuBoff and Christy O. King.-- 1st ed.
     p. cm.
  Includes bibliographical references and index.
  ISBN-13: 978-1-57248-523-5 (pbk. : alk. paper)
  ISBN-10: 1-57248-523-X (pbk. : alk. paper)
 1. Restaurants--Law and legislation--United States--Popular works. 2.
Restaurateurs--Legal status, laws, etc.--United States--Popular works. 3.
Food law and legislation--United States--Popular works. I. King, Christy
O., 1969- II. Title.

KF2042.H6D83 2006
344.7304'64--dc22   2005035094

Printed and bound in the United States of America.
SB — 10 9 8 7 6 5 4 3 2 1

To my partner in law and in life,
Mary Ann Crawford DuBoff, for everything good in my life;
and to my children, Colleen Rose, Robert Courtney, and Sabrina Ashley;
and to my grandchildren, Brian Michael and Taliek Isaiah,
for completing the circle.
—Leonard D. DuBoff

For Andrew, a gifted reader, and for Annalise, an outstanding writer.
—Christy O. King

CONTENTS

Preface . . . . **xiii**

Foreword . . . . **xvii**

Introduction . . . . **xix**

Chapter 1: Organizing Your Business **1**
    Sole Proprietorships
    Partnerships and Joint Ventures
    Limited Partnerships
    Unintended Partners
    Corporations
    S Corporations
    Limited Liability Companies
    Precautions for Minority Owners
    Hybrids

Chapter 2: Business Organization Checklist. 17
Accountant
Business Name
Business Structure: Partnership
Business Structure: Corporations and LLCs

Chapter 3: The Business Plan 27
Executive Summary
History
Nature of the Business
The Market
The Competition
Source of Supplies
Management
Financial Data
The Business Plan Team

Chapter 4: Borrowing from Banks 33
Starting Your Search
The Loan Proposal
Repayment
Analyzing Your Business Potential
Options for Owners of New Businesses
Lender's Rules and Limitations
Details of the Agreement
The Loan Application
Importance of Communication when Problems Arise

Chapter 5: Going Public. 51
Advantages of Going Public
Disadvantages of Going Public
The Initial Public Offering
Federal and State Securities Laws

The Attorney's Role
The Accountant's Role
The Banker's Role
The Underwriter's and Selling Agent's Roles
Privatization

Chapter 6: Contracts. **59**
What Is a Contract?
Types of Contracts
Contracting Online

Chapter 7: Franchising **73**
Franchises
What to Look For

Chapter 8: Patents and Trade Secrets **79**
Patent Protection
International Patents
Trade Secrets
Patent or Padlock Dilemma
Trade Secret Protection

Chapter 9: Trademarks **87**
The Need for a Recognizable Mark
Prohibited Trademarks
Protecting a Trademark
Federal Registration of a Trademark
Trademark Loss and Infringement
International Protection
State Registration
Using an Attorney

Chapter 10: Copyrights **103**
What Can Be Copyrighted
Scope of Protection
Ownership of Copyright
Works Made for Hire
Derivative Works
Collective Works
Copyright Protection for Utilitarian Objects
Notice Requirement
Filing an Application and Depositing the Work
Period of Protection
Infringement
Fair Use

Chapter 11: Advertising **119**
Government Regulation
Comparative Advertising
Publicity and Privacy
Unauthorized Use of Trademark or Copyrighted Material
Geographic Locations
Trade Dress

Chapter 12: Commercial Opportunities and Activities **127**
Licensing Trademarks
Licensing Copyrights
Licensing Other Intellectual Property
Licensing Cautions
Consignment

Chapter 13: The Internet **133**
Intellectual Property Protection
Domain Names
Internet Advertising

Other Intellectual Property Issues
Server Protection
Email
Viruses

Chapter 14: Warranties and Consumers 145
Elements of an Express Warranty
Implied Warranties
Disclaimers
Legal Advice Regarding Risks

Chapter 15: Product Liability 155
History of Liability Law
Product Liability
Federal Laws
Think Before You Pour
Liability Insurance

Chapter 16: Business Insurance 161
Expectations vs. Reality
Scheduling Property
When to Insure
Keeping the Cost Down

Chapter 17: People Who Work for You 169
Independent Contractors
Employees
Employment Contracts
Other Considerations in Hiring
Hazards in the Workplace
Discrimination
Job Descriptions
Employee Handbooks

Zero Tolerance Policies
The Family and Medical Leave Act
Minimum Wage and Overtime
Tips
Termination of Employment

Chapter 18: Keeping Taxes Low **189**
Income Spreading
Taxes on Accumulated Earnings and Passive Investment Income
Qualifying for Business Deductions
Special Rules for Payroll Taxes on Tips
Deductions for the Use of a Home in Business
Other Professional Expenses
Travel Expenses
Entertainment Expenses
Expenses the IRS Scrutinizes
Recordkeeping
Charitable Deductions
Health Insurance

Chapter 19: Renting Commercial Space and Zoning Issues **209**
Who Pays for What?
Security and Zoning
Home-Based Operations

Chapter 20: Pension Plans **217**
Defined Benefit Plans
Defined Contribution Plans
Designing and Documenting a Plan

Chapter 21: Estate Planning **225**
The Will
Disposition of Property Not Willed

Advantages to Having a Will
Estate Taxes
Distributing Property Outside the Will
Probate
Conclusion

Chapter 22: How to Find a Lawyer and an Accountant **239**
Finding a Lawyer
Finding an Accountant

Glossary **245**

Appendix: Restaurant Associations **271**

Index **277**

About the Authors. **283**

PREFACE

When I began writing *The Law (In Plain English)*® series more than a quarter of a century ago, I was a full-time law professor and practicing lawyer. As an academic, I felt that my mission included providing educational tools for my students. In my role as a practicing attorney, I realized the importance of having material available for nonlawyers to help them understand the complex legal rules they are required to follow. It was my belief that *The Law (In Plain English)*® series would serve these goals, and over the years, my expectations were realized.

The books in *The Law (In Plain English)*® series have been used as educational textbooks in law schools and in other educational institutions, as well as for purposes of enlightening nonlawyers about the businesses in which they are involved. As of this writing, the series includes books for writers, craftspeople, gallery owners, healthcare professionals, high-tech entrepreneurs, photographers, and business owners in general. They have received numerous favorable reviews, and I have personally been provided with a great deal of useful feedback regarding the books.

Over the years, as a practicing attorney, I have had the privilege of working with numerous restaurant and food-based business owners. I have also been privileged to address professional restaurant associations at their annual conventions. I have, through these interactions, learned a great deal about the industry. It has also become clear that most, if not all, restaurant professionals have a strong desire to do their best to comply with the law in order to enhance their businesses. It is for these reasons that I began writing this volume in *The Law (In Plain English)*® series and enlisted the aid of my colleague, Christy King, another principal in our law firm, so that our combined knowledge of the field could emerge on these pages. The experience I have gained in representing restaurants, gourmet food companies, and others in this industry for almost three decades has enabled me to appreciate the many legal issues that regularly confront restaurant professionals. It is my hope and desire that the extensive experience Christy and I have in working with restaurant professionals will provide you with the ingredients for a useful, practical, and understandable book about the legal issues that confront you in your food-based business.

It must be emphasized that no book, no matter how well researched and written, can serve as a substitute for the skill of an attorney. The purpose of this volume is to provide you, the restaurant professional, with an opportunity to identify problems so they can be avoided, or if unavoidable, effectively communicated to your attorney. By educating yourself about the problems that can and do arise in your unique business, you will be better able to interact with your attorney. It is for this reason that a chapter on how to find an attorney is included in the text.

It is virtually impossible for a book such as this to be written without the support, help, and involvement of numerous individuals. Regrettably, it may be impossible to identify all of the people who have contributed to the success of this volume, but it is essential to identify some of the most important. Christy and I would, therefore, like to thank Lynn Della for her tireless work in assisting us with the numerous necessary revisions to refine the manuscript. We would also like to thank Peggy Reckow of The DuBoff Law Group, LLC, our legal assistant, for her help in coordinating the components of this book into a publishable work. Jodee Durbin, also of The DuBoff Law Group, has been extremely helpful in transcribing many of my ramblings into something that could serve as the foundation for portions of this text.

We are indebted to Mary Culshaw for the extraordinary work she has performed in helping us construct a tax chapter that captures the complexity of the Internal Revenue Code, while converting that law into practical information for restaurant professionals.

Jed Macy, a lawyer and accountant, has once again assisted us in understanding the complexity of the pension laws. His aid in writing the chapter on pension plans is greatly appreciated.

Marisa James, another attorney with The DuBoff Law Group, has contributed her experience, knowledge, and expertise of complex business arrangements. Her insight has added to the luster of this work.

My brother, Michael DuBoff, a well-respected business lawyer and litigator, has been involved in the practice of law for more than three decades. His knowledge, experience, and professional intuition have been invaluable. We appreciate his input and recommendations with respect to legal issues covered in this book, and his help in bringing this work to completion.

My daughters, Colleen and Sabrina, were a tremendous aid in proofing this work and verifying much of the material that appears in this text. My son, Robert, was extremely helpful in educating me on the intricacies of the World Wide Web and new computer technology. My grandson, Brian, has provided his own special kind of assistance and understanding. There are many days when I would have preferred to play with him rather than remain closeted with this text; yet, he encouraged me to complete this work before enjoying our time together.

Finally, I would like to recognize the aid of my partner in law and in life, Mary Ann Crawford DuBoff, for all of her work on this text. Words are inadequate to express the appreciation I feel for all she has contributed to this and all of my projects.

Leonard DuBoff
Portland, Oregon

FOREWORD

The dream of owning your own restaurant has become an alluring fantasy for millions. From new immigrants to foodies to Hollywood stars, it seems at times that everyone you know or ever heard of wants to open a restaurant (or a catering business or even a food cart).

The goal may be simple and small—a change of career, enough money to support a family, a chance to be your own boss. The dreams may be lofty, for from humble beginnings financial empires grow, bestowing fortune and celebrity status on the "chosen." Even as you read this, almost certainly tomorrow's success on the scale of Starbucks or Cheesecake Factory or McCormick & Schmick's is percolating in someone's head—maybe yours.

This is the part where you have to stop dreaming and get practical. How will you organize your business? Are there partners? Are there investors? Who is entitled to share in your success?

The name of your business has enormous impact on your trademark, branding and future rights of expansion—but you can't use just any name. The fact is, you may not even have the right to use your own name, even if it is McDonald.

Is there a chance you may one day expand? Franchise? Go public? Who will examine your contracts for loans, for services from vendors, for leases? Do your key employees—or *you*—need a contract with your business?

Who will you hire? How will you hire them? Hiring practices can be a legal minefield. If you have a secret recipe that gives you an edge in your market, how can you protect it? Can someone copy your menu? Can someone steal your restaurant design?

How do you plan to keep taxes low? Do you know who's responsible for payroll taxes if employees do not declare tips as income?

We live in an increasingly litigious society, and you are about to enter into real and implied contracts with banks, landlords, vendors, employees, contractors, and even customers. You need a lawyer. You may need more than one.

So do yourself a favor. Just in case you make your dream a reality, and that reality defies all odds and becomes a success, protect yourself. Don't let the dream become a nightmare. Read this book before you do anything else.

Stephen and Bo Kline
Typhoon!

Bongoj (Bo) Kline is executive chef and president of *Typhoon!*, with six restaurants in Oregon and Washington. Since founding the company with her husband, Stephen, in 1995, she has emerged as one of the leading Thai chefs in the world.

Stephen Kline is a former writer and producer who worked on a number of TV series in Hollywood, ranging from *Lou Grant* to *The Cosby Show*. He met Bo while working on a movie of the week filmed on location in Thailand.

INTRODUCTION

When I began my law practice in New York more than thirty years ago, I learned about the restaurant business from the supplier's side. As an attorney who worked on matters for our firm's restaurant supply client, I was provided with an opportunity to see how demanding the restaurant business is.

Later, as a law professor specializing in business and intellectual property law, I continued to develop an understanding for the unique aspects of the restaurant business. My practice included representation of many participants in the restaurant and hospitality industry, from small corner establishments to larger, more prominent restaurant chains. Indeed, I have been fortunate enough to obtain a lawyer's perspective on much of the industry.

This text is the product of that experience and the suggestions of several well-respected clients who felt there was a need for a book such as this. My collaborator, Christy O. King, and I have worked together on several other books in *The Law (In Plain English)*® series, and this volume joins that user-friendly series.

The earlier books in the series were written to educate and assist craftspeople, writers, gallery owners, photographers, healthcare professionals, high-tech entrepreneurs, and others involved in small businesses. Reviewers have praised our efforts in providing our readers with tools that are intended to sensitize them to the many legal issues that can and do arise in their chosen specialties. It is hoped that this volume will continue that tradition by providing those in the restaurant and hospitality industry with a readable book to aid in identifying legal issues that are encountered on a regular basis in their industry. Armed with this educational tool, you will be better able to communicate with an attorney, avoid a host of legal problems, and be in a better position to deal with those that do arise.

This book is not intended to replace an attorney; rather, it is designed to inform those in the food industry so that they can more effectively communicate with their attorneys and better insulate themselves from legal problems.

1 ORGANIZING YOUR BUSINESS

Everyone in business knows that survival requires careful financial planning; yet, few fully realize the importance of selecting the best form for the business. Small businesses have little need for the sophisticated organizational structures utilized in industry. However, since all entrepreneurs must pay taxes, obtain financing, and expose themselves to potential liability with every sale they make, it only makes sense to structure your restaurant business to address these issues.

Every business has an organizational form that best suits it. When counseling people on organizing their restaurant businesses, I usually adopt a two-step approach. First, discuss various aspects of taxes and liability in order to decide which of the basic forms is best for those in the restaurant industry. There are only a handful of basic organizational forms: sole proprietorships, partnerships, corporations, limited liability companies, limited liability partnerships, and a few hybrids. Once you decide which of these is the best form for your business, consider the appropriate documents, such as partnership agreements, corporate bylaws, or operating agreements. These documents define the day-to-day operations of a business and must be tailored to each business's individual situation.

Offered here is an explanation of the features of these kinds of organizations, including their advantages and disadvantages. This should give you an idea of which form might be best for your business. Potential problems are discussed, but you should consult an experienced business attorney before deciding to adopt any particular structure. This information will facilitate your communication with your lawyer and enable you to better understand the choices available.

SOLE PROPRIETORSHIPS

The technical name *sole proprietorship* may be unfamiliar to you, but chances are, you or someone you know is operating under this form now. The sole proprietorship is an unincorporated business owned by one person. Though not peculiar to the United States, it was and still is the backbone of the American dream. As a form of business, it is elegant in its simplicity. All it requires is a little money and work. Legal requirements are few and simple. In most localities, you must obtain a business license from the city or county, and if you wish to operate the business under a name other than your own, register the name with the appropriate state or county agency in which you are doing business. With these details taken care of, you are in business.

Disadvantages of Sole Proprietorship

There are many financial risks involved in operating your business as a sole proprietor. As a sole proprietor, your personal assets are at risk. In other words, if for any reason you owe more than the dollar value of your business, your creditors can force a sale of most of your personally-owned property to satisfy the debt.

For many risks, insurance is available that shifts the loss from you to an insurance company, but there are some risks for which insurance simply is not available. For instance, insurance is generally not available to protect against a large rise in the cost or sudden unavailability of supplies. In addition, the cost of liability insurance—particularly in the restaurant industry—has become so high that, as a practical matter, it is unavailable to many businesses. These liability risks, as well as many other uncertain economic factors, can drive a restaurant business and its sole proprietor into bankruptcy. If you recognize any of these dangers as a real threat, you should consider an alternative form of organization.

Taxes for the Sole Proprietor

The sole proprietor is personally taxed on all profits of the business and may deduct losses. Of course, the rate of taxation changes with increases in income. Fortunately, there are ways to ease this tax burden. For instance, you can establish an approved Individual Retirement Account (IRA) or pension plan by deducting a specified amount of your net income for placement into a pension plan, an interest-bearing account, an approved government securities, or mutual funds. Those funds can then be withdrawn later when you are in a lower tax bracket. (There are severe restrictions on withdrawal of this money prior to retirement age. See Chapter 20 on pension plans for a more complete discussion of this subject.)

For further information on tax planning devices, contact your local Internal Revenue Service (IRS) office or **www.irs.gov** and obtain its free pamphlets on a variety of tax-related topics. Better yet, use the services of an accountant experienced in dealing with tax planning for the restaurant industry.

PARTNERSHIPS AND JOINT VENTURES

A *partnership* is defined by most state laws as an association of two or more persons to conduct, as co-owners, a business for profit. No formalities are required. In fact, in some cases, people have been held to be partners even though they never had any intention of forming a partnership. For example, if your friend lends you some money to start a restaurant and you agree to pay the friend a certain percentage of whatever profit is made, your friend may be your partner in the eyes of the law, even though he or she takes no part in running the business. This is important to realize, because each partner is subject to unlimited personal liability for the debts of the partnership. Each partner is also liable for the negligence of another partner and of the partnership's employees when a negligent act occurs during the usual course of business.

A *joint venture* is a partnership for a limited or specific purpose, rather than one that continues for an indefinite or specified time. For example, an arrangement whereby two or more persons or businesses agree to jointly cater a single event and share the profits is a joint venture, whereas an agreement to go into the catering business together is a partnership.

The economic advantages of doing business as a partnership include the pooling of capital, collaboration of skills, easier access to credit, and, potentially, a more efficient allocation of labor and resources. A major disadvantage is, as previously noted, that each partner is fully and personally liable for all the debts of the partnership, even if not personally involved in incurring those debts.

This means that if you are getting involved in a partnership, you should be especially cautious in two areas. First, since the involvement of a partner increases your potential liability, you should choose a responsible partner. Second, the partnership should be adequately insured to protect both the assets of the partnership and the personal assets of each partner.

Since no formalities are required to create a partnership, if the partners do not have a formal agreement defining the terms of the partnership, such as control of the partnership or the distribution of profits, state law dictates the terms. State partnership laws are based on the fundamental characteristics of the typical partnership as it has existed throughout the ages and are thought to correspond to the reasonable expectations of the partners. The most important of these legally presumed characteristics are the following.

- No one can become an actual member of a partnership without the unanimous consent of all partners.
- Every member has an equal vote in the management of the partnership, regardless of the partner's percentage interest in it.
- All partners share equally in the profits and losses of the partnership, no matter how much capital each has contributed.

- A simple majority vote is required for decisions in the ordinary course of business, and a unanimous vote is required to change the fundamental character of the business.
- A partnership is terminable at will by any partner. A partner can withdraw from the partnership at any time, and this withdrawal will cause a dissolution of the partnership.

Most state laws contain a provision that allows the partners to make their own agreements regarding the management structure and division of profits that best suit the needs of the individual partners.

Major Items of the Agreement

A comprehensive partnership agreement is no simple matter. Some major considerations in preparing a partnership agreement include the name of the partnership, a description of the business, contributions of capital by the partners, duration of the partnership, distribution of profits, management responsibilities, duties of partners, prohibited acts, and provisions for the dissolution of the partnership. (These items are detailed in Chapter 2.) It is essential for potential partners to devote time and considerable care to the preparation of an agreement and to enlist the services of a competent business lawyer.

IN PLAIN ENGLISH

The expense of a lawyer to help you put together an agreement suited to the needs of your partnership is usually justified by the economic savings recouped in the smooth organization, operation, and when necessary, the final dissolution of the partnership.

Taxes

A partnership does not possess any special tax advantages over a sole proprietorship. Each partner pays tax on his or her share of the profits, whether distributed or retained, and each is entitled to the same proportion of the partnership deductions and credits. The partnership must prepare an annual information return for the IRS known as Schedule K-1, Form 1065, which details each partner's share of income, credits, and deductions. The IRS uses it to compare against the individual returns filed by the partners.

LIMITED PARTNERSHIPS

The *limited partnership* is a hybrid containing elements of both the partnership and a more formal business entity. A limited partnership may be formed by parties who wish to invest in a business and share in its profits but who seek to limit their risk to the amount of their investment. The law provides such limited risk for the limited partner, but only so long as the limited partner plays no active role in the day-to-day management and operation of the business. In effect, the limited partner is very much like an investor who buys a few shares of stock in a corporation but has no significant role in running the business. In order to establish a limited partnership, it is necessary to have one or more general partners who run the business and have full personal liability. The limited partners play a passive role.

Forming a limited partnership requires a document to be filed with the proper state agency. If the document is not filed or is improperly filed, the limited partner could be treated as a general partner and would lose the benefit of limited liability. In addition, the limited partner must refrain from becoming involved in the day-to-day operations of the partnership. Otherwise, the limited partner might be found to be actively participating in the business and thereby held to be a general partner with unlimited personal liability.

IN PLAIN ENGLISH

A limited partnership is a convenient form for securing needed financial backers when forming a corporation or limited liability company (LLC) may not be appropriate.

A limited partnership can be used to attract investors when credit is hard to get or is too expensive. In return for investing, the limited partner may receive a designated share of the profits. From the entrepreneur's point of view, this may be an attractive way to fund a business. The limited partner receives nothing if there are no profits, but had the entrepreneur borrowed money from a creditor, he or she would be at risk to repay the loan regardless of the success or failure of the business.

Another use of the limited partnership is to facilitate reorganization of a general partnership after the death or retirement of a general partner. Remember, a partnership can be terminated upon the request of any partner. Although the original partnership is technically dissolved when one partner retires, it is not uncommon for the remaining partners to agree to buy out the retiring partner's share—return that person's capital contribution—and keep the business going. Raising enough cash to buy out the retiring partner, however, could jeopardize the business by forcing the remaining partners to liquidate certain partnership assets. A convenient way to avoid such a detrimental liquidation is for the retiree to step into limited partner status. Thus, the retiree can continue to share in the profits, which, to some extent, flow from that partner's past labor, while removing his or her personal assets from the risk of partnership liabilities. In the meantime, the remaining partners are afforded the opportunity to restructure the partnership funding under more favorable terms.

UNINTENDED PARTNERS

Whether yours is a straightforward general partnership or a limited partnership, one arrangement you want to avoid is the unintended partnership. This can occur when you work together with another person and your relationship is not described formally. For example, if you and another person decide to import and sell gourmet foods, it is essential for you to spell out in detail the arrangements between the two of you. If you do not, you could find that the other person is your partner and entitled to half the income you receive, even though his or her contribution was minimal. You can avoid this by simply hiring the other person as an employee or independent contractor. (see Chapter 17.) Whichever arrangement you choose, you should have a detailed, written agreement.

CORPORATIONS

The word *corporation* may call to mind a vision of a large company with hundreds or thousands of employees. In fact, the vast majority of corporations in the United States are small- or moderate-sized companies. There are, of course, advantages and disadvantages to incorporating. If it appears advantageous to incorporate, you will find it can be done with surprising ease and little expense. You should, however, use the services of a knowledgeable business lawyer to ensure compliance with state formalities and completion of corporate mechanics, and to obtain advice about corporate taxation.

Corporations vs. Partnerships

In describing the corporate form, it is useful to compare it to a partnership. Perhaps the most important difference is that, like limited partners, the owners of the corporation—commonly known as shareholders or stockholders—are not, as a rule, personally liable for the corporation's debts. They stand to lose only their investments. Unlike a limited partner, a shareholder is allowed full participation in the control of the corporation through the shareholder's voting privileges. The higher the percentage of outstanding shares owned, the more significant the control.

For the small corporation, however, limited liability may be something of an illusion, because creditors often require the owners to personally cosign for any credit extended. In addition, individuals remain responsible for their own wrongful acts; thus, a shareholder who negligently causes an injury while engaged in corporate business has not only subjected the corporation to liability, but also remains personally liable. If the other party to a contract with the corporation has agreed to look only to the corporation for responsibility, however, the corporate liability shield does protect a shareholder from liability for breach of contract.

The corporate shield also offers protection in situations in which an agent hired by the corporation has committed a wrongful act while working on the corporation's behalf. For example, if a restaurant consultant negligently injures a pedestrian while driving on corporate business, the consultant will be liable for the wrongful act and the corporation may be liable, but the shareholder who owns stock in the corporation will probably not be personally liable.

The second major difference between a corporation and a partnership relates to continuity of existence. Many of the events that can cause the dissolution of a partnership do not have the same effect on a corporation. In fact, it is common for *perpetual existence* to be specified in the *articles of incorporation* (or other corporate formation documents). Shareholders, unlike partners, cannot decide to withdraw and demand a return of capital from the corporation. All they can do is sell their stock. A corporation may, therefore, have both legal and economic continuity. This can be a tremendous disadvantage to shareholders or their heirs if they want to sell stock when there are no buyers for it.

IN PLAIN ENGLISH

Agreements can be made that guarantee return of capital to the estate of a shareholder who dies or to a shareholder who decides to withdraw.

The third difference relates to *transferability of ownership*. No one can become a partner without unanimous consent of the other partners, unless otherwise agreed. In a corporation, however, shareholders can generally sell all or any number of their shares whenever and to whomever they wish. If the owners of a small corporation do not want it to be open to outside ownership, transferability may be restricted by agreement of the owners.

The fourth difference is in the structure of management and control. Holders of *common stock* are given a vote in proportion to their ownership in the corporation. Other kinds of stock can be created, with or without voting rights. A voting shareholder uses the vote to elect a board of directors and to create rules under which the board will operate.

The basic rules of the corporation are stated in its *articles of incorporation*, which are filed with the state. These serve as the constitution for the corporation and can be amended by shareholder vote. More detailed operational rules—*bylaws*—should also be adopted, but are not filed with the state. Both shareholders and directors may have the power to create or amend bylaws. This varies from state to state and may be determined by the shareholders themselves. The board of directors then makes operational decisions for the corporation and might delegate day-to-day control to a president or chief executive officer.

A shareholder, even one who owns all the stock, may not preempt a decision of the board of directors. If the board has exceeded the powers granted it by the articles or bylaws, any shareholder may sue for a court order remedying the situation. If the board is within its powers, the shareholders have no recourse except to remove one or more board members. In a few more progressive states, a small corporation may entirely forego having a board of directors. In these cases, the corporation is authorized to allow the shareholders to vote directly on business decisions, just as in a partnership.

The fifth distinction between a partnership and a corporation is the greater variety of means available to the corporation for raising additional capital. Partnerships are quite restricted in this regard—they can borrow money or, if all the partners agree, they can take on additional partners. A corporation, on the other hand, may issue a variety of stock to raise additional capital.

A means frequently used to attract a new investor is the issuance of *preferred stock*. The corporation agrees to pay the preferred shareholder some predetermined amount, known as a *dividend preference*, before it pays any dividends to other shareholders. It also means that if the corporation goes bankrupt, after the corporation's creditors are paid, the preferred shareholders will generally be paid out of the proceeds of liquidation before the common shareholders.

In most cases, the issuance of new stock merely requires approval by a majority of the existing shareholders. In addition, corporations can borrow money on a short-term basis by issuing notes, or for a longer period by issuing debentures or bonds.

IN PLAIN ENGLISH

As a practical matter, a corporation's ability to raise additional capital is limited only by its lawyer's creativity and the economics of the marketplace.

The last distinction is the manner in which a corporation is taxed. Under both state and federal laws, the profits of the corporation are taxed to the corporation before they are paid out as dividends. Then, because the dividends constitute income to the shareholders, they are taxed again as the shareholder's personal income. This *double taxation* constitutes the major disadvantage of incorporating.

Avoiding Double Taxation

There are several methods of avoiding double taxation. First, a corporation can plan its business so it does not show much profit. This can be done by drawing off what would be profit in payments to shareholders for a variety of services. For example, a shareholder can be paid a salary, rent for property leased to the corporation, or interest on a loan made to the corporation. All of these are legal deductions from the corporate income.

A corporation can often get larger deductions for the various benefits provided for its employees than can a sole proprietorship or a partnership. For example, a corporation can deduct all its payments made for certain qualified employee life insurance plans, while the employees pay no personal income tax on this benefit. Sole proprietors or partnerships, on the other hand, may not be entitled to deduct these expenses.

A corporation can also reinvest its profits for reasonable business expansion. This undistributed money is not taxed as income to the shareholders, though the corporation must pay corporate tax on it. By contrast, the retained earnings of a partnership are taxed to the individual partners even though the money is not distributed.

Corporate reinvestment has two advantages. First, the business can be built up with money that has been taxed only at the corporate level and on which no individual shareholder must pay tax. Second, within reasonable limits, the corporation can delay the distribution of corporate earnings until, for example, a time of lower personal income of the shareholder, and therefore, lower personal tax. If, however, the amount withheld for expansion is unreasonably high, then the corporation may be exposed to a penalty. Working with an experienced tax planner on a regular basis is the best way to avoid tax-related issues.

S CORPORATIONS

Congress created a hybrid organizational form that allows the owners of a small corporation to take advantage of many of the features described for a regular corporation (*C corporation*) but that is taxed in a manner similar to a sole proprietorship or partnership, thus avoiding most of the double-taxation problems. In this form of organization, called an *S corporation*, income and losses flow directly to shareholders, and the corporation pays no income tax. This form can be particularly advantageous in the early years of a corporation, because the owners can deduct almost all the corporate losses from their personal incomes, which they cannot do in a standard corporation. An S corporation provides this favorable tax situation while simultaneously granting the limited liability of the corporate form.

IN PLAIN ENGLISH

If the corporation is likely to sustain major losses and shareholders have other sources of income against which they wish to write off those losses, the S corporation is probably a desirable form for the business.

An S corporation is sometimes referred to as a *small corporation*. However, as defined by the tax law, a small corporation does not refer to the amount of business generated; rather, it refers to the number of owners. In order to qualify for S status, the corporation may not have more than one hundred owners, each of whom must be an individual or a certain kind of trust or nonprofit corporation. Additionally, there cannot be more than one class of voting stock, and the business must be an active one.

Taxes

S corporations are generally taxed in the same way as partnerships or sole proprietorships. Unfortunately, the tax rules for S corporations are not as simple as those for partnerships or individuals. In general, the owner of an S corporation can be taxed on his or her *pro rata* share of the distributable profits and may deduct his or her share of distributable losses. Work with an experienced tax planner on a regular basis to avoid tax-related problems.

LIMITED LIABILITY COMPANIES

As a business form, a *limited liability company* (LLC) combines the limited liability features of a corporation with all the tax advantages available to the sole proprietor or partnership. An entrepreneur conducting business through an LLC can shield his or her personal assets from the risks of the business for all situations except the individual's own wrongful acts. This liability shield is identical to the one offered by the corporate form. The owners of an LLC can also enjoy all the tax features accorded to sole proprietors or partners in a partnership.

Limited liability companies do not have the same restrictions imposed on S corporations regarding the number of owners and the type of owners (i.e., human beings or specified business forms). In fact, business corporations, partnerships, and other business entities can own interests in LLCs. LLCs may also have more than one class of voting ownership and may even have passive income.

The LLC form is still relatively new by legal standards, so there is not yet a significant body of case law interpreting the meaning of the statutes that created it. It is, however, extremely flexible, and the Internal Revenue Code permits LLCs to be taxed either like C corporations or like sole proprietorships, partnerships, or S corporations. This means that, if desired, owners of an LLC that has chosen to be taxed as a C corporation can file the appropriate form and switch to be taxed as an S corporation, so long as the organization otherwise qualifies as an S corporation under the appropriate tax laws. The benefit of choosing this structure is that while money paid out of an LLC taxed as a S corporation in the form of income to employees will be subject to all employment-related taxes, distributions to owners on account of their ownership interests is considered passive income and not subject to all employment-related taxes. That is, the passive income is not subject to FICA tax and may avoid state taxes that would otherwise be imposed on employees.

PRECAUTIONS FOR MINORITY OWNERS

Dissolving a corporation is not only painful because of certain tax penalties, but it is almost always impossible without the consent of the majority of the owners. This may be true of LLCs as well. If you are involved in the formation of a business entity and will be a minority owner, you must realize that the majority owners will have ultimate and absolute control unless the minority owners take certain precautions from the start. There are numerous horror stories relating to what some majority owners have done to minority owners. Avoiding these problems is no more difficult than drafting an appropriate agreement among the owners. You should always retain your own attorney to represent you during the business entity's formation, rather than waiting until it is too late.

HYBRIDS

In addition to the business forms discussed, many states have enacted laws that permit the creation of hybrid forms of business organization, such as limited liability limited partnerships (LLLPs) and business trusts. It is important for you to consult with an experienced business lawyer in order to determine which business forms are available in your state and would best serve your business objectives.

2

BUSINESS ORGANIZATION CHECKLIST

As discussed in the previous chapter, there is a host of business forms available for the restaurant industry. These forms range from the simplest—sole proprietorship—to more complex organizations like partnerships, corporations, and limited liability companies. The structure of your business will depend upon a number of considerations. Creating any of these business forms is a rather simple process, but to do it right and enjoy all the advantages, it is highly recommended that you consult a competent business lawyer. Of course, a lawyer's time is money, but you can save some money if you come properly prepared. Use this chapter as a checklist of some of the points to discuss with your lawyer.

ACCOUNTANT

Other than yourself, the most important person with whom your attorney will work is your accountant. The accountant should be prepared to provide valuable input on the business's financial structure, funding, capitalization, allocation of ownership, and other issues.

BUSINESS NAME

Regardless of its form, every business will have a name. Contact your attorney ahead of time with the proposed name of the business. An inquiry to the corporation commissioner or secretary of state can establish whether the proposed name is available. Many corporation division offices have online services that enable you to begin the process yourself. Your attorney may be able to reserve your chosen business name until you are ready to use it. You will also have to consider whether the business will have a special mark or logo that needs trademark protection. (See Chapter 9 on trademarks.)

BUSINESS STRUCTURE: PARTNERSHIP

If it is determined that you will conduct your business in the partnership form, it is essential that you have a formal written agreement prepared by a skilled business attorney. The more time you and your prospective partners spend discussing these details in advance of meeting with a lawyer, the less such a meeting is likely to cost you. A discussion of the major items of a partnership agreement that you should consider follows.

The Name of the Partnership

Every business will have a name. Some partnerships simply use the surnames of the principal partners to name the business. The choice in that case is nothing more than the order of the names, which depends on various factors from prestige to the way the names sound in a particular order. If, however, the name does not include the partners' full names, it will be necessary to file the proposed business name with the appropriate agency.

Care should be taken to choose a name that is distinctive and not already in use. If the name is not distinctive, others can use it. If the name is already in use, you could be liable for trade name infringement.

A Description of the Business

In describing their business, the partners should agree on the basic scope of the business—its requirements in regard to capital and labor, each party's individual contributions of capital and labor, and perhaps some plans regarding future growth.

Partnership Capital

After determining how much capital each partner will contribute, the partners must decide when it will be contributed, how to value the property contributed, and whether a partner can contribute or withdraw any property at a later date.

Duration of the Partnership

Sometimes partnerships are organized for a fixed amount of time or are automatically dissolved on certain conditions, such as the completion of a project.

Distribution of Profits

You can make whatever arrangement you want for distribution of profits. Although ordinarily a partner does not receive a salary, it is possible to give an active partner a guaranteed salary in addition to a share of the profits. Since the partnership's profits can be determined only at the close of a business year, distributions are not usually made until that time. It is possible, however, to allow the partners a monthly draw of money against their final share of the profits. In some cases, it may also be necessary or desirable to allow limited expense accounts for some partners.

Not all the profits of the partnership need to be distributed at year-end. Some can be retained for expansion, an arrangement that can be provided for in the partnership agreement.

Whether or not profits are distributed, all partners must pay tax on their proportionate shares of the profit. The tax code refers directly to the partnership agreement to determine what that share is, which demonstrates the importance of a partnership agreement.

Management

The power in the partnership can be divided many ways. All partners can be given the same voice or some may be given more than others. A few partners might be allowed to manage the business entirely, with the remaining partners being given a vote only on specifically designated issues.

Besides voting, three other areas of management should be covered. First is the question of who can sign checks, place orders, or enter into contracts on behalf of the partnership. Under state partnership laws, any partner may do these things so long as they occur in the usual course of business. Such a broad delegation of authority can lead to confusion, so it might be best to delegate this authority more narrowly. Second, it is a good idea to determine a regular date for partnership meetings. Finally, some consideration should be given to the possibility of a disagreement arising among the partners that leads to a deadlock. One way to avoid this is to distribute the voting power in a way that would make a deadlock impossible. In a two-person partnership, however, this would mean that one partner would be in absolute control, which might be unacceptable to the other partner. If, instead, the power is divided equally among an even number of partners, as is often the case, the agreement should stipulate a neutral party or arbitrator who could settle any dispute, thereby avoiding a dissolution of the partnership.

Prohibited Acts

By law, each partner owes the partnership certain duties by virtue of being an agent of the partnership. First is a *duty of diligence*. This means the partner must exercise reasonable care in acting as a partner. Second is a *duty of obedience*. The partner must obey the rules of the partnership and, most importantly, must not exceed the authority that the partnership has vested in him or her. Finally, there is a *duty of loyalty*. A partner may not, without approval of the other partners, compete with the partnership in another business. A partner also may not personally seize upon a business opportunity that would be of value to the partnership without first telling the partnership about it and allowing the partnership to pursue it if the partnership desires. A list of prohibited acts should be made a part of the partnership agreement, elaborating and expanding on these fundamental duties.

Dissolution and Liquidation

A partnership is automatically dissolved upon the death, withdrawal, or expulsion of a partner. Dissolution identifies the legal end of the partnership, but need not affect its economic life if the partnership agreement has provided for the continuation of the business after a dissolution. Nonetheless, a dissolution will affect the business. The partner who withdraws or is expelled, or the estate of a deceased partner, will be entitled to a return of the proportionate share of capital that the departing partner contributed. Details such as how this capital will be returned should be decided before dissolution, because it may be impossible to negotiate at the time of dissolution. One method of handling this issue is to provide for a return of the capital in cash over a period of time. Some provision should be made so that each of the remaining partners will know how much of a departing partner's interest he or she may purchase.

After a partner leaves, the partnership may need to be reorganized and recapitalized. Again, provisions for this should be worked out in advance, if possible. Finally, since it is always possible that the partners will eventually want to liquidate the partnership, it should be decided in advance who will liquidate the assets, which assets will be distributed, and what property, if any, will be returned to its original contributor.

BUSINESS STRUCTURE: CORPORATIONS AND LLCS

There are usually two reasons for creating a business form such as a corporation or LLC—limiting personal liability and minimizing income tax liability. The second reason is generally applicable to a business that is earning a good deal of money. Even if you are not in that category, you may nevertheless want to consider creating a business entity in order to limit your personal liability.

Corporations and LLCs are hypothetical *legal persons*, and as such, are responsible for their own acts and contracts. Thus, if a patron in a restaurant slips on a piece of lettuce, a consultant's car negligently injures a pedestrian, or the food your restaurant served causes food poisoning, the corporation or LLC—not its owners—will be liable, assuming the proper formalities in setting up and maintaining the business structure have been adhered to. It should be noted that any individual personally responsible for a wrongful act will also be liable.

Officers

State statutes generally require a corporation or LLC to have a chief operating officer, such as a president or manager. In addition, state statutes may require other administrative officers, such as a secretary. One matter to decide is who will be the company officers, or in the case of an LLC electing centralized management, who will be the LLC's manager. It may be that the corporate *bylaws* or the LLC's *operating agreement* should have a separate description for specialized officers.

Owners

How many shares of stock should your corporation be authorized to issue? Limited liability companies sometimes use *certificates of ownership*, which resemble shares of stock in a corporation, and the same considerations for their issuance are present. How many units should be issued when the business commences operations and how many should be held in reserve for future issuance? Should there be separate classes of corporate shareholders or LLC owners?

If the corporation or LLC is to be family owned, ownership may be used to some extent as a means of estate planning or wealth shifting. You might, therefore, also wish to ask your attorney about updating your will at the same time you incorporate or create an LLC. (see Chapter 21.)

Owner Agreements

If your corporation has several shareholders, or if the LLC has several owners, a method must be established to prevent an owners' voting deadlock. You may also wish to discuss with your lawyer the possibility of creating owner agreements that govern employment status of key individuals or commit owners to voting a certain way on specific issues.

Buy-Sell Agreements

The first meeting with your lawyer is a good time to discuss *buy-sell agreements*. A buy-sell agreement will direct what happens when one of the owners wishes to leave the business, and describe under what circumstances owners are able to sell their interest to outsiders. In closely held corporations, the corporation or other shareholders are generally granted the first option to buy the stock. In these cases, the law requires a restriction on transferability of ownership. The same kind of procedure can be implemented for LLCs.

Other issues that can be addressed by a buy-sell agreement include the circumstances that will trigger the right of the company or other owners to buy the interest, such as death, disability, retirement, or termination. Further, you must decide if the buy-sell agreement will be tied to *key-person insurance*, which would fund the purchase of ownership interests by the corporation or LLC in the event of a key owner's death. A buy-sell agreement can also be used to identify the mechanism for valuing the stock or LLC interest—annual appraisal, book value, multiple earnings, arbitration, or some other method.

Planning for Future Owners

Articles of incorporation or operating agreement may be used as an important planning tool for the future. You can make plans at the onset to take on new investors, shareholders, or owners in the future. You may have plans for converting the entity into one that is publicly held someday (ownership interests in LLCs may not be publicly traded, but it is possible to bring in some additional owners). You and your attorney should discuss the best method to accomplish these goals during the initial planning to make it easier in the future.

Capitalization

At this point, your attorney will likely work closely with your accountant to establish the initial *capitalization* of the organization. The amount of the initial capitalization, or funding, must be determined, and how it will be paid must be decided. Such practical considerations include the following.

- What is being contributed by owners in exchange for their interests—money, past services, equipment, assets of an ongoing business, licensing agreements, or other things?
- What value will be placed on assets that are contributed to the business?
- Will owners make loans to the business and contribute the rest in exchange for ownership interest?

Governing Board

Additional initial decisions will revolve around the organization's governing board. You must decide who will be on the board of directors of a corporation or the governing board of an LLC, and how many initial directors there will be. You should also establish in the beginning whether owners will have the right to elect members of the board based on their percentages of ownership or by some other method.

IN PLAIN ENGLISH

It is a good idea to have an odd number of directors in order to avoid the potential for a voting deadlock.

Housekeeping

Your attorney will need to know several other details. For instance, the number of employees the business anticipates for the coming twelve-month period must be stated on the application for a federal taxpayer identification number. Other questions that must be answered include the following.

- Will the business tax year end on December 31ˢᵗ or on another date? (S corporations and LLCs that are not taxable entities must use the calendar year as their tax year.)
- Will the business accounting be on a cash basis or accrual basis?
- Will the business authorize salaries for its officers or managers?
- What will be the date for the annual meetings of the governing board and owners?
- Who will be the registered agent? (Often, your attorney will assume this role.)
- Which bank will your business use?
- Who will be the authorized signers on the bank account?

Employee Benefits

Be prepared to consider employee benefit plans, such as life and health insurance, profit-sharing, pension or other retirement plans, employee ownership programs, and other fringe benefits. Even if you do not plan to implement such programs when the corporation or LLC is created, it is nonetheless a good idea to consider whether such programs may be instituted in the future.

Tax Treatment

Lastly, you must make some decision regarding how you want your organization set up for tax purposes. You can elect to have your corporation be an S corporation, where income and most losses flow directly to shareholders and the corporation pays no income tax. If the corporation is likely to sustain major losses and shareholders have other sources of income against which they wish to write off those losses, chances are the S election would be appropriate. Similarly, LLCs can elect to be taxed as entities (like a C corporation) or choose to be mere conduits (like S corporations and partnerships). This choice may be made when the entity is first created or when the first year's tax return is filed.

• • • • •

As you can see, there is much to discuss at the first meeting with your lawyer. A little time and thought prior to that meeting will prove to be a worthwhile investment.

3
THE BUSINESS PLAN

In order to establish a viable restaurant business, it is essential to plan. You must have some guide as to where you intend to have the business go and some method by which to judge your success at reaching your goals.

In addition, every business needs capital at one time or another. This funding might be sought as bank loans, other conventional forms of financing, or as venture capital. It might also be obtained through a public sale of securities. (see Chapters 4 and 5.) No matter what the source of financing, an important first step is the preparation of a *business plan*. This can aid a banker, venture capitalist, or prospective owner in evaluating your company.

A business plan may be considered a roadmap to determine the course your business will travel from start-up to full operation. The structure and content of your business plan will vary depending upon such factors as the company's stage of development, the nature of the business, and the type of markets it will serve. There is a host of different formats that have been used for business plans. Although the order of presentation is by no means standard, each of the following topics should be addressed in structuring any business plan. In addition, there are numerous software packages available to assist in creating your business plan.

EXECUTIVE SUMMARY

The *executive summary* section of the plan provides the reader with a short overview of the key elements of the business plan. Since sophisticated business-people are turned away by exaggeration, the summary must provide an accurate assessment of your business while distinguishing your restaurant business from others that are competing in the same market. The summary should also describe your management team, emphasizing experience and skills. This description should not, however, ignore weaknesses but should explain how you expect to overcome them. Another important part of the summary will be your key financial projections and funding requirements to meet those projections.

Above all, the summary must be designed to catch the reader's attention. Unless the summary inspires one to read further, it has not served its purpose and the remainder of the plan may go unread.

HISTORY

Businesspeople want to know about the past performance of a business before they assess its potential. Toward this end, the business plan should provide a brief history of the business (including when it was founded or if just now start-ing up), subsequent development and growth (or the market research for poten-tial subsequent development and growth), how it has been organized (for example, as a sole proprietorship, partnership, corporation, or LLC), and how well past performance foretells the future. If you have good reasons to believe that the past performance is not indicative of the business's potential, be sure to state those reasons in this section.

NATURE OF THE BUSINESS

The next section describes in detail the *nature of your business*. It should include a summary explaining any unique features and any special services provided, such as catering or merchandising of signature products. It should also contain statements about performance and present status.

Keep in mind, however, that investors may not have expertise with your business or even familiarity with your industry. This section should be written in language that is easily understood by businesspeople without backgrounds in the restaurant industry.

THE MARKET

A section that contains a comprehensive description of the *market* your business targets must be included. If the market niche is innovative, such as a theme restaurant or an unfamiliar cuisine, independent market research may need to be conducted to define both the initial and future markets. If comparable restaurant businesses have been around for some time, the market has most likely already been defined and you may be able to rely on available data from similar businesses, industry professional associations, the Small Business Administration, chambers of commerce, and the like.

IN PLAIN ENGLISH

For purposes of obtaining investment capital, the market section may be the most important part of your business plan.

To the banker, venture capitalist, or prospective owner, a business without a strong understanding of the targeted market is a bad risk, even if the concept is first-rate. Consequently, the market description should be more detailed than the business description. This will indicate to potential investors that you understand the priority of market over product or service.

THE COMPETITION

Identify your competitors. Discuss their relative strengths and weaknesses, and indicate the market share likely held by each. Include a forecast of the market share you expect to capture in the first three to five years and the sources from which you expect to draw customers. Be sure to spell out your rationale for each projection—an innovative approach or creative promotion, marketing, favorable reviews, price, service, or other factors. As with all projections in the business plan, do not understate the strengths of your competition while overstating your own. Sophisticated businesspeople will not back a company that does not have a realistic view of its competition.

SOURCE OF SUPPLIES

Obtaining sought-after supplies or services at an economical price and having the ability to service patrons expeditiously are key to making a profit. The *source of supplies* section should discuss the trade shows that you attend, detail your suppliers, and identify those with whom you have exclusivity or other agreements. Additionally, you should explain the steps taken by you to expand your business operation, as well as your backup suppliers in the event of unavailability of key ingredients.

In some restaurant businesses, merchandising may be important. If that is part of your business, it would be appropriate to discuss that in your business plan. For example, many restaurants sell packaged signature dishes for home consumption, which may or may not be produced by the restaurant.

You should also present information about the reputation of the products sold, including favorable reviews and relevant data from recognized publications, such as *Consumer Reports* or *Money* magazine.

MANAGEMENT

As a general rule, bankers, venture capitalists, and prospective owners favor investing in a start-up business with first-rate management over an established business with mediocre management. This priority should be reflected in your business plan.

In this section, emphasize the experience of each key management executive. Include job descriptions and salaries, and provide résumés detailing each executive's past business experience, education, publications, and any other information that will indicate to potential financiers that you have a qualified management team. If your current management team has weak spots, define them and explain how they will be overcome.

FINANCIAL DATA

Superior products or services and top-flight management count for nothing if your financial projections do not allow for a substantial return on investment. Consequently, this section is the bottom line of your business plan. Begin by summarizing previous financial performance. If your business is new, be sure that all financial projections are realistic. Remember that most prospective investors and lenders are sophisticated and will check out other restaurant businesses. If your projections deviate widely from the industry norm, you will likely lose credibility and jeopardize the financing you seek.

IN PLAIN ENGLISH

Do not inundate your reader with pages of computer-generated spreadsheets. Your financial data should be concise and easy to understand.

Finally, your financial section should discuss the financing itself. Indicate how much money the business seeks, the form of financing sought, and how the money is to be used. Most important, discuss the projected return within the next five years of operation. As with all financial information, be realistic and support your projections with solid data and a sound rationale.

THE BUSINESS PLAN TEAM

The development of a well-written business plan is a considerable undertaking. It forces you to focus your ideas, ferret out weak spots in your organization, and turn abstract concepts into a concrete plan. Experienced professionals, such as lawyers and accountants, can provide invaluable assistance in putting together a sound and attractive business plan. Your lawyer can help your business obtain the legal protection that it needs, while steering you away from the legal pitfalls that face all new or expanding businesses. Your accountant can assist you with the myriad financial assessments you must make. A knowledgeable and respected lawyer and accountant can lend credibility to your numbers and projections. Beyond this, experienced lawyers and accountants often have contacts within the venture capital and banking communities. They can tell you who has the capital, where it is being invested, and how you can best get a share. By enlisting the help of experienced professionals and following the suggestions presented here, you can develop a business plan that will help you attract the financing you need for your new or expanding business.

4

BORROWING FROM BANKS

Commercial loans can be a valuable source of needed capital for qualified business borrowers. Since other sources of funding, such as venture capital or loans from institutional lenders other than banks, are typically not available to a new restaurant, the focus of this chapter will be on bank lending, though you should consider these other sources of funds when seeking additional capital. Most institutional lenders follow the same procedures as banks and demand the same type of information.

STARTING YOUR SEARCH

Lending policies vary dramatically from institution to institution. Therefore, you should talk to several banks to determine which might be likely to lend to your business and which have the most favorable loan terms. While lenders are generally conservative in their lending policies, you may discover some to be more flexible than others. To save time and increase the chances of loan approval, it makes sense to first approach those banks that are most likely to view your proposal favorably and whose lending criteria you feel you can meet.

IN PLAIN ENGLISH

Restaurant businesses may wish to begin their search with a smaller community bank that is more familiar with the community and local economic issues.

Through local newspapers, community involvement, and reputation, your business may already be known to a local banker. Once this resource has been exhausted, then a wider search would be appropriate. You should also contact your local office of the Small Business Administration to determine whether you qualify for an SBA loan. A statewide, regional, or even national search may be necessary before you find the right combination of a willing lender and favorable terms. With the World Wide Web, this is not as difficult as it once was.

After having shopped the marketplace and decided on a particular bank, you will be ready for the next step—preparing the loan application. The importance of being properly prepared before taking this critical step cannot be overemphasized. Loan officers are not likely to be impressed by a hastily prepared application containing vague, incomplete information or unsubstantiated claims. Many loan requests are doomed at this early stage because ill-prepared applicants fail to adequately present themselves and their businesses to the lender, even though the proposed ventures are, in fact, sound.

THE LOAN PROPOSAL

Inexperience with the bank's lending procedures can result in an unexpected denial. Knowing the bank's lending policy, and what it looks for in a loan application, and following its procedure, is essential. At a minimum, a borrower should be prepared to satisfactorily address each of the following questions.

- Is your business creditworthy?
- For what purpose is the money sought, and do you desire a short- or long-term loan?

- How much money do you really need?
- What kind of collateral do you and your business have to secure the loan?

The lender's decision to grant or refuse the loan request will be based on your answers to these questions, among other criteria.

Creditworthiness

The ability to obtain money when you need it may be as important to the operation of your business as having a good location and the right personnel. However, before an institution will agree to lend you money, the loan department must be satisfied that you and your business constitute a good risk—that you are *creditworthy*.

Good Character

The lender will want to know what sort of person you are. Do you have a good reputation in the community and in the restaurant industry? Are you known in the community? What is your past credit history and what is the likelihood that you will repay the loan if your business falters or even fails?

IN PLAIN ENGLISH

It is not uncommon for a loan to be denied, irrespective of the applicant's qualifications on paper, if the loan officer is not convinced of the borrower's good character.

Despite its subjective nature, this character factor figures prominently in the lender's decision making. Even for *signature loans* (which require only the applicant's signature and are available only to businesses and entrepreneurs with the highest credit standing, business integrity, and management skills), the applicant's character will affect the institution's decision to make a loan.

Purpose

Once the bank has evaluated the creditworthiness of your restaurant business, you should be ready to explain the appropriateness of the kind of loan requested. The *purpose of the loan*, such as whether the money is needed to purchase supplies or to acquire fixed assets, such as kitchen equipment or furnishings, will determine what type of loan—long- or short-term—the applicant should request. It is important to be able to convince the lender that your proposed use of the borrowed money will generate the additional revenue needed to pay the loan during the agreed repayment period.

Short-term loans are appropriate for purchasing supplies or funding a specific event, such as a large catered function. They are expected to be repaid as inventory is sold or when the business is paid for the event. Generally, repayment must be made within one year or less, because the bank will likely anticipate repayment from the sale of the assets financed by the loan.

Intermediate-term loans, which require payment in between one and five years, and long-term loans, which extend payments beyond five years, are more appropriate for purchases of fixed assets, since repayment is expected to be made not from the sale of these assets but from the earnings generated by the company's ongoing use of them. Bear in mind that commercial lenders are interested in offering funds to successful businesses in need of additional capital to expand and increase profitability. They are not particularly inclined to make loans to restaurants or other businesses needing the money to pay off existing debts.

Loans that are characterized as *lines of credit* basically provide the business with the opportunity to borrow up to a specified amount at any given time. These can be used to facilitate purchases, help pay salaries when the business is experiencing cash flow problems, and so on. A line of credit is typically available on a long-term basis, though most lenders require the line to be paid off at least once a year even though the money may be borrowed again.

Depending upon your credit reputation, short-term loans may be available with or without security. It is more likely that long-term loans will require adequate security (which may include securing the asset to be acquired) and necessitate a pledge of personal, as well as business, assets.

Amount

The lender is also concerned about the amount of the loan being adequate, since an undercapitalized business is more likely to get into financial trouble. Similarly, a lender will be reluctant to approve a loan that is excessive, since the debt service may result in an unnecessarily high cash drain on the business. The loan should net the borrower the amount necessary to accomplish the desired goal with a slight cushion for error and no more. If the borrower has not included in the loan request a suitable allowance for unexpected business developments, thus leaving no margin for error, so repayment can be made only if the business is successful, the lender may consider the loan too risky.

Estimating the amounts needed to finance building construction, remodeling, or expansion—long-term loans—is relatively easy, as is estimating the cost of fixed-asset acquisition. On the other hand, working-capital needs—short-term loans—are more difficult to assess and depend upon the type and location of the business. To plan your working-capital requirements, it is important to know the cash flow of your business—present and anticipated. This involves a projection of all the elements of cash receipts and disbursements at the time they are likely to occur. These figures should be projected on a monthly basis to aid the bank in its evaluation.

Collateral

Sometimes loans will be made solely on the borrower's signature. More frequently, banks will require *collateral* to secure the loan. Acceptable collateral can take a variety of forms. The type and amount of collateral necessary in a given situation will depend on the particular bank's lending policies and the borrower's financial state. In general, banks will accept the following types of collateral as security for business loans.

Endorsers', Comakers', or Guarantors' Promises to Pay

You may have to get other people to sign a note in order to bolster your credit. These people—*sureties*—may cosign your note as endorsers, comakers, or guarantors, as designated by the lender. While the law makes some subtle distinctions as to when each of these sureties becomes liable for the borrower's debt, in essence, these parties will be expected to pay back the borrowed funds if the borrower fails to do so. The bank may or may not require sureties to pledge their own assets as security for their promise to pay upon the borrower's default. This will depend to a great extent on the surety's own creditworthiness.

Assignment of Leases

Assigning a lease as a form of security is particularly appropriate for franchise situations. If the bank lends a business franchise money for a building and takes back a mortgage, that mortgage may be secured by assigning to the lender the lease entered into between the franchisor and the franchisee that will occupy the building. If the franchisor fails to meet mortgage payments, the bank can directly receive the franchisee's lease payments in satisfaction of the franchisor's debt.

Security Interests

Equipment loans may be secured by giving the bank a *lien* on the equipment you are buying. The amount loaned will likely be less than the purchase price. How much less will be determined by the present and future market value of the equipment and its rate of depreciation. You will be expected to adequately insure the equipment, to properly maintain it, and to protect it from damage. As noted, restaurant equipment frequently becomes a *fixture* belonging to the landlord, and therefore, is unavailable to secure a loan. In addition, even if available, the resale value is generally quite low.

Real Estate Holdings

You may be able to borrow against the equity in your personal real estate holdings, as well as those of your business. Again, you will likely be required to maintain the property in good condition and carry adequate insurance on the property for the benefit of the lender, at least up to the amount of the loan.

Savings Accounts, Certificates of Deposit, and Life Insurance Policies

Sometimes you may get a loan by assigning your savings account or certificate of deposit (CD) to the lender. The lender will then keep your passbook or certificate, while notifying the account holder of the existence of the debt in order to ensure that the account will not be diminished during the term of the loan. In addition, the lender will likely prohibit the use of debit cards and the like during the term of the loan. Most banks will not provide this type of lending unless the savings account or CD is at their institution.

Loans can also be made up to the cash value of a life insurance policy, but you must be prepared to assign the policy over to the lender. Talk to your insurance agent if you are interested in borrowing against any life insurance policy you may have.

Stocks and Bonds

Stocks and bonds may be accepted as collateral for a loan if they are readily marketable; however, banks will typically lend no more than 75% of the market value of a high-grade security. If the value of the securities drops below the lender's required margin, the borrower may be asked to provide additional security for the loan.

Supplies and Inventory

As discussed, business supplies and inventory, either on hand or to be acquired in the future, can be used as security for short-term loans. The lender will expect the loan to be repaid from the revenues generated by the sale of inventory on a timely basis.

Intellectual Property

Patents, copyrights, trademarks, and other forms of intellectual property may be used as collateral for loans. There is an increasing body of case law surrounding the methods by which these assets may be secured. Unfortunately, many lenders are unfamiliar with methods of valuing the potential worth of intellectual properties, and thus, may not be willing to attribute a meaningful value to them. If you plan to pledge your intellectual property as security for a loan, it would be beneficial for you first to attempt to obtain an independent appraisal of it.

REPAYMENT

When and how the loan will be repaid is closely associated with the questions of how much money is sought and for what purpose. The lender will use judgment and professional experience to assess your business acumen and the likelihood of the business's future success. The lender will want to know whether or not the proposed use of the borrowed funds justifies the repayment schedule requested. As the borrower, you must be able to demonstrate that the cash flow anticipated from business operations will be adequate to meet the repayment terms if the loan is granted.

Business Outlook

The lender will be evaluating the *business outlook*, both for your company in particular and the restaurant industry in general, in light of contemporary economic realities. The lender must determine if your proposed use of the loan can reasonably be expected to produce the anticipated increase in revenues for your business. While your proposed plan may appear viable on paper, it may not be realistic given the state of the economy within which your company operates.

Financial Evidence

Remember that bankers prefer to make loans to solvent, profitable, growing businesses. They seek assurance that the loan will contribute to that growth, since repayment ability is directly related to business success. Bankers are generally not interested in lending money so that a business can pay off existing loans.

To aid the bank in understanding the financial health of your restaurant business, you probably will be asked to provide specific financial data. Two basic financial documents are customarily submitted for this purpose—a balance sheet and a profit-and-loss statement. The *balance sheet* will aid the bank in evaluating your business's viability, while the *profit-and-loss statement* summarizes the business's current performance. Unless yours is a new venture, you should be prepared to submit these financial reports for at least the past two or three years, since they are the principal means for measuring your company's stability and growth potential. Ideally, an independent accountant will have prepared these statements. The lender may also request copies of the business's recent tax returns.

ANALYZING YOUR BUSINESS POTENTIAL

In interviewing loan applicants and in studying the financial records of businesses, the bank is especially interested in the following facts and figures.

General Information

A key area that the bank reviews is your records and recordkeeping. Are the company books and financial records up to date, accurate, and in good condition, or are they incomplete, infrequently maintained, and in disarray? Haphazard recordkeeping not only fails to reflect the business's true financial state, but demonstrates poor management skills. For obvious reasons, banks are reluctant to back poorly run businesses, viewing them as too risky.

The lender will also be interested in the current condition of your business liabilities. Are your accounts payable and notes payable being paid in a timely fashion, or are they overdue? If you are not presently able to meet existing debts, the lender will be hard-pressed to understand how you expect to be able to meet any additional obligations. Perhaps the requested funds will solve cash flow problems you now have and will also increase earnings so that you will be able to bring past-due accounts current, while adequately handling the added debt.

IN PLAIN ENGLISH

You might overcome the lender's skepticism by presenting a well-thought-out, solid business plan that clearly demonstrates how the new loan will solve rather than add to the business financial problems and will boost revenues.

Additionally, the lender will likely want to know the salaries of the owners, managers, and other company officers, to see if they are reasonable. Excessive salaries represent an unacceptable drain on company resources and profits that may adversely affect the company's ability to meet debt obligations.

The lender will also be interested in the size of your workforce. Does it seem adequate to maximize the business potential, or does it seem excessive compared to similar restaurant businesses?

You should be prepared to discuss the adequacy of your company's insurance coverage, your present tax situation (whether all taxes are current), and, if your business sells a food or related product, the size, if any, of your order backlog.

All these factors say something about the financial state of your food business. Although the lender may inquire into other areas, the borrower who knows the type of general information of interest to a lender, and can present it articulately, has an increased chance of having the loan approved.

Supplies, Inventory, and Bookings

The prospective lender will be interested in your source of supplies and whether you have an adequate inventory of necessary supplies on hand. The lender will also want to know what alternative plans you have for supplies in the event your primary supplier is unable to meet your needs.

If your business involves the sale of goods, the bank will need to know the state of the current inventory. Banks are interested in unpledged inventory as a possible source of collateral and also as a source of future revenues. The bank may also be interested in the inventory turnover rate, which reflects the demand for your product and aids in evaluating the accuracy of your revenue projections.

Since many restaurant businesses rely on bookings, lenders will want to know how far out and how extensive your bookings are. Is your restaurant booked for the holiday season? Is your catering business busy all summer? Will your business be participating in local food festivals? These are all questions you must be able to answer to the bank's satisfaction.

Fixed Assets

Because fixed assets can be used to secure loans, the bank will likely be interested in the type, condition, age, and current market value of your company's equipment, furnishings, and the like. You should be prepared to explain how these assets have been depreciated, their useful life expectancy, and whether they have previously been mortgaged or pledged as collateral to another lender. It is not uncommon for restaurant kitchen appliances to become leasehold improvements and thereby unavailable to be pledged as security for a loan.

You should also be ready to discuss any need or plans to acquire new assets. On the one hand, this need could mean additional debt obligations in the near future. On the other hand, it could explain and justify your projected growth.

OPTIONS FOR OWNERS OF NEW BUSINESSES

The preceding analysis applies primarily to loan requests made by established, proven businesses. New business loan applicants will probably not be able to supply much of the information previously described. While this will not necessarily preclude having a loan approved, it could make its approval more difficult. You should be aware that new business loans constitute only approximately 5% of all business loans made.

This reluctance to finance unproven businesses, understandably frustrating to new business owners, is consistent with the traditionally conservative nature of banks, which owe a fiduciary duty to their stockholders and depositors to invest funds in a prudent, responsible manner. In light of the extraordinarily high failure rate of restaurant businesses, compounded by the fact that a new business generally cannot provide adequate financial data to evaluate its potential for success, the lender is hard-pressed to justify making high-risk loans. Even when the new business borrower offers more than adequate collateral to secure the loan, the request may be denied.

Banks are comfortable lending money and earning profits from the interest charged on their loans. They are not comfortable in the role of an involuntary partner in the failing business of a delinquent debtor. Even though banks secure loans with a wide range of collateral, they (understandably) are not anxious to have to foreclose on that security. They are not in the business of selling business equipment or inventory, or of trying to run a restaurant. Although banks try to protect themselves by lending only a fraction of the collateral's market value, they still may not obtain the full amount that they are owed in a *distress sale* of that collateral, since this type of sale traditionally attracts bargain hunters who will often buy only at prices well below true market value. With an understanding of these dynamics, a new business loan applicant can better appreciate a bank's hesitation in approving a loan.

Nonetheless, banks do make some loans to new businesses. The entrepreneur will need to demonstrate a good personal reputation for paying debts and offer evidence of business management skills. Emphasize any firsthand knowledge and expertise you may have in the type of business you propose to establish as a result of having been previously employed in the restaurant industry. In addition, provide a sound business plan to support your projections. You can further improve your chances of obtaining a loan if you have invested your own money in the business, thus indicating your confidence in its success. If possible, show that the business has a good debt-to-equity ratio and that it is not saddled with an inordinately high debt.

Even if your loan application is initially refused, it is important to establish a good working relationship with a bank. Any initial business success will impress upon the bank the soundness of your plan, thereby opening the door for future financing, should the need arise.

LENDER'S RULES AND LIMITATIONS

Once the loan has been approved in principle, it is likely that the bank will impose certain rules and constraints on you and your business. These serve to protect the lender against unnecessary risk and against the possibility of your engaging in poor management practices. You, your attorney, and your business advisor should evaluate the terms and conditions of the loan in order to determine whether it is acceptable. If the bank's requirements are too burdensome, it may be appropriate for you to decline this loan and seek alternative financing. Never agree to restrictions to which you cannot realistically adhere. On the other hand, if the terms and conditions of the loan are acceptable, even though they are demanding, it may be appropriate to take the loan. In fact, some borrowers view these limitations as an opportunity for improving their own management techniques and business profitability.

IN PLAIN ENGLISH

Especially when making long-term loans, the lender will be interested in the net earning power of the borrowing company, the capability of its management, the long-range prospects of the company, and the long-range prospects of the restaurant industry.

As a result of the bank's scrutiny of your company, the kinds of limitations imposed will depend to a great extent on the company itself. If the company is a good risk, only minimum limitations need to be set. A poor risk, of course, should expect greater limitations. Three common types of limitations you are likely to encounter are repayment terms, use of pledged security, and periodic reporting.

Repayment Terms

The bank will want to set a loan-repayment schedule that accurately reflects your ability to earn revenues sufficient to meet the proposed obligation. Risky businesses, such as those in the restaurant industry, can expect shorter terms, whereas proven enterprises may receive longer periods within which to repay the loan.

Use of Pledged Security

Once a lender agrees to accept collateral to secure a loan, it will (understandably) be keenly interested in assuring that, should the need arise, the collateral will still be available to satisfy the debt. To this end, the lender may take actual possession of the collateral if it is stocks, bonds, or other negotiable instruments. Of course, a bank is not likely to take physical possession of a business's inventory or fixed assets and remove them to the bank's vault.

There are, however, other ways a bank can secure your fixed assets while allowing you to use them. For example, the lender could *perfect*—legally establish—a security interest in furnishings and intellectual property, as well as equipment used in your restaurant, by filing a *financing statement* in the appropriate state or county office. (A *security interest* is the legal term for a lender's rights in collateral.) Real estate mortgages are perfected by having them recorded in the appropriate government offices, and security interests in inventory can be perfected for most purposes by filing a financing statement. In these situations, the bank may impose restrictions on the use of the collateral and require that it be properly maintained and adequately insured. The bank may further limit or prohibit you from pledging the same collateral for any other business debts or loans.

While this sounds reasonable, you should recognize that such restrictions may seriously hamper your ability to borrow additional funds should the need arise. For example, if inventory is used as collateral, you must find out exactly how much of your inventory is involved. A bank may ask for only a percentage of the total to secure the loan. More likely, though, the bank's security interest will extend to the company's entire inventory on hand at any given time, as well as any later-acquired items. Herein lies the potential problem. The inventory's value may greatly exceed the amount of the loan that it secures. Nonetheless, you may find yourself in the position of not being able to use any of the inventory as collateral for additional loans. If this situation is likely to arise in your business, you are well-advised to consider alternative sources of collateral.

Periodic Reporting

To protect itself, a lender may require you to supply it with certain financial statements on a regular basis, perhaps quarterly or even monthly. From these, the lender can see if the business is performing up to the expectations projected in the loan application. This type of oversight serves not only to reassure the lender that the loan will be repaid, but also to identify and help solve problems before they become insurmountable and threaten the business viability.

DETAILS OF THE AGREEMENT

The loan agreement itself is a tailor-made document—a contract between the lender and borrower—that spells out in detail all the terms and conditions of the loan. The actual restrictions placed on the borrower will generally be found in the agreement under a section entitled "Covenants." Negative covenants are things that you may not do without the lender's prior approval, such as incurring additional debt or pledging the loan's collateral or other business assets to another lender as collateral for a second loan. On the other hand, positive covenants spell out those things that you must do, such as carry adequate insurance, provide specified financial reports, and repay the loan according to the terms of the loan agreement. With the lender's prior consent, the terms and conditions contained in the loan agreement may be amended, adjusted, or even waived. Remember that you can negotiate the loan terms with the lender before signing. While the bank is in the superior position, legitimate lenders are often happy to cooperate with qualified borrowers.

THE LOAN APPLICATION

Having targeted the source for funds and analyzed your business in terms you now know lenders look at, you are ready to develop the loan request. Though most lenders will require the application to include the same standard essential information, they often differ as to the prescribed format of the application. Some lenders may provide suggested formats; others may require a specific format. The actual content, length, and formality will depend on the lender's familiarity with your business, the amount of money requested, and the proposed use of the borrowed funds. A simple application form and a conversation may be adequate for your local banker. The start-up restaurant business seeking substantial funds from lenders unfamiliar with it or the industry will be required to provide much more extensive documentation, including a detailed plan of the entire business.

The business loan applicant is typically asked to submit some or all of the following information.

- *Personal financial statements.* These indicate the applicant's personal net worth. This is helpful to the lender in evaluating creditworthiness and revealing potential sources of collateral, as well as estimating repayment capabilities.
- *Recent and current tax returns* (usually for the last three years, if available). These should include individual and business returns.
- *The business financial statements.* As mentioned, these ideally should extend back for at least two or three years and should have been prepared and authenticated by an independent accountant. The lender may also request cash flow statements and profit projections.
- *A business history.* This should include past profit or loss patterns, current debt-to-equity ratio, current and projected cash flow, and present and projected future earnings.
- *A business plan.* This should explain the proposed use of the requested funds and how the loan will benefit the business. The length and content of this plan will vary according to the financial health of the applicant's business and the amount and type of loan sought. (see Chapter 3.)

Other documentation may also be required. The individual lender will indicate what is needed.

IMPORTANCE OF COMMUNICATION WHEN PROBLEMS ARISE

Once a loan is approved and funds disbursed, the borrower must address a new set of obligations and liabilities. If all goes according to plan, the loan proceeds are invested, the business prospers, the loan is repaid on schedule, and all parties live happily ever after. However, the restaurant industry is fraught with uncertainty. If the business falters and revenues tumble, the borrower may not be able to meet the debt obligations. In this unfortunate event, it becomes imperative that the borrower act responsibly, choosing to view the lender as a potential ally in solving problems, rather than as an adversary.

At least initially, banks are not eager to exercise their right to foreclose on the collateral, securing the loan at the first indication that the debt may not be repaid. They likely have no experience in marketing the types of collateral involved, nor do they want to run a distress sale, which, at best, would probably bring in only a fraction of the money owed. Additionally, foreclosing against the business assets further decreases the bank's chance of recovering any of the unpaid balance, since the borrower, having been stripped of the means to carry on the business, is likely to be insolvent and facing bankruptcy. Even if the lender can liquidate the collateral at its current fair market value, that value may be well below the value agreed upon when the loan was made. For these and other reasons, banks foreclose on collateral only as a last resort.

Bear in mind that, in general, lenders prefer to work with a potentially defaulting debtor to help ease the debt burden so that the borrower can overcome the problems, stay in business, and re-establish the enterprise's profitability. To this end, lenders have learned to identify a variety of red flags as indications that the debtor is experiencing financial difficulty. For example, the alert is sounded when loan payments start to be made later and later each month or when the business's checking account increasingly shows checks being dishonored for insufficient funds.

When the lender sees these signals, the account may be assigned to a separate department set up within the bank to assist borrowers in overcoming problems.

The bank may be willing to offer a variety of accommodations to help the borrower. Repayment terms can be extended, the amount of payment due each month can temporarily be reduced, or the bank may accept repayment of interest only for a specified time. The bank may be in a position to offer advice for ways to help solve the business problems, particularly if poor management is the source of the difficulties.

How far and to what extent the bank will be willing to accommodate or assist a delinquent debtor very often depends on the attitude and degree of cooperation of the debtor. Hard-pressed debtors often fail to understand the importance of establishing a cooperative, rather than an adversarial, relationship with the lender. Expecting a bank to be sympathetic to one's plight and to make concessions seems unreasonable when the borrower waits until the debt is long past due before approaching the lender to explain the problems. Additionally, a bank is not likely to be too sympathetic toward a borrower who fails to return phone calls and virtually disappears or who is always unavailable to discuss the problem.

The lender is likely to be most cooperative with the hard-pressed debtor who alerts the bank to problems early on. The debtor should explain what efforts are being made to remedy the problems and keep in close contact with the bank, informing it of current developments and the progress made toward solution of the problems.

A favorably impressed lender can be an invaluable asset to your business, not only in granting loans, but also in helping you out in difficult times. Do not underestimate the need for establishing a solid, professional relationship with your lender. The ultimate success and growth of your business may depend on it.

5

GOING PUBLIC

At some point, you may determine that you wish to obtain capital from investors rather than borrow from lenders, and you may, therefore, consider having your business conduct a public securities offering. Each year, many private businesses *go public*.

In 2004, 260 companies raised more than $50 billion through their initial public offerings. Some companies that went public have become disillusioned and are returning to their former private status. It is worthwhile to look at the pros and cons of going public and some of the factors to consider before making that crucial decision.

Securities include stocks, bonds, limited partnership interests, and certificates of ownership in LLCs. A general partner's interest in a general partnership may be considered a security, though the law appears to favor a reality test. Any so-called *investment contract* can be deemed to be a security. Even exotic transactions, such as the purchase of profits from the ultimate sale of aged whiskey or profits from the sale of oranges growing on trees in an orange grove, have been declared to involve securities. Whenever one party pledges cash or its equivalent in property in exchange for an interest in a project, a security is involved. Whenever an individual or business sells a passive interest in a business, a security is involved.

Every sale of a security requires the seller or issuer to comply with a host of legal formalities unless an *exemption* from compliance is available. The law governing securities is one of the most technical and complex, and it is essential for you to work with an experienced securities lawyer when attempting to obtain investments in your business.

Even during the creation of a business entity, the securities law should be considered. Your attorney should determine whether an appropriate exemption from securities compliance is available or if you must undertake the time-consuming and expensive process of registering the securities you will be issuing. Most small businesses are exempt from securities compliance, and their formative years will likely not involve a securities registration.

ADVANTAGES OF GOING PUBLIC

Access to capital and increased prestige are the motivating forces behind going public. Issuing stock has the advantage of raising capital without obligating the business to repay loans. The additional capital allows for continued growth, even when earnings and bank loans are insufficient to meet expansion objectives. Also, a successful public offering can improve net worth and debt-to-equity ratio, thereby increasing credibility and financing leverage with lenders.

Public offerings also enhance a company's prestige by increasing its visibility within the business community. The prestige of going public can be an effective device for attracting top-rate management executives. In turn, a strong management team is often the key to both increasing profitability and attracting new investors.

DISADVANTAGES OF GOING PUBLIC

Disadvantages of going public are primarily high costs and diminished control over the company. The costs of going public include printing prospectuses, attorney's and accountant's fees, filing fees, and underwriter commissions. Businesses contemplating a public offering should expect an initial outlay of $50,000 to $250,000. In addition, going public increases a business's administrative costs. Going public has always meant more regulations to adhere to and more paperwork to process. Public corporations undergo extensive auditing, and must gather and disseminate information for their shareholders. They must also comply with a host of regulations that have been adopted in an attempt to cure the ills that have surfaced in recent years. These additional administrative functions add to the overall cost of doing business.

While shareholders supply much needed capital to a growing business, they also usurp a degree of control over the company's operations. Suddenly, management is beholden to investors whose interest in short-term profits may conflict with what is best for the long-term health of the business. Shareholders and the general public (including competitors) must also be apprised of previously private information, such as details about management, organization, executives, products, sales, and profit figures. Public divulgence of this information may put a business at a competitive disadvantage. Furthermore, minority shareholders have certain *dissenter* and *minority rights* that give them a voice disproportionate to the size of their ownership interests.

IN PLAIN ENGLISH

High costs and diminished control over the business must be carefully weighed before undertaking the rigors of going public.

THE INITIAL PUBLIC OFFERING

Deciding to go public and implementing that decision is a time-consuming and complicated task. A company must first determine whether it is in an appropriate position to make a public offering, and then choose the optimal timing. Factors to consider include the availability of other means of financing, the degree of financial need, and the market conditions for the specific product or services being offered. Since an *initial public offering* (IPO) is highly complex, any business proceeding with an IPO needs to assemble a professional team to assist with the myriad legal and financial considerations that are inherent in the process. This support team typically includes experienced legal counsel, independent accountants, investment bankers, underwriters, and selling agents.

FEDERAL AND STATE SECURITIES LAWS

The complex nature of securities law underscores the need for experienced legal counsel. The laws are promulgated under both state and federal statutes. The *Securities and Exchange Commission* (SEC) is responsible for administering the federal securities laws. Its purpose is to assure equal access to and full disclosure of all material facts about a business. However, the SEC recognizes that the burden of disclosure is often excessive and nonessential as applied to smaller businesses. Consequently, special procedures and exemptions have been established for small businesses to simplify and expedite the registration process.

Compliance with federal law does not end the matter. A securities issuer must also comply with state provisions known as *blue sky laws*, which are sometimes even more stringent than the federal statutes. Consequently, stricter state provisions regarding the registration of small issues may offset the benefits of simplified procedures and exemptions under federal law. Nevertheless, the small business must comply with the stricter state provisions.

Violations of securities laws can result in civil and criminal liability. Sanctions include rescission of the entire offering, money damages, injunction against or voiding of business transactions, and even criminal prosecution. Furthermore, all securities, whether registered or exempt, are subject to strict antifraud provisions. Liability of the issuer is unlimited and extends to significant shareholders, as well as to other related persons or entities.

THE ATTORNEY'S ROLE

The complex nature of securities law makes the experienced attorney an indispensable part of any successful public offering. The attorney must ensure adherence to all relevant laws and regulations. The attorney must also make the company aware of possible exemptions, advise on necessary disclosures, and assist in preparing the necessary disclosure documents, such as a prospectus or offering memorandum and a registration statement. Furthermore, an experienced attorney can review existing contracts and advise changes, file necessary documents for the SEC, and review and recommend internal structural changes that will ease the company's transition from private to public.

THE ACCOUNTANT'S ROLE

A significant part of any public offering is the accounting required by the SEC. Accountants must provide audits of the company to be sure that its financial data is current and, when appropriate, prepare earnings projections or forecasts. The accountant will work closely with the attorney during the registration process.

THE BANKER'S ROLE

Many companies will need some interim (bridge) financing before the offering is completed. The banker may assist with this interim financing. In addition, many companies are funded by a combination of financing vehicles, such as conventional loans, lines of credit (secured by inventory, accounts receivable, or both), and traditional equity financing (stock). The banker should assist the company in determining its optimum funding mix. The banker will also aid the company in obtaining loans, when appropriate.

THE UNDERWRITER'S AND SELLING AGENT'S ROLES

Rarely will a company be in a position to sell its own securities. It is, therefore, important for an underwriter to be retained for the purpose of placing the investment. Underwriters generally have a network of sales agents who will assist them in selling the company's securities. Generally, there are three kinds of underwriting.

1. In *firm underwriting*, the underwriter purchases the entire offering at a discount and resells it to investors. This is customarily used for very large, established companies with an existing public market.

2. In *standby underwriting*, the underwriter commits to sell a certain amount of the offering and agrees to purchase up to that portion if it is not sold to investors. Again, this form of underwriting is customarily confined to large, established companies with an existing public market in their securities.

3. *Best efforts underwriting* is the most common for IPOs, smaller companies, and private placements. In this form of underwriting, the underwriter merely agrees to use its best efforts to sell the offering. There is no assurance, however, that any securities will actually be sold, and there is no obligation on the underwriter to purchase unsold securities.

PRIVATIZATION

While many companies go public in order to satisfy business and other needs, some publicly traded companies have *gone private*. The process of *privatizing* a public company is complex, but typically involves a situation whereby an individual company or group offers to purchase the stock or ownership interest from public holders for a price that exceeds the then-trading price of that security. This type of transaction is more likely to occur when it is believed that the publicly traded company's potential value could be enhanced if the individual or group acquiring these securities had more control.

The process of taking a business private is as technical and demanding as the process of taking it public. Compliance with the laws surrounding so-called *tender offers* and the rules imposed by the SEC also necessitates the skills of experienced securities lawyers, investment bankers, underwriters, and the like.

IN PLAIN ENGLISH

The law surrounding securities is pervasive. It touches every transaction in which businesses obtain investments. Determining whether your business must comply with some or all of the federal and state securities laws is essential. You should work with your attorney, accountant, and business advisor in order to make this determination and avoid the undesirable consequences that may result from violating the securities laws.

6

CONTRACTS

Contracts are an essential part of virtually every business, including those in the restaurant industry. Clearly, the entire field of contract law cannot be covered here, but you should be aware of some of the ramifications in contract law to see where you need to be cautious.

WHAT IS A CONTRACT?

A *contract* is a legally binding promise or set of promises. The law requires that the parties to a contract perform the promises they have made to each other. In the event of nonperformance—usually called a *breach*—the law provides remedies to the injured party. (For the purposes of this discussion, it is assumed that the contract is between a business and a person, though it frequently involves person-to-person or business-to-business arrangements as well.)

The three basic elements of every contract are the *offer*, the *acceptance,* and the *consideration.* Suppose a restaurant patron orders a salad (the offer). The server brings the salad (the acceptance). The menu stated the price (the consideration). That is the basic framework, but many variations can be played on that theme.

TYPES OF CONTRACTS

Contracts may be express or implied, and they may be oral or written. Generally, at least two types of contracts must be in writing if they are to be legally enforceable:

- any contract that, by its terms, cannot be completed in less than one year, and
- any contract that involves the sale of goods for over $500.

An *express contract* is one in which all the details are spelled out and can be either oral or written. If you are going to the trouble of expressing contractual terms, though, you should put your understanding in writing. For example, you might make a contract with a supplier for six dozen gallons of apple cider to be delivered to your restaurant on October 1, at a price of $1.75 per gallon, to be paid within thirty days of receipt. This scenario is fairly straightforward. If either party fails to live up to any material part of the contract, a breach has occurred and the other party may withhold performance of its obligation until receiving assurance that the breaching party will perform. In the event no such assurance is forthcoming, the aggrieved party may have a cause of action and sue for breach of contract.

If the apple cider is delivered on October 15 and your restaurant had advertised the availability of the special apple cider during the month of October, time was an important consideration and the restaurant would not be required to accept the late shipment. If time is not a material consideration, however, then even with the slight delay, this probably would be considered *substantial performance*, and your restaurant would have to accept the delivery.

Implied contracts are customarily not reduced to writing and need not be very complicated. An example might be if you call a supplier to order new table linens without making any express statement that you will pay for them. The promise to pay is implied in the order and is enforceable when the linens are delivered.

With implied contracts, however, things can often become much stickier. Suppose a law firm has your restaurant cater a business lunch to try out your service. You deliver a first-class meal. The law firm likes the food and is overheard commenting how great it tastes. Is there an implied contract to pay for the meal in this arrangement? That depends on whether you are normally in the business of giving away large, free samples of food.

You enter into many contracts without thinking much about them, such as the exchange of promises that takes place between your business and the company supplying your telephone service. (The telephone company agrees to provide certain telecommunications services in exchange for your promise to pay for those services under certain agreed-upon terms.) Even the issuance of coupons implicates contract law because a coupon is a written offer, which, once accepted by the customer, must be honored by the restaurant. It is, therefore, important to state all relevant terms on the coupon, including the expiration date.

In order to examine the principles of offer, acceptance, and consideration, some examples are in order. For these examples, a hypothetical business owner Pat Smith owns a restaurant that is decorated with original art by local artists that is for sale. In the following situations, see whether an enforceable contract comes into existence.

- At a reception hosted at the restaurant, Jones expresses an interest in one of the pieces of art. "It looks like the market value of work by local artists is going up," Jones tells Smith. "I'd like to buy one of your pieces while I can still afford it."

  Is this a contract? If so, what are the terms of the offer—the particular piece, the specific price? No, this is not really an offer that Smith can accept. It is nothing more than an opinion or a vague expression of intent.

- Brown offers to pay $400 for one of the works in Smith's restaurant that is listed at $450, and Smith agrees to accept the lower price.

Is this an enforceable contract? Yes. Brown has offered in unambiguous terms to pay a specific amount for a specific item, and Smith has accepted the offer. A binding contract exists.

■ One day Jones shows up at Smith's restaurant and sees a particular painting, for which he offers $450. Smith accepts and promises to transfer title the next week, at which time Jones will pay for it. An hour later Brown shows up. She likes the same painting and offers Smith $600 for it.

Can Smith accept the later offer? No—a contract exists with Jones. An offer was made and accepted. The fact that the object has not yet been delivered or paid for does not make the contract any less binding.

■ Smith discusses certain repairs he would like Green to perform on an expensive painting that was damaged while on display in Smith's restaurant. He offers to pay $600 for the work if the restoration is satisfactory to him. Green completes the work, but when Smith arrives to pick up his painting, he refuses to accept it because the restoration work does not satisfy him.

Smith is making the offer in this case but the offer is *conditional* upon his satisfaction with the completed work. Green can accept the offer only by producing something that meets Smith's subjective standards—a risky proposition for Green. There is no enforceable contract for payment until such time as Smith indicates that the completed work is satisfactory.

Suppose Smith comes to Green's studio and says that the restoration work is satisfactory, but then, when Green delivers the restored painting to the restaurant, Smith says he has changed his mind. Is there an enforceable contract? Yes, the contract became binding at the moment he indicated the work to be satisfactory. If he then refuses to accept it, he would be breaching the contract.

As previously stated, contracts for goods over $500 must be in writing. The last example described was for services only. If the agreement involved both sale of the painting and its restoration, it would be a hybrid sale, for goods and services. Assuming the painting was over $500 in value, the contract should be in writing to ensure enforceability. If, however, the contract had been one for performance of personal services only—say, for restoration to be performed by Green on a painting in Smith's personal art collection, the *Uniform Commercial Code* (UCC) would not apply and the contract would be enforceable whether it was reduced to writing or not. (The UCC is a compilation of commercial laws enacted in some form in every state that establishes rules for commercial transactions.)

Oral vs. Written Contracts

Contracts are enforceable only if they can be proven. All the hypothetical examples previously mentioned could have been oral contracts, but a great amount of detail is often lost in the course of remembering a conversation. The best practice is always to put your understanding in writing. The function of a written contract is not only that of proof, but to make very clear the understanding of the parties regarding the agreement and the terms of the contract.

Some business owners prefer to do business strictly on the basis of a handshake, particularly with their suppliers. The assumption seems to be that the best business relations are those based upon mutual trust alone. Although there may be some validity to this, business owners nevertheless really should put their agreements in writing. Far too many trusting people have suffered adverse consequences because of their reliance upon the sanctity of oral contracts.

Under even the best of business relationships, it is still possible that one or both parties might forget the terms of an oral agreement. It is also possible that both parties might have quite different perceptions about the precise terms of the agreement reached. Thus, a written contract generally functions as a safeguard against subsequent misunderstandings or forgetful minds.

IN PLAIN ENGLISH

When the agreement is put into writing, there is much less doubt as to the terms of the arrangement.

Perhaps the principal problem with oral contracts lies in the fact that they cannot always be proven or enforced. Proof of oral contracts typically centers around the conflicting testimony of the parties involved. If one of the parties is not able to establish by a *preponderance of evidence* that his or her version of the contract is the correct one, then the oral contract may be considered nonexistent—as though it had never been made. The same result might occur if the parties cannot remember the precise terms of the agreement.

Of course, in your restaurant business, some contracts will nearly always be oral, such as when a customer makes a reservation. Although you may not have thought of a reservation as a contract, once your restaurant has accepted the customer's request for a reservation, legally your restaurant has established a contract with the customer. If your restaurant accepts reservations only if they are guaranteed with a credit card, then the contract will not exist until the customer has supplied the credit card number. Although you are not likely to require written contracts for reservations, you should have written policies regarding reservations, cancellations, no-shows, and so on, and ensure that they are followed by your staff.

When Written Contracts are Necessary

Even if an oral contract is established, it may not always be enforceable. As already noted, there are some agreements that must be in writing in order to be legally enforceable.

An early law that was designed to prevent fraud and perjury, known as the *Statute of Frauds*, provides that any contract that, by its terms, cannot be fully performed within one year, must be in writing. This rule is narrowly interpreted, so if there is any possibility, no matter how remote, that the contract could be fully performed within one year, the contract need not be reduced to writing.

For example, if your restaurant agreed to cater a corporation's holiday party each year for a period of five years, the contract would have to be in writing. By the very terms of the agreement, there is no way the contract could be performed within one year. If, on the other hand, the contract called for the restaurant to cater five events within a period of five years, the contract would not have to be in writing under the Statute of Frauds. It is possible, though perhaps not probable, that the five events could occur within the first year. The fact that the restaurant does not actually complete performance of the contract within one year is immaterial. So long as complete performance within one year is within the realm of possibility, the contract need not be in writing to be enforceable— it may be oral.

The Statute of Frauds further provides that any contract for the sale of goods valued at $500 or more is not enforceable unless it has been put into writing and signed by the party against whom enforcement is being sought. The fact that a contract for a price in excess of $500 is not in writing does not void the agreement or render it illegal. The parties are free to perform the oral arrangement, but if one party refuses to perform, the other will be unable to legally enforce the agreement.

The law defines *goods* as all things that are movable at the time the contract is made, except for the money used as payment. The real question becomes whether a particular contract involves the sale of goods for a price of $500 or more. Although the answer would generally seem to be fairly clear, ambiguities may arise.

For example, if a supplier agrees to provide a restaurant with all its produce needs for the coming year, how is the price to be determined? If the wholesaler delivers produce from a number of sources and the total purchase price exceeds

$500 but the price of the individual components is less than $500, which price governs? In light of these possible ambiguities, the safest course is to put all oral agreements into writing. Most states list additional circumstances requiring contracts to be in writing, so you should contact your attorney before entering into any important oral contract.

No-Cost Written Agreements

At this point, owners of small restaurant businesses might object, asserting that they do not have the time, energy, or patience to draft contracts. After all, they are in business to provide a service, not to formulate written contracts steeped in legal jargon.

Fortunately, the businessperson will not always be required to do this, since the vendor may be willing to draft a satisfactory contract. However, be wary of signing any form contracts. They will almost invariably be one-sided, with all terms in favor of whoever paid to have them drafted.

As a second alternative, the businessperson could employ an attorney to draft contracts, but this might be cost-effective only for substantial transactions, such as your lease, and for agreements you can use multiple times, such as catering and employment agreements. With respect to smaller transactions, the legal fees may be much larger than the benefits derived from having a written contract.

The Uniform Commercial Code provides businesses with a third and perhaps the best alternative. Remember, however, that the UCC applies only to the sale of goods. In situations where the UCC applies, your business need not draft contracts or rely on anyone else (a supplier, retailer, or attorney) to do so.

The UCC provides that where both parties are merchants and one party sends to the other a written confirmation of an oral contract within a reasonable time after that contract was made, and the recipient does not object to the confirming memorandum within ten days of its receipt, the contract will be deemed enforceable.

A *merchant* is defined as any person who normally deals in goods of the kind sold, or who, because of occupation, represents him- or herself as having knowledge or skill peculiar to the practices or goods involved in the transaction. Most people in the restaurant industry will be considered merchants.

It should be emphasized that the sole effect of the *confirming memorandum* is that neither party can use the Statute of Frauds as a defense, assuming that the recipient fails to object within ten days after receipt. The party sending the confirming memorandum must still prove that an oral contract was made prior to or at the same time as the written confirmation. However, once such proof is offered, neither party can raise the Statute of Frauds to avoid enforcement of the agreement.

The advantage of the confirming memorandum over a written contract lies in the fact that the confirming memorandum can be used without the active participation of the other contracting party. It would suffice, for example, to simply state: "This memorandum is to confirm our oral agreement."

Since you would then still have to prove the terms of that agreement, it would be useful to provide a bit more detail in the confirming memorandum, such as the subject of the contract, the date it was made, and the price or other consideration to be paid. Thus, you might draft something like the following.

> *This memorandum is to confirm our oral agreement made on July 3, 2006, pursuant to which supplier agreed to deliver to purchaser on or before September 19, 2006, five thousand sheets of letterhead for the purchase price of $600.*

The advantages of providing some detail in the confirming memorandum are twofold. First, in the event of a dispute, you could introduce the memorandum as proof of the terms of the oral agreement. Second, the recipient of the memorandum will be precluded from offering any proof regarding the terms of the oral contract that contradicts the terms contained in the memorandum. The recipient or, for that matter, the party sending the memorandum can introduce proof only regarding the terms of the oral contract that are consistent with the terms, if any, found in the memorandum. Thus, the purchaser in the above example would be precluded from claiming that the contract called for delivery of ten thousand sheets of letterhead because the quantity was stated in the written memo and not objected to. On the other hand, the purchaser would be permitted to testify that the oral contract required the supplier to engrave the letterhead in a specific way, since this testimony would not be inconsistent with the terms stated in the memorandum.

One party to a contract can prevent the other from adding or inventing terms that are not spelled out in the confirming memorandum by ending the memorandum with a clause requiring all other provisions to be contained in a written and signed document. Such a clause might read like the following.

> *This is the entire agreement between the parties and no modification, alteration, or additional terms shall be enforceable unless in writing and signed by both parties.*

If you use such a clause, be sure there are no additional agreed-to terms that have not been included in the written document. A court will generally be confined to the *four corners of the document* when trying to determine what was agreed to between the parties. An exception to this rule is that a court may allow oral evidence for the purpose of interpreting ambiguities or explaining the meaning of certain technical terms. The court may also permit the other party to introduce evidence of *past practices* in connection with the contract in question regarding other agreements between the parties or even in connection with contracts between other parties.

To sum up, you should not rely on oral contracts alone, since they offer little protection in the event of a dispute. The best protection is afforded by a written contract. It is a truism that oral contracts are not worth the paper they are written on. If drafting a complete written contract proves too burdensome or too costly, the restaurant businessperson should at least submit a memorandum in confirmation of the oral contract. That at least surpasses the initial barrier raised by the Statute of Frauds. Moreover, by recounting the terms of your agreement in the memorandum, you are in a much better position to prove the oral contract at a later date.

Essentials to Put in Writing

A written contract rarely needs to—or should—be a long, complicated document written in legal jargon designed to provide a handsome income to lawyers. A contract should be written in simple language that both parties can understand and should spell out the terms of the agreement.

A contract should include the following:

- the date of the agreement;
- identification of the parties, e.g., the buyer and seller in the case of sale of goods or services;
- a description of the goods or services sold;
- the price or other consideration; and,
- the signatures of the parties involved.

To supplement these basics, an agreement should spell out whatever other terms might be applicable, such as pricing arrangements, payment schedules, and insurance coverage. Many transactions are important enough that additional clauses covering certain contingencies should be added, as well.

Finally, it should be noted that a written document that leaves out essential terms of the contract presents many of the same problems of proof and ambiguity as an oral contract.

IN PLAIN ENGLISH

The terms of the contract should be well conceived, clearly drafted, conspicuous (i.e., not in tiny print that no one can read), and in plain English, so everyone can understand them.

CONTRACTING ONLINE

On June 30, 2000, President Clinton signed the *Electronic Signatures in Global and National Commerce Act* (E-SIGN), which became effective in October of that year. This Act was intended, among other things, to encourage online commerce and provide the parties who take advantage of it the ability to contract in cyberspace.

When a contract is required to be in writing, parties can decide to contract electronically by affirmatively agreeing to do so. When a company dealing with a consumer is required to provide a contract or notice in writing, that company must both seek the customer's consent to receipt of an electronic document and verify that the document can be accessed and retained by the consumer. For example, the company must notify the customer of the hardware and software requirements for accessing the document.

Once a consumer consents to electronic receipt of documents, the consumer must notify the company of any change in email address. If the customer desires to withdraw his or her consent to electronic receipt, the location where documents can be sent must be disclosed to the company as well.

Online contracting is available only when there is a method for preserving the electronic contracts and other relevant data electronically. This will eliminate the need for warehousing hard copies of the documents for online contracting. No special technology must be used for online contracting, and the parties are free to establish their own vehicle for accomplishing the Act's requirements. Electronically signed documents can be encrypted if the parties agree. In fact, this is likely to be the standard procedure, at least at the initial stages of the development of the online process of contracting.

7

FRANCHISING

Most successful hospitality businesses begin with a novel idea that is nurtured and grows into a profitable enterprise. The entrepreneur invests time, money, and energy into developing the concept—perhaps an innovative theme or unusual menu. The entrepreneur may also have worked on expanding the business when and where appropriate.

FRANCHISES

An alternative for some restaurant businesses is the franchise. A *franchise* is a right, or license, to follow an established, successful pattern. It allows the business to use the trademarks, recipes, advertising, and training provided through the franchisor. Those who purchase franchise opportunities are often more likely to succeed than those who start from scratch, since many of the mistakes that dissipate resources can be avoided. The purchaser of a franchise is literally acquiring the goodwill, know-how, and intellectual property of an established business.

Perhaps the best source today for looking into franchises is the Internet. Attending *franchise expos*, where a number of companies offering franchises present opportunities, is another method of gathering information. There are also a number of books on franchising available at public libraries and bookstores.

The *Federal Trade Commission* (FTC) has adopted regulations for companies offering the sale of franchise opportunities. In addition, most states have adopted some sort of franchise regulations. For example, many states require franchise opportunities to be registered prior to sale. A typical franchise statute defines a franchise as an agreement by which:

- a franchisee is granted the right to engage in the business of offering, selling, or distributing goods or services under a marketing plan or system formulated by a franchisor;
- the operation of the franchisee's business pursuant to such a plan or system is substantially associated with the franchisor's trademark, service mark, trade name, logo, advertising, or other commercial symbol designating a franchisor; and,
- the franchisee is required to give to the franchisor a payment or something of value (in legal terms, a *valuable consideration*) for the right to transact business in accordance with the marketing plan.

Companies that offer franchise opportunities are required to file with the appropriate regulatory agencies. They must also prepare extensive disclosure statements for publication in the FTC's *Uniform Offering Circular*. By obtaining a copy of the Uniform Offering Circular, those interested in a franchise will find a wealth of material, including:

- information identifying the franchisor, its affiliates, and the affiliates' business experience since joining the franchise;
- information describing the business experience of each of the franchisor's officers, directors, and those management personnel responsible for franchise services, training, and other aspects of the franchise program;
- a description of any lawsuits in which the franchisor or its officers, directors, and management personnel have been involved;

- information about any bankruptcies in which the franchisor or its officers, directors, and management personnel have been involved;

- information about the initial franchise fee and other payments that are required to obtain the franchise;

- a description of the continuing payments franchisees are required to make after a franchise is acquired;

- information about any restrictions on the quality of goods and services used in the franchise, where those goods and services can be purchased, and any restrictions requiring that purchases be made from the franchisor or its affiliates;

- a description of any assistance available from the franchisor or its affiliates in financing the purchase of the franchise;

- a list of restrictions on the goods or services franchisees are permitted to market;

- a description of any restrictions on the customers with whom franchisees may deal;

- a description of any territorial limitations affecting the franchisee;

- a list of the conditions under which the franchise may be repurchased or refused renewal by the franchisor, transferred to a third party by the franchisee, or terminated or modified by either party;

- a description of the training programs available to franchisees;

- a statement regarding the involvement of any celebrities or public figures in the franchise;

- a description of any assistance the franchisor will provide in selecting a site for the franchise;

- statistical information about the present number of franchises, the number of franchises projected for the future, the number of franchises terminated, the number the franchisor has decided not to renew, and the number repurchased in the past;

- the financial statements of the franchisor;

- a description of the extent to which franchisees must personally participate in the operation of a franchise;

■ a complete statement of the basis for any earnings claims made to the franchisee, including the percentage of existing franchises that have actually achieved the results that are claimed; and,

■ a list of the names and addresses of other franchisees.

After reviewing the information in the offering circular, the potential franchisee should ask some hard questions about the opportunity. What sort of controls will the franchisor have with respect to sale of product, territory, and so on? What controls over advertising or promises regarding advertising does the franchisor have? Has the franchisor appropriately protected the trademark in the federal trademark office and at the state level? Has the franchisor secured the appropriate domain name? Is the franchise for an indefinite term, or must it be renewed on a periodic basis? What are the terms of renewal? Does the franchisor's system seem to be workable, understandable, and able to provide benefits necessary to justify the expense of paying a franchise fee? Many franchisors have websites, which should be reviewed before considering the franchise. In fact, many of these websites contain information about obtaining a franchise.

You must determine whether you are willing to pay the expense of acquiring a franchise rather than creating your own business identity. There are pros and cons to both approaches, and it is important for you to consider the costs, benefits, risks, and rewards before undertaking either course.

One of the major sacrifices to be made when acquiring a franchise opportunity is creating your own business identity and perhaps franchising it to others. By acquiring a franchise, you are purchasing some degree of security in exchange for the potential that might be realized from your own creation.

You should also be aware of some franchise abuses that have surfaced. Many franchisees have been injured when the franchisor has permitted competition within a comparatively small geographic area, or established a company owned and operated in close proximity to an existing franchise operation, known in the trade as *cannibalizing*.

It is quite clear that the purchase of a franchise ranks as a significant investment. Before you make that investment, you should check out the pertinent information exhaustively, including consulting your business attorney and accountant, and contacting other franchisees to learn about their experiences with the franchisor.

WHAT TO LOOK FOR

The FTC has attempted to identify bogus opportunities, but the rate at which they emerge continues to outpace the regulators' resources. Particular care should be paid to Web-based offerings, since it is often impossible to determine the location of the franchisor and to obtain any relief if and when problems arise.

IN PLAIN ENGLISH

Before advertising your business opportunity or buying into someone else's, you should consult with an attorney experienced in this field of law.

There are many opportunities for developing or expanding a thriving business. Each has some potential for success and some risk of failure. Good sense, careful evaluation, and use of skilled professionals will aid you in making an informed decision.

8

PATENTS AND TRADE SECRETS

Ordinarily, before a business can achieve a market edge, something must distinguish it from other businesses in the same general category. Of course, you will want to protect that *something* that sets your restaurant apart, so that others cannot exploit its uniqueness. Several bodies of law may help you obtain this protection. The *copyright law* (discussed in Chapter 10) grants, in a tangible form, the right to prevent others from copying an original work to the author of that work.

Copyright protection is not granted to items of utility. If your restaurant's interior decorator commissions a decorative carved brick or block for use in an archway, no matter how beautiful, creative, original, or well-executed, that brick is not likely to be protected under the copyright laws of the United States. *Patent laws*, which allow an inventor the right to prevent others from exploiting a patented invention, do cover utilitarian objects.

PATENT PROTECTION

Decorative utilitarian objects may be granted protection under the design patent laws. For example, the design of a particular sofa or chair may be granted a design patent, though only the aesthetic and not the utilitarian features are protected. A so-called *mechanical* or *utility patent*, the one with which you are probably most familiar, may be obtained for any new and useful process or product that is a substantial technological innovation. Unfortunately, patents are quite costly and difficult to obtain. It often takes an inordinate period of time for the patent document to be issued, and the period of protection is comparatively short (only twenty years from the date of application). Despite this fact, many food-based businesses have been successful in exploiting their patented innovations. For example, spiral slicing around the bone of Honey-Baked Ham enjoyed a market edge during the period when the process was under patent protection.

INTERNATIONAL PATENTS

Generally speaking, each country administers its own patent system. The businessperson who wishes to obtain a patent in a foreign country must file for a patent in that country. One exception to this general rule is the *European patent regime*. A European patent application, which is filed at the *European Patent Office* in Munich, can designate almost any country in Europe. Once a European patent is obtained, the patent can be translated into the language of any other designated European country. By filing it in that country, the European patent may be registered in that country without going through another examination process. The official languages of the European Patent Office include English, so Americans can prosecute their patents in the English language.

TRADE SECRETS

Another form of protection, known as *trade secret law*, allows exploitation of a particular innovation and may afford even greater protection than the copyright or patent laws. A *trade secret* may loosely be defined as anything that has not been revealed and could give you a competitive advantage. The secret should cover something that you actually use in your hospitality business and that you take some reasonable steps to protect. A trade secret may be lost if the owner fails either to identify it or take reasonable steps to protect it. Otherwise, the trade secret protection is perpetual. In fact, one of the most famous trade secrets is the recipe for Coca-Cola, which is more than one hundred years old. Another famous example of successful trade secret protection is the herb-and-spice mixture used by KFC in its fried chicken recipe.

PATENT OR PADLOCK DILEMMA

The determination of whether patent or trade secret protection is most appropriate is sometimes referred to as the *patent or padlock dilemma*. You cannot obtain both kinds of protection, since achieving one will render the other impossible. The patent-versus-padlock decision must be made within one year after disclosure, since the patent laws provide that a patent can be obtained only when the invention in question has not been in public use or on sale for more than one year before application is made. Furthermore, use by the inventor for commercial purposes, even in secret, is considered a disclosure within the meaning of the patent law. The inventor must decide how the innovation will be protected during the first year. If trade secret protection is selected, then patent protection is probably lost forever.

Selecting a patent is also exclusive and will destroy trade secret protection, since the patent application must contain a full description of precisely what was invented. Once issued, the patent application will disclose the invention to the public and the patent may be viewed at **www.pto.gov**.

IN PLAIN ENGLISH

It is impossible both to get a patent and to keep some aspect of the invention secret.

Provided that the applicant files a non-publication request at the time of filing the patent application, and does not withdraw the request or file a corresponding foreign patent application, the applicant may withdraw the application at any time before the patent is issued without jeopardizing trade secret protection. In order to determine which of these methods of protection should be elected, you should consult an attorney or patent agent who specializes in intellectual property. (see Chapter 22.)

TRADE SECRET PROTECTION

All that is necessary for something to be protected as a trade secret is the following.

- It gives you a competitive advantage.
- You do, in fact, treat it as a secret.
- It is not generally known in your industry or business.

The fundamental question of trade secret law is: *What is able to be protected?* The way you use knowledge and information, the specific portions of information you have grouped together, and the mere assembly of information itself may all be trade secrets, even if what you consider important for your secrets is publicly available information. For example, if there are numerous recipes for a particular dish and you have selected one of them, the mere fact that you have selected this method may itself be a trade secret. The identity of your suppliers may be a trade secret, even if they are all listed in the phone book. The fact that you have done business with these people and found them to be reputable and responsive may make the list of their names a trade secret.

Many trade secrets will be embodied in some form of document. One of the first things you should do is to mark any paper, photograph, or the like, identifying it as *confidential*. You should also take steps to prevent demonstrations of your methods, preparations, and so on. Taking these steps will not create trade secret protection, but the fact that an effort has been made to protect the ingredients and methods you consider secret will aid you in establishing that you treated them as trade secrets, should litigation ever occur. In this area, a little thought and cleverness will go a long way toward giving you the protection of the trade secret laws.

First, you should have some degree of physical security. It has been said that physical security is 90% common sense and 10% true protection. You should restrict the access to the area in which the trade secret is used. Some precaution should be taken to prevent visitors from peering into your kitchen, where your secret recipes are used. The credentials of delivery and service persons should be examined. The donning of a disguise to gain entry into a restricted area is a favorite ploy of business spies. Employee access to trade secret information should be on a need-to-know basis. Employees should not be granted automatic free access to the information you desire to keep as a trade secret.

As noted, documents, pictures, or sketches containing trade secrets should be clearly labeled. A procedure should be established for controlled employee access to the documents. For instance, one person could be responsible for granting access, and a sign-in/sign-out process could be instituted for those permitted access to the documents, though less formal arrangements can be implemented for smaller operations.

If possible, the information that you consider to be a trade secret should be fragmented. This means no one employee should have possession of the entire secret; thus, no one person will have sufficient information to hurt you. This is the procedure adopted by Coca-Cola and the reason that its trade secret-protected recipe has lasted for so long. In a small restaurant, however, this may be impractical. It is also a good idea to have employees sign a confidentiality and nondisclosure agreement when hired. An attorney who deals with intellectual property can prepare agreements for use within your business.

If it ever becomes important for you to reveal a secret to an outsider, such as when you wish to have your recipe prepared by a commercial kitchen for retail sales, a different form of confidentiality agreement is in order. These agreements generally provide that, in exchange for disclosure of the confidential trade secret information, the party receiving such information will keep it in confidence and will not use or disclose it without the express written permission of the person making the disclosure. Again, your intellectual property lawyer can prepare such an agreement for you.

Another method of protecting your trade secret is to engage in some vague labeling. For example, if your trade secret consists of a unique recipe for a meat glaze, then instead of having the ingredients bear their true names, label them "Ingredient A," "Ingredient B," "Ingredient C," and so on. Then, if an employee quits or if a stranger happens into your kitchen, all they will learn is that by mixing some portion of A with some portion of B, combined with some portion of C, the desired result will be achieved. This will not be very useful information. Similarly, if the trade secret is the temperature at which a brownie is baked, instead of actually marking the thermometer, you may wish to have the original temperature marks removed and replaced by colored zones.

IN PLAIN ENGLISH

If you are publishing in or contributing to industry or trade journals, take care not to reveal trade secrets. Occasionally, restaurant owners or their employees inadvertently disclose valuable information in an attempt to impress their colleagues, competitors, or consumers.

In order to avoid the charge that you are stealing someone else's trade secret, you should question employees who come to work for you after working for a competitor. Ask if they are bound by any confidentiality agreements or if there is any possibility that their former employer might be concerned about the disclosure of proprietary information. If there is any possibility of a new employee using the competitor's trade secret information, the new employee should meet with the former employer and get written permission to use that information while working for you.

In the restaurant industry, many chefs have their own trade secrets. Whether these trade secrets will become the property of your restaurant or remain those of the chef should be the subject of negotiation between the parties and determined at the time the chef is hired. The agreement regarding ownership should be in writing.

Trade secrets have been deemed so important that, in the mid-1990s, the U.S. Congress passed a federal law making it a crime to misappropriate another's trade secret. Since its enactment, there have been several high profile cases underscoring both the importance of trade secrets and the federal government's efforts to help protect them.

Trade secret laws may be the only protection available for your business secrets. Therefore, care should be taken to restrict access to the information and to treat the information as truly secret. Contractual arrangements, both with employees and outsiders, are quite useful. These, coupled with your common sense in the day-to-day operation of your hospitality business, will go a long way in protecting your intellectual property.

9

TRADEMARKS

Branding has become a part of the lexicon of business terms. In fact, virtually every restaurant business strives to develop its brand and the awareness that results from this process. One of the most important aspects of branding is the establishment of a means of identifying a product or service by use of a name, symbol, logo, device, or combination of these items, known as *trademarks* and *service marks*. A trademark is a mark that is affixed to goods and a service mark is a mark that is used in connection with services, though both are commonly referred to as *trademarks* or *marks*. Currently, there are thirty-four international classifications for goods and twelve for services.

Although modern trademark law has broadened the protection available for trademark owners, its historical antecedents date back to medieval England. In those days, certain craft guilds often required members to place their individual marks on their products so that, in the event a product proved defective, the guild could trace its origins to a particular craftsman and impose appropriate sanctions. The use of marks enabled the guild to maintain the integrity of its name. Moreover, merchants would often affix marks to their products for purposes of identification. Should the product be stolen or misplaced, the merchant could prove ownership by the mark.

The use of marks for purposes of identification would no doubt have worked quite well in an ideal society where all the citizens led principled and moral lives, but this was not the case. It is not particularly surprising that unscrupulous merchants quickly realized that there was easy money to be made by using another's mark or one confusingly similar. The shoddy merchants could more readily sell their products by affixing to them the marks belonging to quality manufacturers.

It was in response to this problem of consumer fraud that the first trademark laws developed. Initially, the emphasis was on prevention of one person passing off products as that of another. In contrast, modern American law focuses upon whether one mark is sufficiently similar to another to cause confusion in the minds of the buying public. The emphasis has shifted from the subjective intent of a dishonest manufacturer or merchant passing off goods as those of another to the objective determination of consumer confusion.

Despite this shift, the essential purpose of trademarks and trademark laws has changed little since the days of the craft guilds. Trademarks still function primarily as a means of identifying the source of a particular product or service. Trademark laws are also designed to enable the trademark proprietor to develop goodwill for the product or service, as well as to prevent another party from exploiting that goodwill—regardless of whether that exploitation is intentional or innocent.

THE NEED FOR A RECOGNIZABLE MARK

What exactly is a trademark? A simplification of the federal definition follows.

> *Any word, name, symbol, device, or any combination thereof, adopted and used by a person, or that a person has a bona fide intention to use in commerce and subsequently does use, that identifies and distinguishes his or her goods or services, including a unique product or*

service, from those manufactured or sold by others, and indicates the source of those goods or services, even if that source is unknown.

A trademark owner may be a franchisee, licensee, broker, or distributor. The term *use in commerce* means the bona fide use of a mark in the ordinary course of trade—not a use made merely to reserve a right in the mark. Reservation of a mark prior to its use can be achieved by filing an *intent-to-use application* with the Patent and Trademark Office (PTO).

The key concept of trademark law is that the trademark must be *distinguishable*. In order to secure trademark protection, one must develop a distinctive mark. The most distinctive trademarks are those that are purely arbitrary or fanciful—those that have no meaning or connotation other than identifying the source of a particular product. For example, the trademark Häagen-Dazs to identify a brand of ice cream or Fuddrucker's as a restaurant chain is purely arbitrary. Less distinctive are trademarks that have another meaning, such as the trademark Sonic to identify a fast-food restaurant. Although trademarks such as Sonic are not purely arbitrary, they are nevertheless afforded substantial protection, since the other meaning bears no resemblance to the product identified.

PROHIBITED TRADEMARKS

Generic and descriptive names are not considered distinctive enough to be granted trademark status. A *generic* word merely identifies the product for what it is. Thus, the use of the name "Beer" to identify a brand of beer is generic and would not be accepted as a trademark. Similarly, a *descriptive* name only characterizes the attributes or qualities of the product. For example, using the name "Raisin Bran" to identify a cereal is merely descriptive of the product's ingredients, and such a mark might have difficulty gaining trademark status.

Generic words are never afforded trademark protection. Descriptive trademarks, however, may be protected in limited circumstances. A descriptive mark may be protected if the proprietor of the mark can prove that it has acquired a *secondary meaning.* Secondary meaning will exist when the public no longer connects the words of the trademark with the literal, dictionary meaning, but rather with a unique product. For example, the descriptive term "The Melting Pot" also has a secondary meaning as the (registered) trademark of a restaurant that serves fondues.

In the *Leathersmiths of London* case in the mid-1980s, however, the question was whether the name "Leathersmiths of London" was a protected trademark. The court held that the word "leathersmith" is generic, at least when used to describe someone who is in the business of working with leather, and therefore, is not entitled to trademark protection.

Some trademarks, even though they are considered distinctive, are nevertheless prohibited by statute or public policy. Obscene or scandalous trademarks are generally denied trademark protection. Trademarks that are deemed deceptive and misleading, such as the mark Idaho Potatoes to identify potatoes grown in some area other than Idaho, are also denied protection.

PROTECTING A TRADEMARK

Common law is the body of law developed from court decisions rather than from state or federal statutes. Federal or state registration of a trademark has certain advantages, but is not necessary. Common law protection of a trademark will suffice, and has the benefit of not requiring any interaction with governmental agencies.

In order to secure trademark protection, it is not sufficient merely to adopt a distinctive mark. The trademark must be used in the ordinary course of trade, or *used in commerce.* The use requirement is fundamental to trademark law and is necessary for common law protection, as well as federal and state registration. A trademark is deemed to be *used* when it has been placed in any manner on the product or its containers, the displays associated with it, or on any of the tags or labels affixed to the product. It is not always necessary that the trademark actually be physically affixed to the goods. As long as the trademark is associated with the product at the point of sale in such a way that the product can be readily identified as coming from a particular manufacturer or source, the trademark may be protected. It should be noted, however, that the mere listing of a trademark in a catalog, the ordering of labels bearing the trademark, the use of the trademark on invoices, or the exhibition of trademarked goods at a trade show may not be sufficient in and of itself to constitute use, since the use of the trademark is not associated with the point of sale.

IN PLAIN ENGLISH

To ensure trademark protection, the trademark proprietor would be well-advised to physically affix the trademark to the product. In this way, the product is certain to bear the trademark when it is sold. Proper use of a service mark is accomplished by identifying the service by the mark in advertising, signs, brochures, receipts, and the like.

Common law protects the trademark proprietor against someone else subsequently using a trademark that is confusingly similar. This raises the question of when trademarks are considered confusingly similar. Generally, trademarks will be confusing if they are similar in sound or appearance, particularly if the trademarks are affixed to or associated with similar products or services, or if products or services are marketed throughout the same or similar geographic areas. On the other hand, if two products or services bearing similar trademarks are not related or are marketed in different geographic areas, there may not be any infringement. However, with the advent of advertising on the World Wide Web, problems may occur. As discussed in Chapter 13, care must be taken to alert website visitors to the physical location of the advertised restaurant.

Thus, a Northwest restaurant chain could probably adopt and use a trademark already used by a restaurant in Maine, provided the mark of the Northwest business does not adversely affect the value of the trademark used by the Maine company. Moreover, a Northwest restaurant chain could probably adopt and use a trademark used by a Northwest chainsaw manufacturer. In these situations, there may be no infringement, since it is not likely that the use of the mark by the restaurant would confuse chainsaw purchasers. Here again, appropriation of another's trademark may be wrongful if the use, even by a non-competing business, would dilute the value of the mark to the original owner.

FEDERAL REGISTRATION OF A TRADEMARK

As noted earlier, the trademark proprietor can procure greater protection under federal or state statutes than under the common law. The federal statute governing trademarks is known as the *Lanham Act of 1946*. It is not the function of the Lanham Act to grant trademark rights, since those are secured by the common law principles, but rather, to provide a central clearinghouse for existing trademarks via registrations.

The *Trademark Law Revision Act of 1988* (TLRA) made substantive changes to the previous trademark laws, and the trademark law was amended in 1996 to add a federal *antidilution* provision. Though the Lanham Act provides much of the skeleton of trademark law, amendments have added the needed detail to make trademark law a more complete body of law.

It should be noted that there are two official registers for trademarks, the *Principal Register* and the *Supplemental Register*. The following sections on how to register a trademark apply to the Principal Register. A separate section included later in this chapter describes what the Supplemental Register covers and how it may be used.

Prior to enactment of the TLRA, a mark could be registered only upon actual use in interstate commerce. This requirement was satisfied when an applicant sold a few units of the product bearing the trademark in an interstate transaction. A mark could essentially be reserved for later use by making a *token use* at the time of application. The minimum token use requirement allowed the registering of trademarks that might never be used and possibly prevented other proprietors from legitimately using the mark. This judicially sanctioned practice also clogged the federal register with unused marks.

Under the TLRA, token use is no longer permitted. *Actual use* of the mark is required in order for a trademark to be registered, although an application can be filed based on a bona fide intention to use a mark in the future. This reserves and protects a mark for a limited time and to a limited extent prior to its being used in commerce. If the mark is not actually used within the prescribed time period, the trademark registration will be denied.

Applications Based on Actual Use

The use requirement is met if the mark is protected as a common law trademark. Once the proprietor has established a mark's actual use in commerce, the mark can be registered by filing an application with the Patent and Trademark Office. This process entails filling out an application, sending in a drawing of the mark (including specimens of the mark used in commerce), and paying the required fee, currently $375 (unless the registration is filed electronically, in which case the fee is reduced to $325). If the examining officer at the PTO accepts the application, the trademark will appear shortly thereafter in the *Official Gazette*. Anyone who believes that he or she would be injured by the issuance of the registration has thirty days to file a written notice stating the reasons for opposition. If nobody objects or if the objections are found to be without merit, a certificate of registration will be issued.

Applications Based on Intent to Use

Under the TLRA, a right to a particular mark can be preserved for future use through the so-called *intent-to-use* provision. This does not remove the requirement of actual use in commerce, which is still necessary for registration of the mark. Protection of a mark for future use can be accomplished by filing an application based on the applicant's *bona fide intent to use* the mark in commerce. An intent-to-use registration should not be requested merely for the purpose of attempting to reserve a mark. The statute does not explicitly define bona fide intent, but the good faith of the applicant will be determined from the circumstances surrounding the application and the applicant's conduct with respect to the mark. The history behind the statute's enactment suggests that the applicant's conduct concerning the intent to use the mark will be measured against standards accepted in the trade or business.

If the intent-to-use application satisfies the requirements of the PTO regulations, it will receive approval for publication in the Official Gazette. Upon such publication, a thirty-day period for opposition to registration of the mark begins to run. This period is similar to the one given to applications for registration of marks that are in actual use. Applications that go unopposed receive a *notice of allowance*. The date the notice is issued is very important, because the reservation of the mark is limited to a period of six months from the date of allowance, during which time actual use of the mark in commerce must begin or the trademark application will lapse.

If an applicant fails to commence using the mark in commerce within the allowable six-month period, it is possible to obtain an extension for another six months. This extension is automatic upon application and payment of fee only if submitted before the original six-month period expires. Four additional six-month extensions are also possible, but require, in addition to application and fee submission before expiration of the current six-month period, approval by the PTO upon a showing of good cause why such extension should be granted. In no event is the period between the date of allowance and the commencement of use of the mark in commerce permitted to exceed thirty-six months. In making a request for extension, the applicant must include:

- a verified statement of continued bona fide intent to use the mark in commerce;
- specification as to which classification(s) of goods and services the intent continues to apply; and,
- inclusion of the required fee, which is currently $150 per extension per classification of goods or services.

Once actual use of the mark in commerce has occurred, the applicant must file a *verified statement of use*. If everything is in order, the mark will be registered for use in connection with the goods or services that the statement of use indicates. The Commissioner for Trademarks will notify an applicant as to whether a statement of use has been accepted or refused. An applicant will be allowed to amend the statement of use if the mark was not used on all the goods initially identified.

IN PLAIN ENGLISH

Application forms may be obtained by calling the PTO at 800-786-9166, or from its website at **www.uspto.gov**.

Constructive Use

An important concept found in the Lanham Act and improved by later amendments is that of *constructive use*. This concept, which has been called the cornerstone of the intent-to-use method, applies to use-based applications, as well. When an application to register a mark is filed under the doctrine of constructive use, filing constitutes use of the mark as of the filing date. When the application to register is filed, a right of priority to exclusive use of the mark is created throughout the United States. This is true only if the mark is filed for registration on the Principal Register. The constructive use doctrine does not apply to applications on the Supplemental Register.

This doctrine gives applicants a strong incentive to file for registration as early as possible. The constructive use statute provides priority-filing protection and prevents others from acquiring the mark by simply using it before the intent-to-use applicant does. Constructive use greatly reduces disputes regarding which party has priority, thus saving costs and limiting uncertainty in infringement or opposition proceedings.

Exceptions to the priority right of use are marks used prior to the applicant's filing date and intent-to-use applications filed prior to the applicant's filing date. Applications for registration filed by foreign applicants are also excepted if the foreign application was filed prior to the constructive use application.

The current law generally prohibits *assignment* of intent-to-use applications, thereby preventing applications for marks being filed by individuals for the sole purpose of selling them. However, an intent-to-use application may be assigned to the applicant's business.

Benefits of Registration

First, registration enables a proprietor to use the "®" symbol or the phrase "registered trademark" in conjunction with the mark, which may deter others from using the mark. Proprietors of marks that have not been registered are prohibited from using the above designations with their marks. Commonly, "™" for trademarks and "SM" for service marks are used in conjunction with unregistered marks during the application period. These designations have no official status, but they do provide notice to others that the user is claiming a property right in the mark.

Second, registration on the Principal Register is *prima facie* evidence of the validity of the registration, the registrant's ownership of the mark, and the exclusive right to use the mark on identified goods in commerce.

Finally, a registered trademark that has been in continuous use for a period of five consecutive years may become incontestable. By registering the trademark, the proprietor may secure rights superior to those of a prior—but unregistered—user, but only if the original user does not object to the registrant's use within five years.

Under the trademark law, registration remains in effect for a period of ten years, and may be renewed in additional ten-year increments by filing an application for renewal during the six months prior to the expiration of the existing ten-year term. Registrations issued prior to November 16, 1989 received a first-term registration of twenty years. All subsequent registrations are for ten-year renewals. The registrations that issue from applications filed with the PTO and that were pending as of the effective date of the 1989 amendment have a first term of only ten years, even though filed under the previous law.

The Supplemental Register

Supplemental Register applications may be made directly if the applicant believes that registration on the Principal Register is unlikely or in response to the PTO's final refusal to register the mark on the Principal Register. This registration provides protection for individuals capable of distinguishing their marks from those of others, but whose marks do not comply with the requirements for registration on the Principal Register. Marks for the Supplemental Register are not published for or subject to opposition. They are, however, published as registered in the Official Gazette. If a person believes that she or he will be damaged by the registration of another's mark on the Supplemental Register, that person may, at any time, petition for cancellation of the registration.

Applications filed on the Supplemental Register cannot be based on intent to use and do not enjoy the benefits of constructive use. Under the Lanham Act, an application filed on the Supplemental Register has to be in lawful use for one year prior to the filing of the application. For a mark to be eligible for registration on the Supplemental Register under the 1989 amendment, the domestic applicant's mark must merely be in lawful use in commerce, meaning a bona fide use in the ordinary course of trade.

TRADEMARK LOSS AND INFRINGEMENT

Use or intent to use is a prerequisite to trademark protection. It should be noted that some forms of use might result in the loss of a trademark. A number of well-known trademarks—such as Aspirin, Thermos, and Escalator—have been lost as a result of improper usage. Trademark protection is lost because the mark is used in some capacity other than as an adjective modifying a noun. When a trademark is used as a noun or a verb, it no longer functions to identify the source of the product or service, but instead becomes the name of the product or service itself. At that point, the mark becomes generic and is not subject to protection.

Abandonment of a mark will also result in loss of protection. A trademark is deemed abandoned when it has not been used for two years and there is no intent to resume its use. Token use will not be sufficient to avoid abandonment. To avoid abandonment, the proprietor does not have to use the mark in interstate commerce in the ordinary course of trade or business, but the mark should be used in intrastate commerce.

Infringement

A trademark that is in use and has been infringed upon allows the trademark proprietor to sue the infringing party either for monetary damages or for an injunction prohibiting the infringing use, or sometimes for both. *Monetary damages* may be measured either by the plaintiff's losses resulting from the infringement or by the defendant's profits. In certain exceptional circumstances, such as when the defendant's conduct is willful and flagrant, the plaintiff might also be entitled to *exemplary damages* equal to three times the actual damages, as well as attorneys' fees.

The relevant sections under the Lanham Act provide remedies for infringement of marks that are actually in use. This effectively precludes an intent-to-use applicant from suing for infringement because use has not been made of the mark. The law permits anyone who feels that he or she will be damaged by acts that are likely to cause confusion, mistake, or deception as to the origin, sponsorship, or approval of the complainant's goods or services with those of another to sue for unfair competition. Under the Act, all remedies available for infringement actions are also available for actions of unfair competition.

Antidilution

In 1996, the federal trademark law was amended to provide special protection for *famous marks*. The statute does not define famous mark, though case law has adopted much of the legislative history that suggests that a famous mark is a mark that has been around for a long time and enjoys extensive notoriety.

In the past, it was possible to appropriate a mark for use in connection with goods or services that did not compete with those of the mark's owner, so long as there was no likelihood of confusion. As a result, it was possible, for example, to call a dog food "Cadillac," intending to suggest that it was the elite form of canine fare, despite the fact that the automobile manufacturer Cadillac did not have anything to do with the dog food. The likely intent of the dog food company was to suggest that it was the Cadillac of dog foods, and thus, the top of the line. Under the 1996 amendment, this type of use probably would not be permitted, since the dog food manufacturer's use of the mark Cadillac would likely be considered a dilution of the General Motors trademark.

While *antidilution statutes* had been in effect in several states, they were not universal. Now, the federal statute provides such protection, at least for famous marks. The remedies available for violations of the antidilution statute are comparable to those that are provided for trademark infringements. However, when the mark that is causing the dilution is not identical, it may be necessary to prove actual confusion.

INTERNATIONAL PROTECTION

In 2003, the United States became a party to the *Madrid Accord*, which is the closest this country has come to providing its citizens with international trademark protection. Under the Madrid Accord, Americans can apply for trademark protection in up to seventy countries by filing the appropriate application and paying the required fees to the United States Patent and Trademark Office. It is thus no longer necessary for Americans to hire specialists in every country in which trademark registration is desired. Under this new arrangement, the application filed with the U.S. Patent and Trademark Office can identify the member countries in which registration is sought, and the classes of goods or services to be covered. The registration can then be prosecuted through the PTO, although the application will be reviewed and accepted or denied by the Patent and Trademark Office in each country in which registration is sought. The savings in costs for Americans using this process is significant, and the convenience provides American businesses with a more efficient method of obtaining foreign trademark registrations in the Madrid Accord member nations.

STATE REGISTRATION

Trademarks can also be registered under state law. The trademark proprietor may file a trademark application with the appropriate state officer, along with documentation similar to that required by the Lanham Act. State law protection of a trademark does not extend beyond the borders of the state. The number of specimens of the mark needed to complete registration varies from state to state, and the registration fee also differs. Protection under state laws can be broader than what is found under federal laws, and remedies available under state laws are also very likely to be different from those found under the federal statute. If a conflict arises between federal and state trademark law, it is important to remember that, under the supremacy clause of the U.S. Constitution, federal law will supersede state law.

USING AN ATTORNEY

Obviously, registration can be quite beneficial to a restaurant that has invested time, money, and energy in developing a reputation for quality products and services. Procuring trademark protection on either the state or federal level may require a considerable amount of time and skill. In this regard, an attorney may prove invaluable. First of all, an attorney can determine if the benefits to be derived from registration justify the expenses. The total cost of federal trademark registration usually runs about $1,500, not counting any artist's fees for drawing a logo. Second, an attorney can research trademark databases to determine if there are any conflicting marks. Finally, an attorney can complete the application and deal with any problems that may occur while it is being processed for registration.

IN PLAIN ENGLISH

If you are interested in contacting attorneys who specialize in trademark work, you can consult the Yellow Pages of your telephone directory, check online (look under "intellectual property lawyers" or "patent attorneys"), or ask your state bar association for some recommendations.

10

COPYRIGHTS

It is quite common for restaurants to use menus, brochures, computer software, artwork, and similar materials created by others. These materials may be protected by the copyright law, and their unauthorized use may subject the user to liability for copyright infringement. There are, however, some situations in which you may be able to use another's work without obtaining permission. The guidelines for this use are found in the federal copyright law.

Some restaurants develop their own copyrightable brochures, advertising copy, catalogs, posters, and the like, and since businesspeople tend to take a proprietary view of their creations, they may wish to prevent others from using their work without permission. Again, the copyright law provides the vehicle by which these works may be protected.

Copyright law in the United States has its foundation in the Constitution, which provides in Article I, Section 8, that Congress shall have the power "to promote the progress of science and useful arts, by securing for limited time to authors and inventors the exclusive right to their respective writings and discoveries." The first Congress exercised this power and enacted a copyright law. The legislation was periodically revised by later Congresses until 1909. From

1909 until the *Copyright Revision Act of 1976*, which went into effect on January 1, 1978, no major changes were made in the law.

Prior to enactment of the 1976 law, unpublished works were protected by common law copyright governed by state laws. This protection could vary considerably from state to state. Federal protection under the 1909 Act began by protecting a published work to which a copyright notice was attached. The Copyright Revision Act of 1976 preempts the field of copyright law. In other words, it is now the only legislation governing copyright. This law was significantly amended in 1989 when the United States became a party to the international copyright treaty known as the *Berne Convention*.

Publication, within the context of copyright law, is a technical term that applies to all copyrightable material. Under the old law, it meant an unrestricted public display. Today, publication is defined as "the distribution of copies of a work to the public by sale or other transfer of ownership, or by rental, lease, or loan."

WHAT CAN BE COPYRIGHTED

Copyright protection can be granted to original works of authorship fixed in any tangible medium of expression. From the point of view of copyright law, an author is a creator—be it a photographer, sculptor, writer, computer programmer, or musician. Expressly exempt from copyright protection is any idea, procedure, process, system, method of operation, concept, principle, or discovery. In short, a copyright extends only to the expression of creations of the mind, not to the ideas themselves. Frequently, no clear line of division between an idea and its expression exists. For now, however, it is sufficient to note that a pure idea, such as a plan to create an innovative advertising program, cannot be copyrighted—no matter how original or creative that idea is.

The law and the courts generally avoid using the copyright law to arbitrate the public's taste. Thus, a work can be copyrighted even if it makes no pretense to aesthetic or academic merit. The only requirements are that a work be original and show some creativity. *Originality*—as distinguished from *uniqueness*—requires that a work be created independently. Originality, however, does not require that it be the only one of its kind. For example, cartographers who independently create identical maps are each entitled to copyright protection. Because their works often look similar to untrained observers, many cartographers will include an intentional minor error on a map so that if the identical error appears on another map allegedly created independently, this minor error will provide obvious evidence of copying.

SCOPE OF PROTECTION

A copyright is actually a collection of five *exclusive rights*. First is the *right to reproduce* a work by any means. The scope of this right can be hard to define, especially when it involves works such as microfilm or videotape. Under the Copyright Act of 1976, someone may reproduce protected works without permission only if such reproduction involves either a fair or an exempted use as defined by the Act (explained later in this chapter).

Second is the *right to prepare derivative works* based on a copyrighted work. A derivative work is one that transforms or adapts the subject matter of one or more preexisting works.

Third is the *right to distribute copies* to the public for sale or lease. However, once a person sells a copyrighted work or permits uncontrolled distribution, the right to control further uses of that work usually ends. This is known as the *first sale doctrine*. It is superseded in a situation in which the work is merely in the possession of someone else temporarily by virtue of bailment, rental, lease, license, or loan. In these instances, the copyright owner retains the right to control the further sale or other disposition of the work. Moreover, the first sale doctrine does not apply if the copyright owner has a contract with the purchaser restricting the purchaser's freedom to use the work, as is the case with many software programs. In such a case, if the purchaser exceeds the restrictions, he or she may incur liability. In this situation, however, the copyright owner's remedy generally will be governed by contract law rather than by copyright law.

One should distinguish between the sale of a work and the sale of the copyright in that work. If nothing is said about the copyright when the work is sold by the copyright owner, the seller retains the copyright. Since the purchaser of the work may not be aware of this, a seller may wish to call it to the purchaser's attention, either in the sales memorandum or on the work itself. If a license is granted, it should be in writing and should be very specific in the scope of rights being granted. The drafter of the purchase agreement should be clear in defining the boundaries of permissible uses.

IN PLAIN ENGLISH

A restaurant that has purchased a painting for its interior décor generally may not reproduce the painting on its menu unless expressly given that right.

Fourth is *the right to perform* the work publicly, such as to broadcast a film on television or to show it in a lecture room or meeting room.

Fifth is the *right to display* the work publicly. Once the copyright owner has sold a copy of the work, however, the purchaser has the right to display that copy, but is generally still prohibited from reproducing it.

These rights are *divisible*, which means they can be transferred in whole or in part. If the copyright owner takes no special action upon selling the work, he or she is presumed to have retained all rights. If desired, however, the copyright owner may explicitly transfer any one or more of these rights.

OWNERSHIP OF COPYRIGHT

As a general rule, the creator of a work owns the copyright, and therefore, owns the exclusive rights previously discussed. Under the old law, when a work was sold, ownership of a common law (*prepublication*) copyright passed to the purchaser unless the creator reserved the copyright in a written agreement. In other words, there was a presumption in the law that a sale included the work itself plus all rights in that work.

The Copyright Act of 1976, as amended, reversed the presumption that the sale of a work carries the copyright with it. Today, unless there is a written agreement to the contrary, the creator retains the copyright when the work is sold.

The creators of a joint work are co-owners of the copyright in the work. A *joint work* is defined as "a work prepared by two or more authors with the intention that their contributions be merged into inseparable or interdependent parts of a unitary whole." Whatever profit one creator makes from use of the work must be shared equally with the others, unless they have a written agreement that states otherwise.

The key point is the intent that the parts be absorbed or combined into an integrated unit at the time the work is created. The intent must exist at the time the work is created, not at a later date. The authors do not necessarily have to work together, work during the same period, or even know each other. However, the joint works definition does not include the situation in which an artist creates a work, such as a piano solo, without intending that the work involve another artist, and later commissions lyrics. If there is no intention to create a unitary or indivisible work, each creator may own the copyright to that creator's individual contribution.

In the case of *Ashton-Tate Corp. v. Ross*, the Ninth Circuit Court of Appeals held that joint authorship was not established by the mere contribution of ideas and guidance for the user interface of a computer spreadsheet, because joint authorship requires each author to make an independently copyrightable contribution.

WORKS MADE FOR HIRE

Works considered to be *works made for hire* are important exceptions to the general rule that a person owns the copyright in a work he or she has created. If a work was created by an employee on the job, the law considers the product a work made for hire, and the employer will own the copyright. However, the parties can, if desired, avoid the application of this rule with a well-written contract. If the employment contract states that creating the copyrightable material in question is not part of the *scope of employment*, the employee retains the copyright and the creation is not a work made for hire.

A work made for hire is defined as "a work made by an employee within the scope of his or her employment." The principle is based on the following grounds.

- The work is produced on behalf of and under the direction of the employer.
- The employee is paid for the work.
- The employer, having paid all the costs and borne all the risks of loss, should reap any gain.

Courts may also consider the amount of an employer's artistic advice before, during, and after the work was created.

Some courts developed a doctrine whereby an independent contractor was considered to be a *special employee* for copyright purposes when a commissioning party had the right to exercise control over the work. This resulted in the commissioning party, rather than the independent contractor, owning the copyright. In 1989, the U.S. Supreme Court, in *Community for Creative Non-Violence (CCNV) v. Reid*, held that unless the party creating the work is an actual employee as that term is defined in the law, the copyright belongs to the creator rather than to the commissioning party. The court left open the question of whether the work could be considered a joint work by virtue of the parties' intent.

If the creator is an independent contractor, a work will be considered a work made for hire only when:

- the parties have signed a written agreement to that effect and
- the work is specially ordered or commissioned as a contribution to a collective work, a supplementary work (one that introduces, revises, comments upon, or assists a work by another), a compilation, an instructional text, answer material for a test or the test itself, an atlas, a motion picture, or an audiovisual work.

It has been held in some jurisdictions that, in order to be valid, the written contract must predate the performance of the work.

IN PLAIN ENGLISH

Unless there is a contractual agreement to the contrary, the independent contractor owns the copyright.

DERIVATIVE WORKS

In the case of a *derivative work*, the contributing author owns only what he or she contributed. A *derivative work* is a work based upon one or more preexisting works, such as translation, fictionalization, motion picture version, sound recording, art reproduction, abridgment, condensation, or any other form in which a work may be recast, transformed, or adapted, or a work consisting of editorial revisions, annotations, elaborations, or other modifications which, as a whole, represent an original work of authorship. Any work based completely or substantially upon a preexisting work, if it satisfies the originality requirement and is not itself an infringing work, will be separately copyrightable.

The distinction between a derivative work and a joint work lies in the intent of each contributor at the time the contribution is created. If the work is created with the intention that the contributions be merged into inseparable or interdependent parts of a *unitary whole*, then the merger creates a joint work. If such intention occurs only after the work has been created, then the merger results in a derivative or collective work.

COLLECTIVE WORKS

A collective work is a work, such as a periodical issue, anthology, or encyclopedia, in which a number of contributions, constituting separate and independent works in themselves, are assembled into a collective whole. The originality involved in a collective work is the collection and assembling of preexisting works, each of which may be independently copyrightable, without any changes in such material. This assemblage of works is copyrightable.

COPYRIGHT PROTECTION FOR UTILITARIAN OBJECTS

Because copyright law was originally intended to protect literary works, earlier versions of the law omitted protection for three-dimensional designs. These designs were not given copyright protection until 1870.

The Copyright Act of 1909 did not contain any protection for utilitarian objects, but the regulations adopted to interpret the law extended copyright protection to the artistic elements of a utilitarian piece. The regulation stated that the aesthetic but not mechanical or utilitarian aspects of the item would be protected.

Despite the lack of specific legislation, some protection is available for manufacturers of utilitarian objects. The copyright law may be relied on to a limited extent. For example, if an individual draws a copyrightable picture and obtains copyright protection for that design, then the copyrighted picture could be used or incorporated into any utilitarian item (such as a restaurant's cocktail glass) and be protected. Similarly, architectural drawings are entitled to copyright protection.

NOTICE REQUIREMENT

The requirement that original works and all copies have a copyright notice affixed to them on publication is basic to both the Copyright Act of 1909 and the Copyright Revision Act of 1976. The notice consists of the international symbol "©" or the word "copyright" (or its abbreviation "Copr."), the name of the author (in the case of works made for hire, this is the employer), and the year of first publication. For example:

Copyright 2006 by John Doe

or

© John Doe, 2006

The order of the words is unimportant.

Under the Copyright Act of 1909, a publication without notice caused the work to fall into the public domain, and once the rights were lost, they could not be retrieved. It was publication with notice that created a federal copyright under this law.

Under the Copyright Revision Act of 1976, a federal copyright is created as soon as an original work is made in tangible form. Until 1989, however, the proper notice had to be attached at publication if you wished to retain copyright after publication. However, a savings clause provided methods for saving a copyright when notice was omitted.

Due to the 1989 amendment to the 1976 Act, notice is no longer required on works created or first published after March 1, 1989. Although notice is not required, notice should still be used to make others aware of your rights. One who copies a work believing it to be in the public domain because there is no notice may be considered an *innocent infringer*. In this situation, the author whose work is copied will likely not recover significant damages. In fact, the court might even allow the copier to continue copying the work.

FILING AN APPLICATION AND DEPOSITING THE WORK

To register a copyright, you must file an application form with the Register of Copyrights. The forms can be downloaded from the Copyright Office's website at **www.copyright.gov** and mailed to the Library of Congress, Copyright Office, 101 Independence Avenue SE, Washington, D.C. 20559-6000. Because of mail screening, be sure to carefully read the instructions provided with your form. A security delivery address must be used if the package is delivered by certain commercial couriers or messengers.

You must also deposit two copies of the work, if published, or if the work is unpublished, one copy. In order to avoid your deposits being damaged by the Copyright Office's screening process, you may want to package your deposits in boxes rather than in envelopes.

Remember, if you have a copyright notice on your work or if your work was published after March 1, 1989, even without a notice, you already have a copyright. Under the Copyright Revision Act of 1976, as amended, registration is necessary only:

- as a prerequisite to commencing an infringement action;
- when the copyright owner wishes to take advantage of the savings provision of Section 405; or,
- if the Register of Copyrights demands registration of published works bearing a copyright notice (which is not likely to happen unless you have been in correspondence with that office).

The current law separates registration from the deposit requirements. Under the 1909 Act, registration involved filing a copyright application, paying a $6 fee, and depositing two copies of the work itself or two photographs of the original. Now, the Register of Copyrights is allowed to exempt certain categories from the deposit requirement or provide for alternative forms of deposit. This has been done in the case of computer software, films, videotapes, and other items.

Under the present law, you should deposit two of the best copies of the work with the Library of Congress within three months of publication. If the objects are bulky, fragile, or valuable, photographs may be deposited instead of the actual work. The same photograph privilege applies to fine prints in editions of 300 or fewer. Filing the application (which includes a $30 fee) need not be done at the time of deposit. When you feel depositing two copies is a hardship, you may apply for a waiver of the two-copy deposit requirement.

Although you can delay registration, there are at least two reasons why you should deposit the work and register the copyright (i.e., file the application) within three months of publication. First, the copyright law prohibits the awarding of attorney's fees and statutory damages for infringements that occur before registration, unless registration took place within three months of publication. Second, if you deposit the required two copies of the work within three months but postpone sending the registration form and fee, the Copyright Office will require two more copies of the work when you eventually do send in the form and money. Finally, if the two copies are not deposited within the requisite three-month period, the Register of Copyrights may demand them. If the copies are not submitted within three months after demand, the person upon whom demand was made may be subject to a fine for each unsubmitted work. In addition, such person or persons may be required to pay the Library of Congress an amount equal to the retail cost of the work. If no retail cost has been established, the costs incurred by the Library in acquiring the work, provided such costs are reasonable, will be substituted. The copyright proprietor who willfully and repeatedly refuses to comply with such a demand may be liable for additional fines.

PERIOD OF PROTECTION

The Copyright Act of 1909 granted copyright protection in a work for a twenty-eight-year period, which could be renewed for one additional twenty-eight-year period. Under the revised law, a work created on or after January 1, 1978, had copyright protection from the instant it was fixed in tangible form until fifty years after the creator's death. This was extended by the *Sonny Bono Term Extension Act* to the life of the creator plus seventy years. If the work was created jointly, the copyright expires seventy years after the last author dies. There are no renewal registrations required for copyrights created under the 1976 Act. Copyrights granted under the 1909 Act that were in effect on January 1, 1978, automatically received an extension to create a term of ninety-five years from the date the copyright was first obtained. It is important to note that this automatic extension applies only to copyrights that were in effect on January 1, 1978. If the copyright on a work had lapsed prior to January 1, 1978, the copyright would not have been revived. In all cases, copyright terms end on December 31st of the given year.

The copyright period of life plus seventy years applies only to works created by human beings using their own names. In other cases, for example, a corporation that obtains a copyright in accordance with the doctrine of works made for hire or for works created anonymously or pseudonymously, the period of protection is either 120 years from creation or ninety-five years from first publication, whichever expires first.

INFRINGEMENT

The federal courts have exclusive jurisdiction over copyright infringement litigation. Under both the 1909 and 1976 Acts, the trial judge has wide discretion in setting damages. Under the 1909 Act, a judge could award either *actual damages* (plaintiff's out-of-pocket losses or defendant's profit) or *statutory damages*. Under the 1976 Act, as amended in 1989, a judge may also award actual damages and statutory damages, the range for which is:

- as little as $200 for innocent infringement;
- between $750 and $30,000 for the typical case; and,
- up to $150,000 for willful infringement.

Both acts allow the awarding of reasonable attorney's fees to the prevailing party. Both acts also provide for injunctions against continued infringement and, in some cases, impoundment. The statute of limitations for both acts allows a plaintiff three years to file a lawsuit after the infringement occurs. This time frame refers to the date the infringement was committed, not the date the infringement was discovered.

In the case of willful infringement for commercial gain, criminal sanctions may also be imposed. The law was amended in 1982 to provide more severe penalties for those who unlawfully reproduce and sell sound recordings, motion pictures, audiovisual works, or phonorecords. Under these provisions, a criminal infringer may be imprisoned, fined, or both.

FAIR USE

Not every copying of a protected work is an infringement. There are two basic types of noninfringing use—*fair use* and *exempted use*.

The Copyright Act of 1976 recognizes that copies of a protected work for purposes such as criticism, comment, news reporting, teaching (including multiple copies for classroom use), scholarship, or research can be considered fair use, and therefore, not an infringement. However, this is not a complete list, nor is it intended as a definition of fair use. The Act cites four criteria to be considered in determining whether a particular use is or is not fair:

1. the purpose and character of the use, including whether it is for commercial use or nonprofit educational purposes;
2. the nature of the copyrighted work;
3. the amount and substantiality of the portion used in relation to the copyrighted work as a whole; and,
4. the effect of the use upon the potential market for, or value of, the copyrighted work.

The Act does not rank these four criteria, and it does not exclude other factors in determining the question of fair use. In effect, all that the Act does is leave the doctrine of fair use to be developed by the courts.

In *American Geophysical Union v. Texaco, Inc.*, the U.S. Court of Appeals for the Second Circuit held that making even one copy of a copyrighted professional journal for purposes of retaining an article in one's file for reference purposes was an infringement. The court pointed out that if the employees of the Texaco research lab desired additional copies of articles in the copyrighted journals, reprints could have been purchased. The making of an unauthorized copy deprived the copyright owner of a sale, and was an infringement. A restaurant that makes even a single copy of a copyrighted review written by someone not affiliated with the restaurant may be an infringer unless the copying can be deemed fair use.

It has also been held that the mere fact that permission to quote from a copyrighted work has been requested and denied does not necessarily mean that a use will be infringing. In *Maxtone-Graham v. Burtchaell*, the defendant, a Catholic priest, requested permission to quote from the plaintiff's book of interviews with women who were, as the title suggests, *Pregnant by Mistake*. Since the priest's intended use of the quoted material was to support his pro-life publication, permission was denied. He nevertheless used the excerpts. In the resulting litigation, the court held that the use was fair since the priest's unauthorized use of the copyrighted material was a productive use and since the plaintiff was not necessarily deprived of sales. It is still relatively unclear how broad or narrow the scope of the fair use doctrine really is.

In many instances, the ambiguities of the fair use doctrine are resolved by statutory exemptions. The exempted uses apply to situations in which the public interest in making a copy outweighs the potential harm to the copyright proprietor. For example, the *library and archives exemption* allows libraries and archives to reproduce and distribute a single copy of a work, provided that certain requirements are met. However, this exemption in no way affects the applicability of fair use, and it does not apply when such copying is prohibited in contractual arrangements agreed to by the library or archive when it acquired the work.

IN PLAIN ENGLISH

If you would like more information, write to the Library of Congress, Copyright Office, 101 Independence Avenue SE, Washington, D.C. 20559-6000, and ask for a free copyright information packet, or visit the Copyright Office's website at **www.copyright.gov**.

11

ADVERTISING

There are many different issues that arise in the context of advertising. In the trademark chapter, the method by which you may protect your restaurant name and logo is discussed. The protection available for restaurant literature, advertisements, and posters is considered in the copyright chapter. In this chapter, several other important legal considerations that may arise when planning an advertising campaign are explained.

GOVERNMENT REGULATION

To begin with, a business may always tout the qualities of its products or services, but those representations must be true. If there are any misrepresentations contained in your restaurant's ads or promotions, the state government, federal government, or a person who has sustained injury as a result of the misrepresentation may be able to file a lawsuit to redress this wrong.

Most states have consumer protection laws, which, among other things, impose fines and other legal sanctions on businesses that engage in misleading advertising. The state attorney general can cause an offending advertisement to be withdrawn. Similarly, the Federal Trade Commission (FTC) is involved in policing businesses that are engaged in interstate commerce. If your restaurant activity extends beyond your state boundaries and either touches or affects another state, then the Federal Trade Commission has jurisdiction over your company. This is also true if you advertise on the World Wide Web. In a particularly egregious case of dishonesty, an East Coast restaurant posted excerpts of reviews of a West Coast restaurant with a very similar name on its website, even going so far as to substitute its restaurant's name and its chef's name for those of the West Coast restaurant.

There are some specific laws and regulations that apply to food businesses. For instance, some jurisdictions (including Florida and New York) require that if a food is advertised as "kosher," such food must, in fact, be prepared in accordance with Jewish religious requirements.

IN PLAIN ENGLISH

Truth-in-Menu laws protect consumers from fraud by food and beverage sellers.

Federal regulations require restaurants to provide customers (upon request) with data to back up claims regarding nutrition or health. Nutrient claims relate to an item's nutrient content (e.g., "high in Omega 3 fatty acids") and health claims relate to the relationship between a nutrient or food and a disease or health condition (e.g., "heart healthy"). If you make any such claims, it would be wise to have them reviewed by both an attorney and a dietician. You should also be sure that customers are charged the amount set forth in the menu and that any mandatory service, cover, or minimum charges are clearly disclosed.

Further, the food served must match the description in the menu—in other words, a hamburger advertised as containing half of a pound of ground beef should contain eight ounces of ground beef. If a geographic source for the food is given ("Maine lobster"), the food must, in fact, be from that geographic area. Also, if a food is advertised as "grilled," it must, in fact, be grilled—manufactured food with grill marks will not meet legal requirements. Likewise, "home-made" products must be made onsite. You should contact an attorney knowledgeable in this area if you have any questions about your menu.

COMPARATIVE ADVERTISING

Restaurants occasionally tout the merits of their food and services by comparing themselves to their competitors. This form of comparative advertising is permissible, provided that the statements made are true. Thus, a restaurant would be permitted to use the name of a competitor and describe the competitor's products in an advertisement, even though the comparison will likely point out the competing food's or service's inferiority, under a few conditions. The use of a competitor's name is permissible, as long as there is no likelihood that a consumer would believe the advertiser is actually selling the competing product or service, and the statements made are accurate. In a leading case, it was held permissible to use the names of famous perfumes in an advertisement that stated that those who like the famous perfume would also like the advertiser's less expensive product. The court felt that there was no possibility of a consumer being confused into believing that the expensive perfume manufacturer was advertising for the cheaper knockoff scent. In addition, since the perfume smelled the same, the statements made were felt to be accurate.

A closely related situation arises when one company makes disparaging remarks about the product of another. In this situation, the one who intentionally or negligently makes untrue, disparaging remarks about the product or service of another business may be held legally accountable to the injured party. It should be noted that for a disparaging remark to be actionable, it must be both untrue and believable by a reasonable person. If the statement made was so outlandish as to be unbelievable, it is unlikely the owner whose product was disparaged will be able to prove any injury. If a car manufacturer claimed its competitor's vehicle was so poorly constructed that it literally fell apart within the first week of use, it is most likely that this gross exaggeration would not be believed, and therefore, the claim would not be actionable. On the other hand, if a restaurant's advertisement claimed that its direct competitor had several incidents of food poisoning, that statement is believable, and unless true, would be actionable.

PUBLICITY AND PRIVACY

A restaurant may use a celebrity to endorse it, provided the celebrity consents to the endorsement. If not, the company may be liable to the celebrity for violating his or her right of publicity. In the overwhelming majority of states and in many other countries, this right is granted to those who commercially exploit their names, voices, or images, such as actors or singers. The use of a look-alike for commercial purposes may be actionable. When businesses used look-alikes for Jackie Onassis, Woody Allen, and the rap group The Fat Boys, liability was imposed.

People who have not achieved notoriety because of their commercial activities may also have a right of privacy, and thus, may have a claim if their names or likenesses are used in an advertisement without their permission. In one curious case, a bank photographed several employees engaged in their day-to-day work. These pictures were displayed as part of the bank's promotional material for a trade show. When the employees were given the day off to see the trade show and saw the photos, they retained an attorney who filed suit on their behalf. The lesson learned is that even employees who are not entertainers must grant permission for their names, voices, or likenesses to be used for advertising purposes.

If an individual's photograph is not the focal point of the ad, but is instead merely an incidental part, such as a head in a crowd or a member of an audience, then an individual's permission may not be essential for the photograph to be used commercially. Even though you may not be required to have permission from an individual before using his or her photograph, it is a good idea to get a signed photo release whenever possible. The release should be worded in such a way as to give your restaurant permission to use the name and likeness—or, where relevant, the person's voice—for any and all purposes, including advertising. This will protect you if, for example, the individual ultimately becomes popular and you wish to use the photographs you obtained at an earlier date before the individual became a celebrity.

UNAUTHORIZED USE OF TRADEMARK OR COPYRIGHTED MATERIAL

An advertiser may be permitted to use the name or logo of another business in its advertisement, as long as there is no likelihood that the average viewer would believe the ad is sponsored by the company whose name or logo is used. For example, it would be permissible for you to have an ad containing a photo of a patron in your restaurant holding a copyrighted publication, the name and logo of which are registered trademarks, such as *USA Today*. Similarly, an automobile advertisement may show the advertised vehicle cruising past your restaurant.

GEOGRAPHIC LOCATIONS

Geographic locations may also be used in advertisements without obtaining the owner's consent. It would be permissible for a company to advertise its product by having someone stand in front of a famous building, such as the Empire State Building or the Sears Tower. Since items of utility are not copyrightable, buildings, parks, and other landmarks are not protected under the copyright laws, and thus, may incidentally be used in advertising programs without the owner's permission. In one case, however, it was held that an architecturally unique, identifiable, and famous building could enjoy the protection of the trade dress laws when it was prominently featured on a poster. Perhaps the distinction between an incidental use of a building as a backdrop and focusing on the prominent identifiable architectural features of a building is significant. Therefore, it would generally not be necessary for you to obtain your landlord's permission to photograph the building in which your restaurant is located for use in an ad or on your website.

TRADE DRESS

A form of advertising that has been given special protection is *package design*. While it is true that the copyright laws do not protect functional items, such as product packaging, the courts have developed a form of protection known as *trade dress*. This means that the design elements of a particular packaging design are protected as long as they are not otherwise functional (e.g., a hanger or a lid). The trade dress form of protection may be automatic and has been extended beyond traditional packaging.

In 1992, the U.S. Supreme Court endorsed the expansion of the trade dress doctrine in *Two Pesos v. Taco Cabana*. In this case, the Court stated that the non-functional aspects of a restaurant might be protected trade dress, provided they are distinctive and identifiable. A restaurant's architectural features, décor, and menu may be protected so long as they have a distinctive *look and feel*, are not functional, and have achieved notoriety. Thus, it is likely that McDonald's golden arches would be considered protected trade dress. The trade dress doctrine has been used to prevent copying of a business's distinctive theme or a food company's packaging.

In 2000, the U.S. Supreme Court clarified the trade dress doctrine by providing that product design trade dress can be established only by conducting an extensive survey of consumers in order to determine that they recognize the unique look and feel of the item involved. As of this writing, the court has not applied the same requirement to package design trade dress.

IN PLAIN ENGLISH

Many businesses have begun to register their trade dress. This is accomplished by registering the distinctive *look and feel* (as discussed in the trademark chapter) of a restaurant or its products. By doing this, the proprietor gains added protection under the Lanham Act and the body of law known as trade dress, and may bypass the Supreme Court's requirement of a survey.

Individuals can also have distinctive styles. For example, when an advertiser hired one of Bette Midler's backup singers to replicate Ms. Midler's distinctive vocal rendition of a song for a commercial, Ms. Midler sued and recovered for the knockoff. It was held that the intentional copying of the singer's famous, distinctive style and voice was a form of infringement and actionable. However, when a manufacturer hired a group that looked and sounded like the group known as The Fat Boys, the federal court in New York held the manufacturer liable only for violating the celebrities' publicity rights. The court refused to impose liability for the unauthorized use of The Fat Boys' sound, since the New York publicity statute extends protection merely to one's "name, portrait, or picture," and not to one's sound. The Midler case relied on a California statute that, among other things, protects a celebrity's voice.

IN PLAIN ENGLISH

While preparing an advertising campaign, it is essential that you take care not to violate the rights of other businesses or individuals. Care should be taken to work with an attorney skilled in advertising law, in order to be assured you have an effective idea that will enable you to promote your restaurant without exposing your business to potential liability. A poorly planned advertising campaign is likely to be more harmful than no advertising at all.

12

COMMERCIAL OPPORTUNITIES AND ACTIVITIES

Since most restaurants will use some form of intellectual property in connection with the business's operations, it is important to be sure that restaurant's rights are properly protected. Once perfected, the restaurant can exploit those rights and expand its financial opportunities.

LICENSING TRADEMARKS

One of the most common methods for exploiting one's trademark is to grant another the right to use that trademark. This permission to use is referred to as a *license*. Since trademarks and service marks are used to identify the source or producer of a particular product or service, it is essential to impose quality control standards on the permitted user of one's trademarks. Trademark law is a form of consumer protection law, and unless the licensor (or owner of the mark) controls its use, a consumer acquiring a product or obtaining a service bearing that mark may not receive the quality expected. In fact, it has been held that granting a license to use a trademark or service mark, without imposing quality control standards and a means for ensuring that those standards are adhered to, is granting a *naked license*, and the trademark may be deemed abandoned.

IN PLAIN ENGLISH

Since some restaurants have expanded their opportunities by selling prepackaged or canned signature dishes for home consumption, their trademarks will likely appear on those products. If the packaged food is prepared in the restaurant's own kitchen, then quality control is assured; however, this is not common. When unaffiliated commercial kitchens are used for purposes of producing the prepackaged dish, it is essential that the restaurant (licensor) establish guidelines and a means for ensuring that those guidelines are followed.

LICENSING COPYRIGHTS

The rules regarding the licensing of copyrights are not as demanding as those for trademarks. In fact, a copyright may be licensed without requiring adherence to quality control standards. However, if the copyright owner's name is used and the licensed item is inferior, the reputation of the owner may be tarnished. Thus, while quality control is not required for a copyright license, it is certainly a good idea for copyright owners to demand the right to preapprove any use of their copyrighted material. Restaurant owners who have developed copyrighted features that they deem important to their restaurant's operation, such as distinctive artwork in their lobbies or the text of their advertising copy, should take steps to both protect them and be prudent about allowing their use by others.

LICENSING OTHER INTELLECTUAL PROPERTY

A restaurant's signature dishes and the distinct characteristics of the food served in the restaurant are likely what establish its position in the marketplace. Recipes may be protected trade secrets and licensing their use is possible, but risky. If a *unique* dish can be obtained at many different restaurants, then it is no longer unique. Similarly, if the quality and character of food offered at your restaurant is virtually the same as that offered by your competitors, you may very well have lost your market edge. While you may be in a position to obtain some royalty payments for the grant of a license to use your recipes and know-how (techniques for preparing certain dishes) protected by trade secret, it may not be prudent to take advantage of this opportunity.

Tools and equipment that are cleverly designed and novel may be patentable. Licensing a patented invention is quite common, and if possible, often lucrative. Few, if any, restaurants manufacture their own tools and equipment; instead, these devices are more often produced by job shops. By working with an intellectual property attorney, you will be able to determine how best to exploit any novel invention.

LICENSING CAUTIONS

As pointed out in Chapter 6, oral contracts are not worth the paper they're written on. It is for this reason that a license, which is a contract, should always be in writing. Care should be taken to define the scope of the license, since problems may very well arise if you find that your restaurant is competing with one or more of its licensees. In addition, your intellectual property (patent, copyright, trademark, or trade secret) may be tarnished if appropriate safeguards regarding quality of use and quality of user are not established and enforced. While licensing can provide you with expanded commercial opportunities, it can also drain your restaurant business of some of its most important assets. In addition, if you are considering franchising your restaurant, then you must protect your trademark and your other intellectual property, and you could have problems with preexisting licensees.

CONSIGNMENT

Many restaurants sell merchandise that is compatible with or complementary to their theme, as a means of enhancing their revenue. This can be accomplished by displaying a few trinkets in the restaurant's lobby, establishing a gift shop, or displaying artwork for sale on the restaurant's walls.

The method of acquiring the items to be sold will likely fall into one of two categories. The restaurant can either purchase the items outright or take them on *consignment*. The difference between these two forms of acquisition is important. By obtaining an item through purchase, the restaurant will own it and generally have complete control over the price and terms of resale. The restaurant will also have to advance the purchase price, and if the market softens, it may find that its profit margin is not nearly as appealing as originally anticipated.

Consignment is an arrangement whereby one party, known as the *consignor* (who is generally the owner of the item) transfers it to another (generally referred to as a *consignee*) for purposes of sale on terms established by the parties. The consignee never owns the property, but merely acts as an intermediary for purposes of facilitating the sale for a commission, usually a percentage of the sale price. Because of the unique character of the consignment arrangement, problems can and do arise. Creditors of the consignee can be misled into believing that the consignee owns the consigned items. Because of this, *Article 2* of the *Uniform Commercial Code* (UCC) provides that when a consignor delivers an item to a business dealing in goods of the kind consigned, the consignor will not have priority over the claims of creditors or a trustee in bankruptcy, unless the consignor:

- complies with the applicable state law providing that the consignor's interest be indicated by a sign on the consignee's premises;
- establishes in court that the consignee is known by its creditors to be substantially engaged in selling goods under consignment; or,
- complies with the filing requirements in Article 9 of the UCC.

Most states do not have sign laws. Even in those states that do, a consignee restaurant must determine whether it wishes to alert its patrons to the fact that merchandise and artwork for sale on its premises are owned by others. The second option is likely not common in the restaurant business since few, if any, restaurants would be known as *substantially* engaged in the business of selling the goods of others. It is, therefore, likely that those consigning items to your restaurant will file a financial statement (known as a UCC-1) with the Secretary of State in the state where the consigned items are being displayed. The current form of UCC-1 is not required to be signed by the consignee, so it is possible that you may not even be aware that such filings have been made. It would, therefore, be a good idea for you to have an appropriate contract with each consignor dealing with, among other things, whether UCC-1 filings will be made.

Some states have enacted special rules for the consignment of artwork. If your restaurant is contemplating or involved with consignment arrangements for merchandise or artwork, you should work closely with your attorney in order to determine what the rules in your jurisdiction are with respect to your situation.

13

THE INTERNET

It has become more and more common for restaurants to establish a presence on the World Wide Web. Technology allows even the smallest businesses to create interactive sites that attract a good deal of positive attention. Elaborate websites have appeared with regularity for not only large, multinational restaurant chains, but for single-location restaurants as well.

The Web is a significant retail marketplace, and the use of websites for commercial activities is continuously expanding. Many businesses encourage Web commerce by providing discounts and exclusive offers for Web-based transactions. In fact, the only limitations in cyberspace are the imaginations of users and the capacity of their equipment.

INTELLECTUAL PROPERTY PROTECTION

The World Wide Web's popularity has raised significant questions regarding the extent of legal and intellectual property protection in cyberspace. One of the earliest cases involved the Church of Scientology, and raised the question of whether U.S. copyright laws and state trade secret laws are enforceable in cyberspace. In that case, several former church members were sued for posting copyrighted material on the World Wide Web that they had received in confidence.

The court held that these traditional forms of intellectual property protection were, indeed, applicable in cyberspace. In addition, it was held that the *Internet service provider* (ISP) could be exposed to liability for merely permitting the infringing material to appear on the Web. As elsewhere, one who facilitates or aids in the commission of an infringing act may be liable as a contributory infringer. Congress later changed this situation for ISPs who do not have control over the content of the material posted.

The Church of Scientology also claimed that the wrongdoers misappropriated the Church's trade secrets, and sought an injunction to have the offending material removed from the Web. It was alleged that the information posted on the Web by the former church members was confidential and protected under trade secret laws. The court rejected this argument, pointing out that once information is posted in cyberspace, it is no longer secret, and the injunction was denied. As a result, anyone who downloaded that information would not be guilty of trade secret misappropriation.

IN PLAIN ENGLISH

If a protected trade secret, such as a special recipe or technique for preparing a signature dish, is posted on a website in violation of an agreement or in breach of one's duty to the owner of the protected information, then the act of posting would be wrongful and the perpetrator would likely be liable for the improper activity.

Cyberspace may be a relatively new medium, but it is still a vehicle of communication and dissemination analogous to broadcasting on television or publishing in a magazine.

DOMAIN NAMES

Characterization of website names has also presented some vexing problems. It is unclear whether a domain name is merely an address used for the purpose of locating the site or whether that name may be characterized as a trademark. In addition, the problem is compounded by the fact that while there is only one World Wide Web, each trademark is distinguished by the classification of goods or services it covers. There are thirty-four international classes of goods and twelve international classes of services. When, for example, the American Bar Association, commonly referred to as the ABA, wished to register its acronym as its domain name, it was not able to do so, because the American Booksellers Association—also commonly known as the ABA—had already registered **www.aba.org**.

Domain names were originally registered with a company called Network Solutions. Today, there are a number of different registrars, and competition for domain name registration is fierce. Prices for securing a domain name have become far more competitive. Generally, domain names are registered on a first-come, first-served basis. Many computer businesses can assist you in obtaining a domain name, which is a *Uniform Resource Locator* (URL). Initially, there were five top-level domain name categories for U.S.-based registrants:

- .com for commerce;
- .org for organizations;
- .gov for government;
- .mil for military; and,
- .edu for educational institutions.

These suffixes were supposed to be made available only to those who qualified for their use. As the availability of popular domain names shrank, it became necessary to create additional opportunities by creating new suffixes, such as .pro for professionals, .biz for businesses, .fm for radio, and the process continues. In fact, the number of suffixes is becoming rather large, though the initial five are still the most popular. In addition to all of the U.S. designators, many other countries have distinctive suffixes as well, such as .uk for the United Kingdom and .ru for Russia.

There are several methods for resolving domain name disputes. These include litigation in federal district court, reliance on the anticybersquatting legislation, and the online arbitration process using the procedure established by *Internet Corporation for Assigned Names and Numbers* (ICANN). A lawyer specializing in online intellectual property issues should be consulted when these issues arise.

Generally speaking, obtaining trademark registration for your restaurant name will also provide you with leverage in both obtaining and keeping the business name as a domain name. For example, Wendy's would likely have success in either obtaining the URL *wendys.com* or in defending that URL against another potential registrant of that domain name because the Wendy's business name is a registered trademark. It is possible today to register trademarks in seventy countries throughout the world pursuant to the Madrid Protocol through the United States Patent and Trademark Office. One of the principal reasons for this expanded opportunity to obtain international trademark protection was the expanded use of trademarks in commerce on the World Wide Web.

Under some circumstances, using your business name as a domain name may be considered adequate for purposes of trademark registration. A number of cases have dealt with trademark issues in cyberspace. In those cases, the applicability of federal trademark law and the question as to which jurisdiction was proper for purposes of litigating the wrongdoing were considered. While the issues have not been definitively resolved, the trend appears to be in favor of extending trademark laws to cyberspace and holding infringers liable wherever their infringing activity can be accessed.

In a landmark case, an enterprising individual residing in Illinois decided to register a number of popular business names as website domain names. When the business owners who had previously registered those names as trademarks attempted to register their company names as domain names, they were told that they were too late. The entrepreneurial registrant then offered to sell these companies the domain names for their own registered trademarks at inflated prices. A number of the companies filed suit in federal court in California, alleging that the appropriation of the protected trademarks as domain names by one who lacks authority from the trademark owner is an infringement. The court agreed and stated that this outrageous conduct would result in liability.

In another case, a European restaurant bearing the same name as a restaurant in the United States established a website. The American company sued, alleging trademark infringement, and the court held that it was unlikely that the European restaurant would cause the kind of market confusion necessary to establish trademark infringement by advertising on the Web and having those advertisements viewed in the United States. This is consistent with intellectual property law in general, since even in cyberspace it will be necessary to establish a *likelihood of confusion* and that the infringer somehow appropriates business from the owner of the protected trademark before liability will be imposed.

A number of other issues have generated Web-based litigation. When Total News, Inc., decided to provide Web surfers the ability to compare data from several news sources, such as The Washington Post and CNN, problems arose. The other services filed suit, complaining that the visual presentation of their material was *framed* within the host's name, and their protected material was thereby being retransmitted without their permission. The case was settled with Total News agreeing to refrain from framing the protected material and the plaintiffs agreeing to grant Total News licenses to link directly to their sites. Later cases have judicially established that framing is unlawful and can be redressed legally.

In the Total News case, the question of *linking*, where one may jump from one site to another by simply clicking on an identifying icon or phrase, was raised but not resolved. More recently, this question has been reconsidered, and some cases have held that linking is unlawful when the link is established without the permission of the proprietor of the linked site, though this is by no means a settled question.

INTERNET ADVERTISING

One of the most important distinctions of advertising on the Internet is the way cyberspace advertising reaches consumers and the ability to provide useful, up-to-date information. Magazine and newspaper ads are fixed in time, whereas the Web can be regularly updated with comparative economy. Radio and print media are, at best, two dimensional, whereas the Web may be multidimensional. As technology evolves, the devices available to website designers increase, and a restaurant's website can provide the visitor with a cybertour of the facility, as well as an opportunity to preview the menu, read reviews, and obtain general information, such as location, hours, and contact information. In fact, a few sites even take online reservations. Restaurants that have gift shops or retail outlets have also taken the opportunity to conduct online sales.

Cyberspace has become a significant marketplace, and laws adopted for purposes of preventing deceptive advertising do apply in cyberspace. The *Federal Trade Commission* (FTC) periodically conducts Internet surf days in conjunction with state attorneys general. The FTC requires certain disclosures in connection with traditional forms of advertising, but these disclosures are easily lost in cyberspace. A disclosure can be bypassed when linking from one site to another, and required legends can be buried in text that users may just scroll through. In contrast, when a disclosure appears in a more traditional advertisement, the viewer sees the entire composite—and required disclosures are unlikely to be bypassed. Users have not uniformly been pressed into having to read disclosures if they do not want to.

IN PLAIN ENGLISH

According to the FTC, it is a good idea to require website visitors to click through required disclosures whenever an advertising site is visited.

The FTC has announced that it will sue a website designer if that designer knows or should have known that the site created violates the law.

Some intellectual property practitioners suggest that an attorney who has expertise in working with websites should be requested to conduct a so-called Internet traffic and Web-content audit. This would include evaluating whether the appropriate permissions to display material have been obtained. For example, if copyrighted material is to be used, the attorney would make sure the copyright owner granted permission for the work to be displayed on the Web. If testimonials are to be displayed, then it is important to get written permission from each individual providing a testimonial.

Internet advertisers also need to determine whether their existing liability insurance covers their activity in cyberspace. One matter that needs to be addressed is whether your business will be protected if your website crashes. Another example includes whether the website designer will be insured if the site contains infringing work, defames another, or otherwise exposes the website owner to liability. A form of errors-and-omissions insurance should be available for this purpose.

Since websites are, by definition, worldwide, it is important to determine whether your site, the content of which is legal in the United States, may subject you to liability elsewhere. For example, comparative advertising is generally permissible and fairly common in the United States, but other countries, such as Germany, are far more restrictive in what they permit in a comparative advertising spread.

In addition, activities that are legal in the United States can nonetheless subject a website owner to liability abroad. One who engages in Internet advertising has, by definition, established a worldwide presence, and must, therefore, comply with worldwide laws—a difficult task even for multimillion-dollar companies.

OTHER INTELLECTUAL PROPERTY ISSUES

The extent of litigation that has resulted from activity on the Internet suggests that care must be taken when establishing your presence in cyberspace. This new dimension gives rise to increased and often desired exposure, but the ramifications of problems can be devastating for a small restaurant business.

Even the simple act of advertising artwork consigned to your restaurant for retail sale could have serious consequences if you are not careful. For instance, if you market or sell a copyrighted item—even if you have obtained permission to advertise this item for sale—you may still not have the right to scan an image of that item into your computer and post it on your website. It may be necessary for you to obtain specific permission to replicate the work in two dimensions before engaging in cyberspace promotional activities.

Downloading and reusing material from other websites may also expose a business to liability. Some businesses have developed electronic *watermarks* to place on the images they post on their websites in order to discourage anyone from attempting to capture and reuse those images without permission.

Similarly, you have to recognize the fact that the Web is worldwide and that your material may find its way into jurisdictions and geographical regions that do not have copyright treaty relations with the United States. In this event, you may find that you have lost control of protected work.

While the *World Intellectual Property Organization* (WIPO) has expanded the extent of protection available for intellectual property with the *WIPO Treaty of 1996* and the *WIPO Performances and Phonograms Treaty*, not all countries have adopted or implemented them. As of the date of this writing, more than one hundred countries belong to WIPO, yet few have ratified these treaties to expand protection for sound recordings, motion pictures, computer software, and other digitally transmitted literary works. Even when the treaties are in force, there is still a risk, since the treaties are limited in scope. Additionally, not all countries can be expected to participate and enact these treaties without reservation. Some countries will remain on the U.S. *watch list*, since they continue to disregard their current treaty obligations, and there is no reason to believe these countries will adopt or respect the WIPO treaties.

SERVER PROTECTION

One significant risk in maintaining a website is that it may serve as a window to your company's computer system. There are some safeguards that should be taken in order to prevent improper access and protect your business's valuable trade secrets.

IN PLAIN ENGLISH

If your business hosts its site on its own server that is networked with your other business computers, hackers could gain access to your entire system and all of your data.

Information you deem to be confidential and sensitive should be encrypted. That is, it should be available only through the use of special software. Similarly, your system should always be protected by a password, which should not be obvious or simple, and should be changed frequently. More and more systems are using *firewalls*, which are electronic blocks preventing access to all but those who have the proper key. Many businesses have been created for the purpose of developing and installing computer security devices or software. You should consult with an expert when designing your website in order to take advantage of the latest technology.

EMAIL

The popularity of the World Wide Web has been paralleled by the expanded use of email. Communications within a business are commonplace and efficient. Internal, paperless transmissions of important messages throughout business help facilitate the day-to-day operations. In addition, more and more businesses are developing intranets, which are available only to a defined network, such as a company's employees. Because of the widespread use of internal email, business handbooks and policy statements should deal with the proper use of email. For instance, it has been held that repeated transmission of sexually or racially explicit email messages by one employee to another may be deemed harassment, and if not controlled by the employer, may render the employer liable as well.

External use of email is also quite common, enabling business users to communicate quickly with customers, clients, suppliers, and the like, including transmitting documents electronically. Here too, security is an issue to consider. Once again, there are a variety of vehicles available for security, such as encryption.

Internet email is often abused. It has been held that persistent transmission of undesired electronic junk mail, commonly called *spam*, continued after a request to stop is an actionable wrong. In response to this problem, most of the major ISPs have developed spam filters and pop-up blockers. Similarly, software can be purchased to serve the same function. Interestingly enough, the word "spam," which has been used to describe bulk email, became the subject of litigation. Hormel, the meat company which first developed the name Spam for its canned meat, filed suit for trademark infringement against a software manufacturer for using the word as part of the name of its spam-filtering product.

Congress reacted to the glut of spam by enacting legislation that requires advertisers to identify the source of an advertisement, as well as the fact that it is an advertisement, and provide recipients the opportunity to *opt out*. Unfortunately, the penalties for violating the anti-spam legislation are paltry, and it is simple to avoid their application by having the spam initiate from sites outside of the United States.

VIRUSES

One of the most serious problems to arise in cyberspace is the prevalence of computer viruses, worms, Trojan horses, traps, and tracking programs. These parasites are intended to interfere with computer use, and in some cases, to damage software or hardware. Briefly, viruses and worms are computer programs, often designed to damage a computer or computer system by compromising or destroying the computer's hard drive. Many have been created with the ability to invade a computer's address book and resend itself to all of the addressees, unbeknownst to the computer owner. The purpose of the retransmission is to invade the recipient's computer and repeat the process in a never-ending progression. Others do not leave the recipient's computer but destroy some or all of the computer's software or hardware. Traps, on the other hand, are website-based programs that automatically spring on a user. They may be as simple as opening dozens of websites within a few seconds to downloading and installing automatic dialers and resetting various computer settings. They also may embed other unwanted software in the victim's computer. These are easy to remove but difficult to identify and locate.

As a result of the breakup of the Soviet Union, the burst of the technology bubble, and widespread unemployment of computer-savvy individuals, *cyberterrorism* has become epidemic. In fact, the United States Department of Homeland Security has identified computer hacking and the infiltration of worms and viruses as one of the more significant problems faced by the free world today.

Although the authorities have been aggressive in identifying and prosecuting the perpetrators of these and other cybercrimes, no computer system is immune from these unwanted intrusions and the havoc they wreak. Even software giants such as Microsoft have been forced to announce the discovery of vulnerabilities in their systems that have been exploited by hackers and those who produce worms and viruses. While hackers typically invade government sites and the computer systems belonging to banks and other large business operations, worms, viruses, and similar programs can interfere with and cause significant damage to even a small business's computer system or an individual's home computer. As quickly as they are identified and software is developed or modified to block them, new ones appear. A number of companies, including McAfee and Symantec, specialize in antivirus and antiworm protection software.

Another reason for ensuring cybersecurity is the expanded use of online commerce. It is now possible to contract online and to engage in other forms of commercial activity, such as credit card purchasing. In the early days of cyber-commerce, there was a great deal of fear among consumers with respect to the security of their credit card information being compromised on the Web. Today, secure sites are the norm, and companies, such as Visa, have established certification programs for ensuring customers of a website's security.

By proceeding with good judgment and consulting with experienced intellectual property lawyers who have been involved with new technology and computer system specialists, you can remain on the cutting edge of cyberspace.

14

WARRANTIES AND CONSUMERS

You may be warranting certain attributes of your restaurant, whether you realize it or not. The rules that govern warranties for products, such as the food you serve, have been embodied in the Uniform Commercial Code, some form of which has been adopted in every state.

A *warranty* is, in essence, a guarantee that an item will be of a certain quality or have particular attributes. Giving a warranty involves certain obligations, so you should be aware of what those obligations are. Any statement of fact or promise that describes the characteristics of an item will create an *express warranty*. In general, you do not need to use the words "warranty" or "guarantee" to create an express warranty. However, the more explicit your statement, the more likely it is that you have, perhaps unwittingly, given an express warranty.

ELEMENTS OF AN EXPRESS WARRANTY

In order to determine whether statements are the type that will give rise to an express warranty—as opposed to mere expressions of opinion, which will not— the courts have developed a test. If the seller makes a statement to the buyer relating to goods about which the buyer is uninformed, that statement is probably an express warranty. On the other hand, if the seller merely expresses a judgment about something on which each party would be expected to have an opinion, no express warranty is given.

For example, if a supplier were to state that a ceramic bowl was safe to put in an oven, this statement would likely be considered an express warranty, since most restaurant buyers cannot easily determine the characteristics of every type of pottery, and the seller would know about this bowl in particular. In order to determine whether a statement will be considered an express warranty, a number of factors are relevant. A written statement, particularly if it is part of a contract or bill of sale, is more likely to be considered an express warranty than an oral statement. How much the seller qualifies the statement is also an indication of whether an express warranty is created.

Another way an express warranty can be created is by giving a description of the item that becomes part of the *basis of the bargain*. For example, the description does not need to be the sole inducement for a customer to order a particular dish in order for it to constitute a warranty. If a contract is involved, any statements must have been part of the contract negotiations, but the precise time a statement is made is irrelevant. The buyer could already have paid for an item and the seller could then make a statement that could be considered part of the basis of the bargain, since, theoretically, the buyer could still decide to return the goods to the seller and get the money back. This could apply, for example, if your restaurant is purchasing a new oven. These post-purchase statements must, however, be made within a reasonable period of time to be considered part of the bargain, and they probably only apply to dealings in person.

An additional problem presents itself if your restaurant sells canned or prepackaged signature dishes, whether through a catalog, ads, or in the restaurant. Catalogs, ads, menus, and your website, and any statements made in them, could be considered part of the basis of the bargain for those making purchases, although buyers would probably have to prove that they relied on those statements in making the decision to purchase.

An express warranty can also be created by the use of samples or models, such as displays of synthetic representations of your dishes. There is a distinction between a sample and a model. A *sample* is drawn from the actual goods that are the subject of the sale. Therefore, the sample embodies the qualities of the goods being offered, unless the seller specifically states otherwise.

IN PLAIN ENGLISH

If you provide a customer with a taste of a dish and the customer does not investigate the other dishes on your menu, an express warranty is created that the remaining items are of similar quality as the one examined.

On the other hand, a *model* may not be drawn from the exact group of goods that are the subject of the sale. A model is, therefore, not quite as descriptive as a sample, but an express warranty can still be created. This might apply in a situation where your restaurant purchases flatware based on a model provided by a salesperson. If the actual flatware delivered does not conform to the model, then the vendor may have breached the express warranty of quality.

While the UCC does not expressly deal with services, most of the rules discussed should apply by analogy. Some state statutes other than the UCC may have more specific laws dealing with services, though they are not common.

IMPLIED WARRANTIES

In addition to express warranties, the Uniform Commercial Code imposes a number of *implied warranties* on the sale of goods, because such warranties are presumed to be part of the sales transaction. One of these, the *implied warranty of merchantability*, applies whenever the seller is a merchant. *Merchants* are defined as people who deal with goods of the kind involved in the sale, or who, by their occupation, hold themselves out as having particular knowledge or skill. Merchants can also be those to whom this knowledge or skill can be attributed, because they are acting as agents or intermediaries for a merchant. Everyone engaged in the restaurant business would be defined as a merchant by the statute.

Various tests for merchantability have been developed, including the following.

- Does the item pass without objection in the trade under the description given in the contract between the buyer and seller?
- Is the item at least fit for the ordinary purposes for which such goods are used?
- Is the item adequately contained, packaged, and labeled as the contract or usage of trade may require?
- Is the item of average quality based on the description given?
- Does the item run within the variations permitted by the agreement between the buyer and seller? Are the items of a consistent kind, quality, and quantity within each unit and among units?
- Does the item conform to any promises made on its container or label?

To be merchantable, an item need not be perfect. *Trade usage*, that is, the norms of a particular trade, will also establish the particular qualities that will be acceptable for items produced by members of that trade. Generally, the higher an item is priced, the more justifiable is the buyer's expectation of high quality.

Where the product is food, it must be *wholesome* to be considered merchantable. Wholesome food is that which is free from foreign materials and dangerous substances (including bacteria that cause food poisoning). In determining whether food is wholesome, reasonable expectations may be considered. Thus, a chicken bone in a chicken potpie, a fish bone in fish chowder, or a walnut shell in a walnut ice cream dish will often be considered risks that should have been expected and guarded against by the consumer. Items such as glass or rocks will, under either test, generally be considered a breach of the warranty of merchantability.

IN PLAIN ENGLISH

Some courts have held that a *natural* harmful substance, such as bones or nutshells, will never be considered a breach of the implied warranty.

When a seller knows of a particular purpose for which the buyer is purchasing the goods and knows the buyer is relying on the seller's skill or judgment to choose something suitable, there is an implied warranty that the goods will fit such a purpose. The usual way this warranty is created is when the buyer asks the seller for assistance.

A *particular purpose* means a specific purpose for a specific buyer's use. Accordingly, purchasing an item because it aesthetically pleases the buyer is probably not a particular purpose—it is an ordinary purpose. A particular purpose must be reasonably specific and explicit in order to assume that the seller has been informed of the buyer's purpose. In this regard, if the buyer is knowledgeable about what you sell, it is less likely that this implied warranty is created. The one exception to this warranty is when a buyer asks for a particular brand or a particular company's product. In that case, the buyer is not relying on the seller's skill and judgment, so no implied warranty is created.

For example, if a patron asks the server for a menu recommendation, an implied warranty is created. The implied warranty would probably include at least two specific attributes: (1) that the dish contains the ingredients represented and (2) that it conforms to the other attributes described. If the patron informs the server that members of the party are allergic to peanuts, providing a dish cooked with peanut oil would breach both the implied warranties of merchantability and fitness for a particular purpose.

A *warranty of title* is implied in every contract for sale of goods. It simply means that the seller has good title, or the right to sell the item, and that the seller is unaware of any outstanding lien against the item. The seller does not need to be a merchant, as previously defined, and is not saved from liability by ignorance of a defect in the title. This warranty is based on the commonsense idea that a buyer should not have to defend ownership of goods against the claims of a third party. This warranty frequently occurs in the restaurant industry when a restaurant purchases equipment. If the seller does not have good title or if the equipment is encumbered by a lien, the warranty is breached. It is, therefore, a good idea for purchasers to conduct a search to determine whether a security interest has been filed against the item to be purchased. These security interests may be filed with the state, the county, or other governmental agency. It is best to work with an experienced business lawyer in order to determine where such liens would be filed and how best to obtain that information.

The most modern of the implied warranties is the *implied warranty against infringement*. When an item is sold, the seller warrants that the item is not infringing any rights protected by patent, trademark, copyright, or trade dress. If the object was created in violation of a third person's intellectual property rights, this warranty is breached.

At one time, there may have been some technical legal defenses available to a defendant who, as a manufacturer or packager, did not directly sell a defective item to a person who was injured by it. It now appears that the vast majority of states would permit a victim to sue the retailer, wholesaler, manufacturer, or component-part manufacturer (packager) for injuries sustained as a result of a defective or injurious product. When a consumer orders a soft drink that contains unsanitary material, such as insects or rodent parts, the patron is permitted to sue the restaurant, the soft drink distributor, and the bottling company.

DISCLAIMERS

What can you do if you do not want to give one or more of these express or implied warranties? You can use a disclaimer, but it must be given in specific ways.

To be safe, you should put disclaimers in *writing*. When you have given an express warranty, it is difficult to disclaim it. It is considered unreasonable to give an express warranty and then turn around and disclaim it. Therefore, an attempt to disclaim an express warranty will usually not be successful. This includes any express warranties that may be set forth in a description of an item.

A common problem results when a customer claims that oral warranties were made before the signing of a written contract. The seller may be shielded from this problem by a rule that sometimes prevents prior oral statements from being considered as part of the contract. There are, however, exceptions of which you should be aware. If there is a written agreement and it is not the final agreement, the written agreement will not supersede prior oral express warranties. Also, if the oral terms are consistent with a written disclaimer, they will be considered binding if the writing was not intended as a complete and exclusive statement of the terms. These types of problems tend to arise most often when someone else sells your goods for you or you purchase goods through an intermediary, such as a wholesale distributor.

IN PLAIN ENGLISH

Since most restaurant owners use waitstaff, any disclaimers should be in the menu.

Implied warranties can also be disclaimed. To exclude or modify the implied warranty of merchantability, the word "merchantability" must be specifically mentioned and the disclaimer must be *conspicuous*. This warranty can be disclaimed orally. The implied warranty of fitness for a particular purpose, however, can be disclaimed only in writing. The implied warranty of title can be disclaimed only by specific language or by circumstances that give the buyer reason to know that the seller does not have title or that the seller's title is subject to a third party's interest.

You are well-advised to consult with an attorney to determine which warranties should be disclaimed and the best method for accomplishing this. The rules on disclaimers are quite technical, and care must be taken in determining how much exposure you may have in a particular situation.

If you decide to give a written warranty or disclaim warranty protection in writing, you should be aware that there are federal regulations promulgated under the *Magnuson-Moss Warranty Act* to cover consumer products. According to the Act, all of the following must be indicated in a written warranty:

- to whom the warranty is extended;
- exactly what parts of the product are covered;
- what the warrantor will do in case of defect;
- when the warranty begins and ends;
- what the buyer has to do to get warranty coverage;
- any limitations on the duration of implied warranties (this is not allowed in some states); and,
- any exclusions or limitations regarding relief.

In the written warranty, you must also specify what you are promising in regards to the material and workmanship, and you must specify that the item is defect-free or will meet a specific level of performance. You must also clearly indicate whether the warranty is full or limited. Under a full warranty, the warrantor agrees to the following:

- to remedy the problem with the product within a reasonable period of time without charge if the product has a defect, malfunctions, or fails to conform to the written warranty;
- not to impose a limitation on implied warranties;
- not to exclude or limit consequential damages unless this is clear on the face of the warranty; and,
- to replace the item or refund the purchase price if the item is unsuccessfully repaired numerous times.

If any one of the above qualifications is not met, you have given a *limited warranty.*

If you breach a warranty and the buyer is damaged by your failure to comply with the warranty obligations, the buyer may sue, and you may be ordered to pay damages, court costs, and reasonable attorney's fees. Since this remedy exists, you should be careful to determine which warranties you are giving and learn how to disclaim them if you do not want to give them.

A disclaimer will not always be sufficient to protect your restaurant business from liability. For instance, state and federal laws regulate food safety, so your restaurant business may be liable for violating those laws even if a disclaimer exists.

LEGAL ADVICE REGARDING RISKS

You should consult with a business lawyer to evaluate the extent of exposure that may be expected as a result of the numerous warranties and consumer protection laws that apply to sales. Where appropriate, warranty disclaimers, as well as limitations of liability, can be used to reduce your exposure, but skilled drafting is necessary for effective protection. In addition, product liability insurance may be procured as a means of insulating yourself from extensive liability.

15

PRODUCT LIABILITY

In November of 1978, a California jury awarded the victim of an automobile accident $120 million after his defectively designed Ford Pinto caught fire and exploded, inflicting serious injury to the victim. The size of this judgment against the Ford Motor Company staggered the nation. Similarly, in 2003, a Florida jury awarded $145 billion to Florida smokers.

Unless your restaurant happens to own a Pinto or manufactures cigarettes, you may ask, "What does this have to do with me?" The answer is that since your restaurant regularly sells a product, you might find yourself in court being sued by one of your customers for an injury if the customer claims that a dish your restaurant served was defective. The same laws that apply to the sale of a Pinto by Ford or the sale of cigarettes by Lorillard Tobacco, Philip Morris, RJ Reynolds, and the Leggett Group apply to a sale of food by your restaurant. In one sense, it seems quite logical and fair that the laws apply equally to all businesses, regardless of size. When we take a closer look at the law, however, we see that it was not designed with the small restaurant business in mind.

HISTORY OF LIABILITY LAW

One of the harshest rules of early product liability cases was that people injured by defective products could not sue the manufacturers unless they purchased directly from them. This technical requirement was carried down the distribution lines so that only individuals who dealt directly with each other had rights against each other, and consumers could not sue anyone but the retailers with whom they had traded.

This doctrine was recognized as harsh and formalistic; thus, it was not followed in a number of situations. For example, a seller, regardless of its position in the chain of distribution, could be sued if negligent and if the product was *inherently dangerous*. The courts struggled for some time over just what was and what was not inherently dangerous. Current law provides that a product is inherently dangerous if injury to the owner is predictable if the item is defective. Where once a car was not deemed inherently dangerous, now negligence suits have been brought for such seemingly innocuous items as a toy top, rubber boots, and a lounge chair.

A manufacturer can be liable for defects in component parts made by another manufacturer if the assembler did not inspect them. As products became increasingly more complex, it is no longer true that the buyer and seller are equally knowledgeable or uninformed. Businesses are large enough to bear the immediate losses and ultimately can spread the risk over a broad number of consumers. Since the majority of the products on today's market are mass produced by large manufacturers, this rule reflects present economic reality.

Unfortunately, this is not the economic reality for many small restaurant businesses. However, they too must learn to cope with these laws in a climate of litigious consumers and generous juries.

IN PLAIN ENGLISH

It is better to learn about these problems while you can still protect yourself, rather than when it is too late.

PRODUCT LIABILITY

In every product liability case, the plaintiff must prove that:

- injury occurred to the plaintiff;
- the injury was caused by some defect in the product; and,
- the defect was present in the product when the defendant had control over it.

Once people are in possession of your product, you will not be able to stop them from injuring themselves. You can control this third element, however, by making sure that no item that leaves your control contains a defect. For example, if your restaurant allows take-out or if your signature dishes are packaged for sale, care should be taken that they are not defective when they leave your business's control.

The area of product liability has evolved to the point where restaurants are being held liable for food poisoning or other claims based on defective food or drink. The doctrines appear to have evolved with an eye to the large manufacturer of a mass-produced item, but the rules are applied with the same vigor to the small restaurant. Since a single lawsuit could ruin a small restaurant business, it is important to be aware of the potential risks involved and to take the necessary precautions.

Wendy's was recently involved in a claim that a severed finger was served in a bowl of its chili; however, it was soon determined to be a hoax. In other cases, foreign matter, including human flesh, has been discovered in restaurant food, and patrons have been scalded by overheated beverages. Similarly, national fast-food chains, such as McDonald's, Burger King, and others, have been charged with exposing their customers to the risk of inordinate weight gain as a result of the alleged unhealthy products they sell. While these claims receive a great deal of media attention, many smaller restaurant operations have been threatened with similar lawsuits, so it is important to be sensitive to these issues if your restaurant business is to survive.

FEDERAL LAWS

Not only is there state legislation pertaining to liability—there is at least one body of federal law that may directly affect your business. The *Consumer Product Safety Act* empowers the Federal Trade Commission (FTC) to regulate the composition, content, and design of any consumer product. The FTC has promulgated regulations for the use of architectural glass in doors, windows, and walls, and has banned the use of surface-coating materials (paints) containing lead. This is a dynamic area, and all manufacturers should check with the FTC to determine whether the materials used in their products are subject to regulation. These regulations would apply to many of the items used in your restaurant's kitchen and service areas.

THINK BEFORE YOU POUR

Restaurants that serve alcoholic beverages should be aware of the extent of their legal responsibility for intoxicated patrons. The amount of potential liability is staggering. In one Michigan case, a tavern owner's insurance company settled a wrongful death claim for more than $10 million. An Ohio bar and its owner were sued for $24 million by the widows of two men killed in a head-on collision.

Liability is generally dependent on the serving of alcohol to someone who is obviously intoxicated or under the legal drinking age. Today, most states have laws regarding the liability for servers of alcoholic beverages. Many states have statutes imposing liability called *dram shop* or civil damages acts. Other states impose liability through the common law. In most states, liquor license holders are responsible for damages if the individual served was intoxicated, the individual was a clear danger to him- or herself or to others, and intoxication was the cause of the subsequent harm. The requirements for liability do vary from state to state.

IN PLAIN ENGLISH

Restaurant owners and managers may even be personally liable for their employees' failure to follow alcoholic beverage regulations and dram shop laws.

Insurance may be available for restaurants that serve alcoholic beverages, but because of the increase in litigation, insurance companies have sharply increased their premiums. Some have dropped liquor liability coverage entirely. Several states, however, require dram shop insurance as a condition of a liquor license. In some states, there are state-operated insurance pools that will divide the risk among participating companies, so that liability coverage will be available to all commercial servers. You should contact your insurance broker or state insurance department for more information.

To reduce the risk of liability, servers should always ask for identification from anyone who appears to be under the age of 30 before serving an alcoholic beverage. It is somewhat more difficult to identify intoxicated guests, but servers should refuse to serve anyone who appears to have had too much to drink. Arrangements should be made for individuals who have had too much to drink to be driven home, either by other guests or by taxi. Some tow companies and mass transit operations offer free or low-cost transportation services for this purpose during holidays. Servers should be trained for such situations, and the training should be both ongoing and well documented.

IN PLAIN ENGLISH

To reduce the risk of liability: always ask for identification; refuse to serve anyone who appears to have had too much to drink; and, arrange transportation for individuals who have had too much to drink.

LIABILITY INSURANCE

Under the current law of product liability, a seller held liable for a defective product may, in turn, seek reimbursement from the manufacturer for the amount paid in damages. This may involve another expensive lawsuit, and if the manufacturer is broke, the seller is out of luck. There are two things that a seller might do for protection. First, incorporate or use another business form that offers limited liability. (see Chapter 1.) The second method of self-protection is to obtain insurance.

In general, the cost of liability insurance is affordable for the small restaurant business. Consult with your insurance broker or agent to ascertain the rates applicable to your business. You should also determine whether this form of insurance is available to you from professional trade or business associations with which you are affiliated. Many trade associations, such as national and local restaurant associations, provide product liability insurance to their members for reasonable prices. You must then evaluate the cost of insurance against the risk of a lawsuit. Many product liability suits are settled for, or are litigated to a judgment of, more than $100,000. You can deduct the cost of this kind of insurance as a business expense for tax purposes. Given these risk factors, since there is a reasonable expectation that a customer in your restaurant could sustain injury from consuming the food or drink your restaurant serves, you should seriously consider obtaining product liability insurance.

16
BUSINESS INSURANCE

Insurance has a certain air of gambling to it. You put down some money, and if a certain event occurs, you get back many times more. If it does not occur, you get back nothing. That is where the similarity ends. Public policy will not permit you to insure something unless you have what is called *an insurable interest*.

To have an insurable interest, you must have a property right, a contract right, or a potential liability that would result in a real loss to you if a given event occurs. This is simply to minimize the temptation you might have to cause the calamity against which you are insured. History contains too many gruesome stories of desperate or disturbed people obtaining insurance on a neighbor's barn or even a neighbor's child. Because of issues like these, most kinds of insurance—particularly liability insurance—do not cover injuries that are intentionally caused by the policyholder.

All insurance is based on a contract between the insurer and the insured, whereby the insurer assumes a specified risk for a fee, called a *premium*. The insurance contract must minimally contain all of the following:
- a definition of whatever is being insured (the subject matter);
- the nature of the risks insured against;

- the maximum possible recovery;
- the duration of the insurance; and,
- the due date and amount of the premiums.

When the amount of recovery has been predetermined in the insurance contract, it is called a *valued policy*. An *unvalued* or *open insurance policy* covers the full value of property up to a specified policy limit.

The insurance contract does more than merely shift the risk from the insured to the insurance company. The insurance industry is regulated by state law, which spreads the risk among those subject to that same risk. The risk spreading is accomplished by defining the method used for determining the amount of the premium to be paid by the insured. First, the insurance company obtains data on the actual loss sustained by a defined class within a given period of time. State law regulates just how the company may define the class. For example, an insurance company may not separate white restaurant owners and nonwhite restaurant owners into different classes, but it may separate drivers with many accidents from drivers with few.

Next, the company divides the risk equally among the members of the class. Then, the company adds a fee for administrative costs and profits. This amount is regulated from state to state. Finally, the premium is set for each individual in proportion to the likelihood that a loss will occur.

The very documents that a company uses to make insurance contracts are also regulated. Sometimes the state requires a standard form from which the company may not deviate, especially for fire insurance. A growing number of states require that *plain English* be used in all forms. Plain English is measured in reference to the average number of syllables per word and the average number of words per sentence. Because of a federal ruling that all insurance contracts are, per se, *fraudulent* if they exceed certain maximum averages, the insurance companies are forced to write contracts that an average person can understand.

EXPECTATIONS VS. REALITY

One frequent result of the excessive language used in most insurance contracts is that the signed contract may differ in some respects from what the agent may have led the insured restaurant owner to expect. If you can prove that an agent actually lied, then the agent will be personally liable to you for the amount of promised coverage. In addition, the insurance company itself may be liable for the wrongful acts of its agent.

Most often, the agent will not lie, but will accidentally neglect to inform the insured of some detail. For instance, if you want insurance for your employees who must drive to pick up unique recipe ingredients or a piece of kitchen equipment, the agent may sell you a policy that covers transport only in public carriers, such as when you rent a truck for the task. In most states, the courts hold that it is the duty of the insured to read the policy before signing. If you neglect to read the clause that limits coverage, such as to a public carrier in the example, you would be out of luck.

In other, more progressive states, this doctrine has been considered too harsh. These states allow an insured to challenge specific provisions in the signed contract to the extent they do not conform to reasonable expectations resulting from promises that the agent made. In the previous example, it might be considered reasonable to expect that you would be insured when you or your employees are engaged in your restaurant's activities. If the agent did not specifically call your attention to this limitation in the contract, odds are that you would have a good case for getting rid of it. In addition, it is common for the insured to receive the policy only after the premium is paid or only after a specific request is made.

Other states follow a different approach for contract interpretation and attempt to ascertain the intention of the parties. The first step in interpreting an insurance policy is to examine the text and context of the policy as a whole. If, after that examination, two or more conflicting interpretations remain reasonable, the ambiguity is resolved against the insurer. A court in these states will assume that parties to an insurance contract do not create meaningless provisions and will favor the interpretation that lets all provisions have meaning.

IN PLAIN ENGLISH

You should read the contract with the agent. If it is unintelligible, ask the agent to list all the important aspects on a separate sheet before signing, and keep that sheet with the policy.

Since you can, at best, break even with insurance, you might think it would be profitable to underinsure your restaurant. You could gain by paying lower premiums and lose only in the event that the damage exceeds the policy maximum. This has been tried and failed.

EXAMPLE: The insured stated the value of her unscheduled property as $9,950 and obtained insurance on that amount. (Unscheduled property means an undetermined collection of goods—for example, a restaurant business's furnishings and equipment—that may change from time to time.) Unfortunately, a fire occurred, causing at least $9,950 damage. The insurance company investigated the claim and determined that the insured owned at least $36,500 in unscheduled property. The company refused to pay on grounds that the insured obtained the insurance fraudulently. The court agreed with the insurance company, stating that the intentional failure to communicate the full value of the unscheduled property rendered the entire contract void. Therefore, the insured could not even collect the policy maximum. All she could hope for, at best, would be to get her premiums back.

Although at first glance this decision may seem harsh, its ultimate fairness becomes apparent with a little analysis. The chance of losing $9,950 out of $36,500 is greater than the chance of losing $9,950 out of $9,950, simply because most accidents or thefts do not result in total losses.

Various tests are used by the courts to determine whether an omission or mis-statement renders such a policy void. In almost all cases, the omission or mis-statement must be intentional or obviously reckless, and it must be *material* to the contract. Materiality is typically measured with reference to the degree of importance that the insurance company ascribes to the omitted or misstated fact. If stating the fact correctly would have significantly affected the conditions or premiums that the company would demand, then the fact is likely material. In the previous example, had the full value of the unscheduled property been stated, the insurer would either have demanded that the full value be insured or that a higher premium be paid for the limited coverage. Thus, the misstatement was clearly material.

Unintentional Undervaluing

It should be noted that not all undervaluations are material. Many insurance contracts do allow some undervaluation when it is unintentional. This provision is designed to protect the insured from inflation, which causes property to increase in replacement value before the policy's renewal date.

A so-called *coinsurance clause* generally provides that the insured may recover 100% of any loss up to the face value of the policy, provided the property is insured for at least 80% of its full value.

> **EXAMPLE:** If a restaurant worth $100,000 was insured for $80,000 and suffered a $79,000 loss from a covered casualty, the insured would recover the full amount of the loss, or $79,000. If the restaurant was only insured for $50,000, then a formula would be used to determine the amount of recovery.

$$\frac{\$50{,}000 \text{ (insurance)}}{\$100{,}000 \text{ (value of restaurant)}} \times \$74{,}000 \text{ (loss)} = \$39{,}500 \text{ (recovery)}$$

This formula requires you to establish a ratio between the amount of insurance coverage and the total value of the restaurant, and then multiply the resulting fraction by the loss to get the recovery.

IN PLAIN ENGLISH

It is important to carry insurance on at least 80% of the value of your restaurant business. Considering inflation, it is wise to reexamine your coverage each year. There are some policies that automatically increase the coverage annually based on some fixed percentage, such as the consumer price index (CPI).

All insurance policies are limited to defined subject matter and to losses to that subject matter caused by specific defined risks. Once the risks are recognized, it is a simple matter to decide whether or not to insure against them. However, correctly defining the subject matter of insurance is tricky business. Mistakes here are not uncommon and can result in anyone finding him- or herself uninsured.

SCHEDULING PROPERTY

The typical insurance policy will include various exclusions and exemptions. For example, most homeowner and auto insurance policies cover personal property, but exclude business property. If a restaurant owner keeps certain kitchen equipment at home for personal enjoyment, is it personal or business property? The answer depends on whether the restaurant owner ever uses this equipment at home for the benefit of the restaurant. If so, this may convert the equipment to business property.

In order to avoid the potentially uninsured loss of such property, the restaurant owner may *schedule* the items that are held for personal enjoyment. Scheduling is a form of taking inventory, in which the insured submits a list and description of all items to be insured with an appraisal of their value. The insurer assumes the risk of loss of all scheduled items without concern as to whether or not they pertain to the business. Insurance on scheduled property is slightly more expensive than that on unscheduled property.

Many battles occur over the value of objects stolen, destroyed, or lost. In anticipation of such battles, you should maintain records of the purchase price to establish the market price of items and an inventory of all items on hand. In the case of certain kinds of property (artwork used to decorate your restaurant, for example), the value must be determined by an expert in the field. However, this will not avoid all problems, because the insurance company can always contest the scheduled value.

WHEN TO INSURE

Three factors should be weighed to determine whether or not to obtain insurance. First, you must set a value on the items that are to be insured. Health is of the utmost value and should always be insured. Material goods are valued according to the cost of replacement. If you keep a large inventory of canned or packaged ingredients, or if you own expensive equipment, it probably should be insured. The most elementary way to determine if the value is sufficiently high to necessitate insurance is to rely on the pain factor—if it would hurt to lose it, insure it.

Second, you must estimate the chances that a given calamity will occur. An insurance broker can tell you what risks are prevalent in your industry or in your neighborhood. You should supplement this information with your personal knowledge. For example, you may know that your restaurant is virtually fireproof or that only a massive flood would cause any real damage. These facts should be weighed in your decision. If the odds are truly slim but some risk is still present, the premium will be correspondingly smaller in most cases.

The third factor is the cost of the insurance. If the cost will put you out of business faster than a fire would, you need to find some more affordable alternatives.

IN PLAIN ENGLISH

Bear in mind that insurance purchased to cover your restaurant business is tax deductible. This means that if you pay tax at a 33% rate, Uncle Sam is theoretically paying for 33% of your premium.

KEEPING THE COST DOWN

As already explained, the premiums charged by an insurance company are regulated by the government. Nonetheless, it still pays to shop around. Insurance companies can compete by offering different packages of insurance and by hiring competent agents to assist you in your choice.

If there are enough restaurants in your region, it may be possible for you to form a *co-op insurance* fund. Similarly, your local restaurant association may also consider the formation of an insurance co-op. To do this, you must estimate the total losses your co-op would sustain in the course of a year. Each member then contributes a *pro rata* share. The money is put into a bank to collect interest. If a disaster occurs and the losses are greater than the fund, each member must contribute to make up the difference. If there is money left over, it can be used to lessen the following year's premiums. This method is cheaper than conventional insurance because it eliminates insurance agents' commissions and whatever you would have paid toward the profit earned by the insurance company. Before you form your co-op, you should contact an attorney to determine what regulations exist in your state.

17

PEOPLE WHO WORK FOR YOU

There comes a time in the life of almost every restaurant business when it is necessary to get help, be it brain or brawn. The help typically needed first is the bookkeeper or accountant to assist in establishing accounting and bookkeeping systems. When things get a little hectic around the restaurant, you might then hire someone to help with serving, cooking, or running errands. If *customer relations* is not your greatest talent, you may wish to engage the services of a host or hostess, and perhaps an advertising professional. If business is really good, you will soon have to hire more employees to keep up with the demand.

INDEPENDENT CONTRACTORS

Someone hired on a one-time or job-by-job basis is called an *independent contractor*. Although paid for their services by the hiring firm or individual, contractors remain their own bosses and may even employ others to do the actual work.

If you occasionally hire a friend as a server, the friend may be an independent contractor. If you hire an accountant once or twice a year to go over your business records, that person too is probably an independent contractor. The fact that the person is independent and not your employee means that you do not have to pay Social Security, withhold income taxes, obtain a workers' compensation policy, or comply with the myriad employment rules imposed on employers.

More importantly, you are generally not liable for injuries to a third party resulting from the independent contractor's negligence or wrongful acts, even while working for you. However, there are situations when, despite your innocence, an independent contractor can render you legally responsible for his or her wrongful acts. Such situations fall into the following three basic categories.

1. If an employer is careless in hiring an independent contractor when a careful investigation would have disclosed facts to indicate that the contractor was not qualified, the employer may be liable when the independent contractor fails to properly perform the job and a third person is injured.

2. If a job is so dangerous as to be characterized as *ultrahazardous* or *inherently dangerous* and is to be performed for the employer's benefit, then regardless of who performs the actual work, the employer will remain legally responsible for any injuries that occur during the performance of the work. A fireworks displayer, for example, cannot escape liability by having fuses lit or rockets aimed by independent contractors.

3. An employer may be required by law to perform certain tasks for the health and safety of the community. These responsibilities are said to be *nondelegable*—that is, an employer cannot delegate them and thus escape liability for their improper performance. Therefore, if a nondelegable duty is performed by an independent contractor, the employer will remain responsible for any injury that results. A good example of a nondelegable duty is the law (common in many states) that business owners and others are responsible for keeping their sidewalks free of dangerous obstacles. If a restaurant hires an independent contractor to fulfill this obligation by removing ice during the winter, the restaurant is still legally liable if someone is injured on the slippery sidewalk, even if the accident resulted from the contractor's carelessness.

EMPLOYEES

The second capacity in which someone can work for you is as an *employee*. This category includes anyone whose work you exercise direct control over—helpers, apprentices, servers, cooks, a bookkeeper who is a member of your staff, and so forth. The formation of this relationship entails nothing more than an agreement on your side to hire someone and an agreement by that person to work. Although a written contract is generally not necessary, putting employment terms in writing so there are no misunderstandings later is always a good idea.

EMPLOYMENT CONTRACTS

While there is no prescribed form that the contract must take, there are, nevertheless, certain items that should be included. The first item should be the term of employment. An *employment contract* may be either *terminable at will* or for a fixed duration. (If the employment is to be for more than one year, there must be a written contract specifying the period of employment; otherwise, either party may terminate the relationship at any time.) Making the contract for a fixed period gives the employee some job security and creates a moral and contractual obligation for the employee to remain for the term. Of course, if the employee chooses to quit or the employer chooses to fire the employee, the law will not compel fulfillment of the contract. Improper, premature termination of a contract for a fixed period will, however, subject the party who is responsible for the wrongful act to liability for damages.

The second item is the *wage*. Unless you have gross sales of $500,000 or more per period or are engaged in interstate commerce, you do not have to comply with federal minimum wage laws. Most states, however, have their own minimum wage laws with which you must comply. Beyond the requirements imposed by law, the amount of remuneration is open to bargaining.

In addition to an hourly wage or monthly salary, other benefits can be offered, such as health and life insurance or retirement pensions, among others. Some professional advice in this area is strongly recommended in order to achieve the most advantageous tax treatment.

Third, it is often wise to spell out your employee's duties in the employment contract. This serves as a form of orientation for the employee and may also limit future conflicts over what is and what is not involved in the job.

Fourth, you may want your employee to agree not to work for someone else while working for you, or more importantly, not to compete against you at the end of the employment period. The latter agreement must be drawn carefully to be enforceable. Such an agreement must not be overly broad in the kind of work the employee may not do; it must cover a geographic area no broader than the one in which your business actually operates; and, it must be for a reasonable duration—a three-year period has been upheld.

Note that some states impose restrictions on *noncompetition agreements*. In Oregon, for example, a noncompetition agreement is unenforceable unless it was entered into either prior to or contemporaneously with the beginning of employment, or unless it became effective simultaneously with a meaningful promotion. Some states refuse to uphold noncompetition agreements. For example, California law states that a noncompetition agreement is generally void, as it is against public policy, unless it is coupled with a business sale or the purchase or sale of stock.

Employers may achieve some form of protection by restricting the use of the business's intellectual property. This should include a prohibition on the use of any company trade secrets, such as special recipes, both during the term of employment and thereafter. These restrictions should be in writing. It has been held that trade secrets may include, among other things, customer lists, supplier lists, recipes, and know-how.

Finally, *grounds for termination* of the employment contract should be listed, even if the contract is terminable at will. You should clearly specify that the contract may be terminated either for the specified causes or at the will of the employer.

Unlike the situation in which you have hired an independent contractor, your restaurant business is *vicariously liable* for the negligence, and sometimes even the intentional wrongdoing, of your employee when the employee is acting on behalf of the business. For example, if your employee is on the job and is involved in an automobile accident that is his or her fault, your business—as well as your employee—is legally liable. It would be wise to be extremely careful when hiring, and to contact your business insurance agent to obtain sufficient insurance coverage for your business resulting from your employees' job-related activities.

OTHER CONSIDERATIONS IN HIRING

There are other issues you should consider when hiring an employee, many of which fall into the realm of accounting or bookkeeping responsibilities. Therefore, you should consult with your accountant or bookkeeper, and in some cases, your attorney, regarding such items as the following.

- A workers' compensation policy for your employees in the event of on-the-job injury or occupational illness. State laws vary on the minimum number of employees that trigger this very important requirement. The workers' compensation laws of many states provide that an employer who has failed to obtain or keep in force required workers' compensation insurance will be strictly liable for on-the-job injury or illness, even in the absence of negligence. This includes not only medical expenses, but also damages for pain and suffering, lost earning potential, and other damages.
- Withholding taxes (federal, state, and local). Here, too, the laws vary and you must find out what is required in your locale. Employers are required to withhold employees' federal taxes, and failure to do so will expose the employer to liability for that amount plus interest and penalties. This tax

obligation is imposed not only on the business entity, but on its principals in their individual capacities.

- Social Security (FICA). There are some exemptions from this body of social legislation. Discuss this with your accountant or payroll service, or contact your local or regional Social Security office to determine how these exemptions may affect you.
- Unemployment insurance (both federal and state). There are also certain technical requirements for subcontractors and the like.
- Municipal taxes for specific programs such as schools or public transportation.
- Wage and hour laws (both federal and state). These include minimum wage and overtime requirements. In some states, the law also regulates holidays and vacations, as well as the method of paying employees during employment and upon termination.

Other items that should be considered when hiring an employee and that usually fall to management include:

- verification of work eligibility (including immigration or citizenship status and compliance with child labor and health and safety laws);
- background checks (which must be done in accordance with the Fair Credit Reporting Act);
- testing (skill tests, psychological tests, drug-screening tests, etc.);
- employee benefits, such as insurance coverage (medical, dental, prepaid legal), retirement benefits, memberships, parking or mass transit subsidies, and so on; and,
- union requirements, if you or your employees are subject to union contracts.

As already noted, the requirements, of these laws vary from state to state, and you are advised to discuss them with your lawyer, accountant, and bookkeeper. In addition, you should find out if any other forms of employment legislation, such as licensing requirements, apply to you, your employees, or your restaurant business.

IN PLAIN ENGLISH

It may be cost-effective for your restaurant business to contract with a payroll service, which will likely be proficient with many of these issues.

HAZARDS IN THE WORKPLACE

Employees are often not aware of the potential hazard that may result from even ordinary use of cleaning supplies and other toxic materials. It is advisable to research the potentially toxic effects of all substances used in your restaurant, whether or not they are labeled for toxicity. You should then disclose pertinent information regarding hazardous substances to your employees when they are hired. You are also required to post manufacturers' *material safety data sheets* (MSDSs), if available.

Congress and federal administrative agencies are becoming more active in the field of regulation of hazardous substances. You should also be aware that your state workers' compensation agency or the *Occupational Safety and Health Administration* (OSHA) may have passed special rules regarding specific workplace substances and activities. It is critical to obtain professional advice as to which of these regulations apply to your restaurant. Your state's labor department will likely be able to give you information regarding applicable workplace regulations.

Even though these laws are being enacted, your lawyer may not be able to tell you exactly to what extent you are legally obligated to advise your employees of potential risks inherent in their jobs. Again, the best course for a restaurant employer in doubt is to advise the newly hired individual of all known hazards that may result from the work, and to disclose the fact that there may be other undiscovered risks in using the particular materials involved in restaurant's activities. If an employment contract is used, a paragraph containing such a disclosure and the employee's acknowledgment of the known risks should be incorporated in the contract. A similar statement should also be included in any employment handbook.

While these documents would not provide a defense to a workers' compensation claim, they would sensitize employees to the need for caution in working with the toxic or hazardous materials. Needless to say, you should take all precautions available to protect the health and safety of those who work for you.

DISCRIMINATION

Restaurant owners and managers must comply with numerous antidiscrimination laws, including the *Civil Rights Act*, the *Equal Pay Act*, the *Age Discrimination in Employment Act* (amended by the *Older Workers' Benefit Protection Act*), and the *Americans with Disabilities Act*. The *Equal Employment Opportunity Commission* (EEOC) is responsible for enforcement of these laws.

Antidiscrimination laws apply not only during the hiring process, but also during the term of employment itself, including considerations for transfer, promotion, layoff, and termination. They apply to job advertisements, recruitment, testing, use of company facilities, training, benefits, and leave. These laws generally prohibit not only intentional discrimination, but also practices that have the effect of discrimination. Many antidiscrimination laws apply to independent contractors as well as employees.

IN PLAIN ENGLISH

Discrimination laws make it clear that members of management may not legally retaliate against employees or job applicants who file discrimination charges against them. If a restaurant is found to have unlawfully discriminated, then it will probably be liable for lost wages, punitive damages, and other damages, including attorney's fees.

Many states, as well as some cities and counties, have also passed laws that reiterate and expand the federal government's protection against discrimination. These laws are often more protective of employees than the federal law. In addition, some categories not covered by federal law, including those with respect to sexual orientation, may be covered by state or local law.

Civil Rights Act

The Civil Rights Act prohibits discrimination based on race, color, religion, sex, or national origin. With regard to *religious discrimination*, employers generally may not treat employees or applicants less or more favorably because of their religious beliefs or practices. Employees cannot be forced to participate or not participate in a religious activity as a condition of employment. Employers must reasonably accommodate employees' sincerely held religious beliefs and permit employees to engage in religious expression if employees are permitted to engage in other personal expressions at work. This law also requires the employer to take steps to prevent religious harassment of their employees, not only by other employees and management, but also by vendors and customers.

National-origin discrimination includes discrimination based on foreign accents and English fluency, as well as English-only rules (though there are exceptions if they are necessary for the safe or efficient operation of the business). *Race-based discrimination* includes discrimination based on skin color, hair texture, and facial features, as well as discrimination based on a person's marriage to or association with those of a different race. It also includes harassment and segregation on account of race.

The prohibitions against *sex-based discrimination* encompass pregnancy, birth, and related medical conditions, as well as sexual harassment. The *Equal Pay Act* (part of the *Fair Labor Standards Act*) also prohibits sex-based discrimination. It prohibits sex-based wage discrimination among persons in the same establishment who are performing under similar working conditions. Virtually all employers are subject to this Act.

More information about the Civil Rights Act and the Equal Pay Act can be obtained at the EEOC's website at **www.eeoc.gov**.

Harassment

One of the legal obligations of all business owners and managers is to create a nondiscriminatory work environment. A policy should be established prohibiting any discriminatory language (i.e., ethnic jokes or racial slurs) or other offensive language or activities.

Sexual harassment is one form of illegal discrimination, though harassment based on race and certain other characteristics also violates the Civil Rights Act. There are two basic types of sexual harassment—*quid pro quo* and *hostile environment*. Quid pro quo refers to either a harasser asking for sexual favors in exchange for some advantage in the workplace, or a harasser penalizing another person for rejecting his or her sexual advances. A hostile environment, on the other hand, is more generalized, in that the harasser creates or permits a hostile work environment through language, activities, or conduct.

An employer is subject to *vicarious liability* for a hostile work environment. Restaurant management will be responsible for the actions and language of a supervisor that results in an employee's injury, harm, or damage. If a supervisor has harassed or permitted harassment of an employee, and this situation has led to that employee's termination, relocation, or the like, the employer will be held liable for the discriminatory sexual actions of its supervisor. To avoid this form of liability, the employer must exercise reasonable care to prevent and promptly correct any harassing behaviors that are reported or otherwise become known. The employee who was harassed must also have taken advantage of all preventive programs or policies provided by the employer. There are a host of training and other resources available to business owners. Check with your business attorney or state employment division.

Many states have anti-harassment policies as well. For example, a relatively new law requires California employers with fifty or more employees to provide certain sexual harassment training and education to supervisory employees. Details of the California sexual harassment laws can be obtained at **www.dfeh.ca.gov**.

IN PLAIN ENGLISH

More information on sexual harassment is available at the EEOC website, at **www.eeoc.gov**.

Age Discrimination

Federal *age antidiscrimination* laws apply to employers of twenty or more employees, as well as to government and union offices. These laws provide that persons 40 years old or older may not be discriminated against due to their age in connection with any term, condition, or privilege of employment, including hiring, firing, layoffs, job compensation, benefits, job training, assignments, tasks, and promotions. More information on age discrimination is available at **www.eeoc.gov**.

Disabilities Discrimination

The *Americans with Disabilities Act* (ADA) prohibits discrimination against disabled persons in public accommodations, transportation, telecommunications, and employment. This Act applies to those who employ fifteen or more individuals. *An individual with a disability* means a person who has a physical or mental impairment that substantially limits one or more major life activities, has a record of the impairment, or who is regarded as having the impairment. A qualified individual with a disability is someone who, with or without reasonable accommodation, can perform the essential functions of the job.

Reasonable accommodation must be made so that a disabled job applicant or employee can perform the necessary and essential work of the job position. Reasonable accommodations include making existing employee facilities readily accessible to and usable by disabled employees, acquiring or modifying equipment or devices, job restructuring, and modifying work schedules.

A restaurant is not required to provide accommodations if to do so will result in an undue hardship. Under the Americans with Disabilities Act, *undue hardship* refers to an action requiring significant difficulty or expense when considered in light of factors such as the employer's size and financial resources.

Under the ADA, complex rules apply to medical examinations and inquiries, so you should contact an attorney for more information if you plan to make such inquiries or require any physical examinations.

For more information concerning the Americans with Disabilities Act, see **www.ada.gov**. Many states have laws that are comparable to or more restrictive than the ADA. You should check with your business attorney or state employment division to determine whether your state has such legislation.

Because employers in the food service industry have obligations under state and local health laws to protect the public from food poisoning and the transmission of disease through contact with food, the EEOC has issued guidelines to assist employers with the interaction of these laws. You can find more information at **www.eeoc.gov/facts/restaurant-guide.html**.

JOB DESCRIPTIONS

It is important that a *job description* be drawn up for each position. The description should include only the tasks necessary to carry out the required responsibilities—that is, only *bona fide occupational qualifications*. These are qualifications that a manager can prove are necessary for the safe and efficient performance of the job, or for the normal operation of the particular business or enterprise. In other words, your chef must be able to actually cook.

Job qualifications can include such mental and physical attributes as previous experience, a minimum age (i.e., in order to serve alcoholic drinks or work after curfew), speaking more than one language, licensure to provide certain services, or certification by a professional organization to perform certain tasks.

EMPLOYEE HANDBOOKS

You should have an *employee handbook* to set forth your restaurant's policies on sexual harassment and nondiscrimination, hours of work, security, overtime, and so on. The handbook should make it clear that it is not an employment contract, and in fact, that employment is *at will*. It should also cover trade secret protection. This document should be drafted or reviewed by an attorney, since there are numerous requirements for legal notices and other areas that a layperson or even a handbook software program may fail to properly address.

If you plan to monitor your employees' Internet usage, emails, computer files, phone calls, voicemails, and the like, use video surveillance, or conduct searches of employees' personal belongings, you should include a specific written employee privacy policy identifying the types of situations where employees should not have an expectation of privacy. Note that your employees do have certain privacy rights, such as privacy in the restroom. Any monitoring must be done in a nondiscriminatory manner, to ensure quality and equitable enforcement of policies and standards.

ZERO TOLERANCE POLICIES

A *zero tolerance* standard will best protect an employer from discrimination claims. An employee handbook containing policies against sexual harassment, offensive behaviors, and the like is a good starting point. A well-drafted discrimination policy will apply to behavior, as well as oral and written (including electronic) communications. It will include procedures that provide employees with a way to confidentially report problems regarding offensive or harassing behavior, and will direct management on how to investigate and resolve the issues. The process should include an employee appeals process for any adverse findings. The complaint and appeals procedures should direct an employee to contact someone other than the employee's immediate supervisor, since that supervisor may be the one responsible for such conduct.

Employees should be advised that both complaints and appeals need to be put in writing so that there can be no misunderstandings, though the first step is often verbal. A well-drafted policy should state that the employer will, whenever possible, provide complaining employees and witnesses reasonable confidentiality. However, it should be made clear that there can be no assurance of confidentiality, since it may become necessary for management to disclose the identity and testimony of relevant parties in any legal proceeding.

IN PLAIN ENGLISH

It is essential for employers to provide employees with ongoing education in respect to employment relations, including harassment and discrimination issues.

THE FAMILY AND MEDICAL LEAVE ACT

The *Family and Medical Leave Act* (FMLA) allows employees to take up to twelve weeks of unpaid leave each year for certain family or medical reasons, as long as they have worked for the employer for a year and meet certain other eligibility requirements. The Act must be followed by private sector employers who employ fifty or more employees during the current or preceding calendar year, and who are engaged in interstate commerce or any activity affecting commerce.

An eligible employee may take his or her twelve-week leave:
- due to the birth and care of his or her newborn;
- when a foster child is placed with the employee;
- to care for a spouse, child, or parent with a serious health condition; or,
- to take care of the employee's own serious health condition.

The Act defines *serious health condition* as an illness, injury, impairment, or physical or mental condition that brings about a period of incapacity, or requires intensive and continual medical treatment, and specifically includes prenatal care. When the worker returns to the job, the job may be the exact job that the employee left or it may be an equivalent job—with equivalent duties, pay, benefits, and so on. The only employees to which this would not apply are key employees whose absence from their positions will cause substantial and grievous economic injury to the employer.

There are certain notice requirements, as well as rules for requiring medical certification of the need for leave. More information can be found at **www.dol.gov**. Many states have supplemental leave acts. Check with your business attorney or state employment division for more information.

MINIMUM WAGE AND OVERTIME

Although employers may generally set compensation, there are federal and state laws that affect compensation rates. The *Fair Labor Standards Act* (FLSA) (as amended), which applies to many restaurants (since it applies to any business with gross sales of $500,000 or more per year or which is engaged in interstate commerce), provides for a federal minimum wage and overtime rates. Many states have passed legislation providing higher minimum wages than the federal government, and if you are operating your restaurant in one of those states, you will need to pay your employees the higher amount.

The Fair Labor Standards Act does not limit the working hours in a day or week for an employee 16 years or older. *Overtime* means any time in excess of forty hours per week, and an employee who works overtime must be paid one-and-one-half times his or her regular rate of pay for all overtime worked. To be exempt from minimum wage requirements and overtime pay, an employee must hold a professional, administrative, or executive position, be an outside salesperson, or work in certain computer-related occupations. Certain other limited categories of workers are exempt from overtime pay, but not from minimum wage requirements.

Note that the FLSA holds salaried managers exempt from overtime pay only if they are paid on a *salary basis*. An exempt, salaried employee who receives a paycheck of a predetermined amount is not subject to having that amount reduced due to variations in the quality or quantity of the work performed. For example, a restaurant must pay its manager his or her full salary, regardless of whether or not that manager works less than forty hours in a given week. A reduction of such a manager's salary resulting from unavoidable absences or cash register shortages would defeat the exempt status of that manager. Recently, both the Long John Silver's restaurant chain and Starbucks Coffee Company have been sued for failure to pay overtime pay.

You should be aware that most states have rules regarding overtime that are more stringent than the FLSA, and those more stringent rules must be followed.

TIPS

Tips are often an important issue in the restaurant industry. The Fair Labor Standards Act defines a tipped employee as one who regularly receives more than $30 per month in tips. The restaurant may consider these tips as part of the waitstaff's wages, but the restaurant must also pay a minimum of $2.13 per hour in direct wages to tipped employees. If the restaurant opts for this tip credit, it must also inform the involved employees in advance of this practice, and must be able to demonstrate that the employees receive at least the minimum wage when their regular wages and the tip credit allowance are combined. Note that this is the federal law only—many states do not allow a tip credit. Additionally, employees must retain all of their tips, except to the extent that they participate in a valid *tip-pooling* arrangement.

A tip is generally given to a waitstaff employee directly and personally by a patron. The tip then belongs to that employee, unless the restaurant has a tip-pooling arrangement, where participating employees share their tips with one another in a predetermined fashion. Tip-pooling is the subject of numerous cases, and the Department of Labor has held that only those who customarily participate in a tip pool may legally be permitted to do so when the tip pool is established by the employer. If an employee participates in a tip-pooling arrangement, the restaurant should document the employee's participation by having him or her sign a tip-pooling consent form.

Note that, by law, tipped employees cannot be required to share their tips with restaurant personnel who do not customarily receive tips, such as dishwashers and cooks. However, the restaurant may reduce the amount of a tip received by a tipped employee on a credit card by an amount equal to the fees levied by the credit card company.

The Department of Labor has also raised questions about whether an employee must be compensated for activities that are merely preparatory, as distinguished from actual time spent on the employer's assigned work. Thus, if an employer requires servers to wear a particular uniform, then the time necessary to don that uniform will be deemed *work time* and the employee must be paid for that time. This should be distinguished from a situation where a server merely changes clothes for his or her own convenience. In this situation, the time used in changing clothes will not be deemed work time and compensation will not be due.

In the event no salary is specified, the law will presume a reasonable wage for the work performed. Thus, you cannot escape paying your employees fairly by not discussing the amount they will earn. If you hire someone to bus the tables, and the accepted salary in your region for such a person is $6 per hour, then it will be presumed that he or she was hired for this amount unless you and that person have agreed to a different amount.

TERMINATION OF EMPLOYMENT

Determining whether someone is an employee or an independent contractor is not always easy. One reason the characterization is important is that employers are responsible for income tax withholding, Social Security, workers' compensation, and the like, while one who hires an independent contractor is not.

There is another reason that the characterization may be important. If the individual working for you is an independent contractor, the contract between you and that person will govern your respective rights regarding termination. On the other hand, if the individual is an employee, care must be taken not to become responsible for a wrongful termination when dismissing the individual.

Historically, an employee who was not under contract could be terminated for any reason whatsoever. Approximately thirty years ago, this right of absolute dismissal was challenged and the rule was modified. At that time, it was held that an employee's job could be terminated for the right reason or for no reason at all, but could not be terminated for a wrong reason. For example, an employee whose job was terminated for refusing to commit perjury before a legislative committee was entitled to recover damages against the employer for wrongful termination. The public policy of having individuals testify honestly was considered more important than the employer's right to control the employment relationship.

Courts have become even more protective of the rights of employees. In a 1983 case, *Novosel v. Nationwide Insurance Company*, the U.S. Circuit Court of Appeals held that the power to hire and fire could not be used to dictate an employee's political activity, and that even a nongovernmental entity is limited by the Constitution in its power to discharge an employee. The court, in essence, held that one's right to exercise constitutionally protected free speech was more important than the employer's right to control an employee's conduct.

Wrongful termination cases fall into at least four general categories. Employers may not legally terminate an employee's job for the following reasons:
1. refusing to commit an unlawful act, such as committing perjury or participating in illegal price-fixing schemes;
2. performing a public obligation, such as serving on a jury or serving in a military reserve unit;
3. exercising a statutory right, such as filing a claim for workers' compensation; or,
4. discrimination.

In a bizarre case, the Arizona Supreme Court held that an employee whose job was terminated for refusing to moon fellow employees in a parody of the song "Moon River" during a company retreat was entitled to damages for wrongful termination. The public policy of protecting her right of privacy was deemed more important than the employer's right to terminate an employee's position for disobedience. The courts appear to go quite far in holding that an employer cannot discharge an employee unless there is *just cause* for termination. Some states may have legislation that would restrict the employer's right to terminate an employee's job to cases in which there was just cause. These laws also contain specific prohibitions on the termination of employment for *whistleblowing* (i.e., cases in which employees notify government authorities of wrongful acts by the employer, such as tax evasion, or cases in which employees tell corporate officers about wrongful acts of immediate supervisors).

Employers should take some precautions to avoid being placed in the untenable position of having bound themselves to individuals in their employment when the relationship has soured. This can result from language in employee handbooks that might be construed as giving rise to a contractual right. It is also possible that oral statements made by recruiters or interviewers could give rise to contractual rights. To avoid this problem, an employer should have a legend placed in any employee handbook making it clear that the material is not an employment contract and that no oral statement by a hiring agent is binding on the company unless it is reduced to writing. It has also become common for employers to require prospective employees to sign a statement making it clear that the employment is at will and does not give rise to any contractual right. If there is a probationary period, the employer should be careful to state that the probationary employee will become a *regular* or *full-time* employee, rather than a *permanent* employee. Further, care should be taken to avoid specifying a fixed probationary period, since it could be argued that the candidate must be retained for at least that period.

In addition, if there is any evaluation of the employee after the probationary period has ended, it should be conducted fairly. When evaluations become merely *pro forma*, problems can and do arise. Employees may argue that they have received sparkling evaluations and are being fired for some invalid reason.

Perhaps an employer who uses evaluations should employ what has been characterized as *progressive discipline*. In this procedure, the employer starts by orally warning a problem employee of the concern, and progressively imposing disciplinary practices until termination becomes the only form of recourse left. Care should be taken not to violate the employee's rights, since the liability for wrongful termination can be catastrophic to a small restaurant business. When in doubt, an employer should contact an attorney with some experience in the field of employment relations. In this area, as with many others, pre-problem counseling can prevent a good deal of time-consuming and costly litigation.

18

KEEPING TAXES LOW

A restaurant business can enhance profitability by increasing sales or reducing expenses. Careful purchasing will go far in expense reduction, but taxes have one of the most profound effects on business profitability. Most business planning is tax driven, and prudent businesspeople are careful to determine the tax consequence of virtually every transaction.

You should have periodic meetings with your business lawyer and tax accountant to determine the most expeditious and cost-effective method of conducting your business. Restaurant businesses should have at least one year-end planning session for the purpose of evaluating business activities and tax planning.

The U.S. Tax Code allows for basic needs through personal exemptions, a narrow list of personal deductions, and a reduced tax rate for those at the low end of the income scale. As of 2005, there are five graduated tax rates for individuals—10% on the lowest taxable income range, 15% and 28% on income in the middle taxable income ranges, and 33% and 35% on income in the highest taxable income ranges.

Capital gains taxes for many long-term investments were cut by the *Jobs and Growth Tax Relief Reconciliation Act*. This applies to sales of capital assets made after May 6, 2003, and is a great tax advantage over the higher capital gains rates in place over the preceding decade.

Note that the tax rates for gains on such items as depreciation recapture and gain on the sale of collectibles remain at the regular ordinary graduated tax rates.

INCOME SPREADING

There are two important means of reducing tax liability. The first is spreading taxable income by the use of several provisions in the Tax Code. The second is the use of tax deductions.

Installments and Deferred Payments

One way a business can spread income is to receive payment in *installments*. Care must be taken with the mechanics of this arrangement. If a business makes a sale for a *negotiable note* due in full at some future date, or for some other deferred payment obligation that is essentially equivalent to cash or that has an ascertainable fair market value, the business may have to report the total proceeds of the sale as income realized when the note is received, not when the note is paid. (A *negotiable note* is a written and signed promise to pay a specified sum of money either on demand or at a specified time, payable either to an identified party or to the bearer.) The *Internal Revenue Code* (IRC) does, however, enable a taxpayer who sells property with payments received in successive tax years to report the income on an installment basis in some situations, if the sale is properly structured. Under this method, tax is assessed only as payments are received.

> **EXAMPLE:** Suppose you remodel your restaurant kitchen and sell your used equipment for $15,000. Ordinarily, the entire $15,000 would be taxable income in the year you received it (not allowing for recaptured depreciation, which is

beyond the scope of this discussion). If, however, you use the installment method, with three annual payments of $5,000, income from the sale will be taxed as the installments are received. In either case, the amount of income is $15,000, but under the installment method, the amount is spread out over three years, and you may be able to take advantage of being in a lower tax bracket than had you taken the full $15,000 in the year you sold the equipment. Be aware that there are special rules for installment sales, which are extremely complex and should be discussed with your tax advisor.

Someone in a high tax bracket might wish to defer income until the future. For example, a popular chef could obtain an agreement from the employer that salary paid would not exceed a certain amount in any one year, with the excess to be carried over and paid in the future. This would result in tax savings to the chef if, when the deferred amounts are finally paid, the chef was semi-retired and in a lower tax bracket.

There are drawbacks to deferred payments. These include the possibility that the party owing the money may not be willing to pay interest on the deferred sums and the possibility that that party could go broke before the debt is fully paid. In addition, the Internal Revenue Service may very well challenge such arrangements as a sham, since the recipient had control over the income. One should consider these risks carefully before entering into a contract for deferred payments, because it might be quite difficult to change the arrangement if the need should arise.

Spreading Income Among Family Members

Another strategy for restaurant owners in high tax brackets is to divert some income directly to members of their immediate families who are in lower tax brackets, by hiring them as employees. Putting dependent children on the payroll can result in substantial tax savings, because their salaries can be deducted as a *business expense*. If the business is unincorporated, then no Social Security and Medicare taxes are required to be withheld from pay relating to these wages. This salary arrangement is permissible as long as the child is under 18 years of age. Your child can earn up to the amount of the *standard deduction* without incurring any tax liability. You, as the taxpayer, can still claim a personal dependency exemption for the child if you provide over half of his or her support and if the child is under 19 years of age at the end of the tax year, or if the child is between the ages of 19 and 24 and is a full-time student. The child, however, may not claim a personal exemption if he or she can be claimed by the parents on their tax return.

There are other restrictions on such an arrangement:

- the salary must be reasonable in relation to the child's age and the work performed;
- the work performed must be a necessary service to the business; and,
- the work must actually be performed by the child.

A second method of transferring income to members of your family is the creation of a family partnership. Each partner receives an equal share of the overall income unless the partnership agreement provides otherwise. The income is taxed once as individual income to each partner. If you are the parent who heads a family business, you can break up and divert your income to your family members so it will be taxed to them according to their respective tax brackets. The income received by children may be taxed at significantly lower rates, resulting in more income reaching the family than if it had all been received by the parent, who is presumably in a higher tax bracket than the children. The law stipulates, however, that if a child is under 14 years of age and receives unearned income from the partnership, any amount over $1,600 (subject to change each year) will be taxed at the parents' highest marginal rate.

IN PLAIN ENGLISH

Although the IRS recognizes family partnerships, it may subject them to close scrutiny to ensure that the partnership is not a sham.

In addition, if partnership capital produces significant income and partners are reasonably compensated for services performed for the partnership, the IRS may opt to forbid the shift in income in accordance with the IRC section that deals with distribution of partners' shares and family partnerships. The same section provides that a person owning a capital interest (or ownership interest) in a family partnership will be considered a partner for tax purposes, even if he or she received the capital interest as a genuine and irrevocable gift.

Incorporating a Family or Setting Up an LLC

Some families have incorporated or created family-owned limited liability companies (LLCs). If the IRS questions the motivation for such incorporation, the courts will examine the intent of the family members. If the sole purpose of incorporating was tax avoidance, this arrangement will not stand. If the IRS successfully contends that the business entity should be disregarded, the IRS can reallocate income from the corporation or LLC to the individual taxpayer. This will be done, for example, if the corporation or LLC does not engage in substantial business activity and does not observe proper formalities, or if its separate status is not otherwise adhered to by the businessperson.

Tax Advantages and Disadvantages

A *bona fide* (genuine) corporation or limited liability company being taxed as an entity may provide some tax advantages for the owner of a small business. As an employee, the owner can control his or her taxable income with a limited salary. Although the corporation or LLC must recognize income whenever a sale is made, the entity can deduct the owner's salary and other business expenses.

Incorporating or creating an LLC should not be done solely for tax reasons, and since individual tax rates are now substantially lower than corporate tax rates, you may actually find that you are paying more tax on any profits left in the corporation than if you had chosen a pass-through type of entity, such as a partnership, S corporation, or LLC electing pass-through tax status. Additionally, there are some unavoidable legal and accounting expenses that will need to be paid to set up and maintain the business entity. If your business operates on very small margins, you should determine whether the possible tax savings to you justify the additional legal and accounting costs associated with creating and maintaining a business entity. The cost to the entity for payroll taxes, unemployment taxes, workers' compensation, and legal and accounting fees can be substantial, though most of these will apply even to a sole proprietor or partnership.

In addition, use of the corporate form is no longer necessary for setting up a retirement plan. Revisions to the rules for pension plans allow a self-employed person to set aside as much money for retirement as could be done through a corporate retirement plan.

IN PLAIN ENGLISH

While creating a business entity may not provide tax benefits in some situations and may even result in added expense, it still may afford you a liability shield. Many businesses are incorporated or created as LLCs primarily for the purpose of obtaining limited liability for their owners.

There are several potential business tax problems that a restaurant owner should carefully consider before forming a corporation or LLC. Making use of a corporation or LLC taxed as an entity means that any distribution of profits to owners in the form of distributions will be taxed twice—once at the entity level as business income and again at the owner level as personal income. This double taxation can often be avoided through careful tax planning and distribution of profits through means other than distributions, such as wages. Although creating a business entity allows income to be shifted from the businessperson to other owners, such as family members, without the use of careful tax planning, the shift may occur at the expense of double taxation. Obviously, it is important to consult with an accountant or tax advisor in order to determine whether the benefit of shifting income to a corporation or LLC taxed as an entity outweighs the effects of double taxation.

Another alternative for the small enterprise is to organize as an S corporation. Income from an S corporation is taxed only once, at the individual level. Although income from a partnership, self-employment, or LLC electing tax pass-through treatment is also taxed only once at the individual level, the tax rates associated with the incomes are different. Income to owners of S corporations is not subject to Social Security and Medicare taxes (or, as it is sometimes called, self-employment taxes).

The tax law allows an LLC to elect to be taxed as an entity (either as a C corporation or an S corporation), or to be taxed as if the business were still run as a sole proprietorship (in states allowing one-person LLCs) or a partnership. If no election is made, the default tax treatment will be that of a partnership if there is more than one member, or that of a sole proprietorship if there is only one member. You should be aware that some states have a gross receipts tax for LLCs that may make an LLC an unattractive option in your state.

TAXES ON ACCUMULATED EARNINGS AND PASSIVE INVESTMENT INCOME

If a business incorporates as a C corporation in order to postpone a significant portion of income, the IRS may impose an *accumulated earnings tax*. The IRC allows a maximum accumulation of $250,000, which is not subject to the accumulated earnings tax. Accumulated earnings beyond the maximum must be justified as reasonable for the needs of the business. Otherwise, the earnings will be subject to a tax of 38.6%, in addition to the regular corporate tax.

The IRC also imposes an additional tax on most types of passive investment income, which is income retained by the corporation or LLC (electing entity taxation) if the business entity is found to be a personal holding company. The current rate is 38.6%. This may occur if 60% of the corporation's income consists of copyright, book, movie, or other royalties; dividends; rents; or, personal service contracts.

Also, if the owner sells his or her stock or ownership interest before the corporation has realized any income, the corporation could become a *collapsible corporation*, causing the gain realized on the sale of the stock to be taxed at ordinary income rates.

QUALIFYING FOR BUSINESS DEDUCTIONS

Another means of reducing tax liability involves making use of various tax deductions. For this, you must keep full and accurate records. Receipts are a necessity. Even if your business is based at home, as are some start-up food businesses (such as catering), you should have a separate checking account and a complete set of books for all the activities of your food-based business. A hobbyist or dilettante is not entitled to trade or business deductions in excess of earnings, except in very limited circumstances.

Tax laws presume that a person is engaged in a business or trade, as opposed to a hobby, if a net profit results from the activity in question during three out of the five consecutive years ending with the taxable year in question. For instance, if the food-based business owner does not have three profitable years in the last five years of working as such, the IRS may contend that the work merely constitutes a hobby. In this case, the taxpayer will have to prove profit motive in order to claim business expenses in excess of income for that year. Proof of a profit motive does not require proof that a profit would actually be made—it requires proof only of intention to make a profit.

The *Treasury Regulations* call for an objective standard on the profit-motive issue, so statements of the taxpayer as to intent will not suffice as proof. The Regulations list the following nine factors to be used in determining profit motive.

1. The manner in which the taxpayer carries on the activity (e.g., effective business routines and bookkeeping procedures).
2. The expertise of the taxpayer or the taxpayer's advisors (e.g., study in an area, awards, prior publication, critical recognition and membership in professional organizations).
3. The time and effort expended in carrying on the activity (i.e., at least several hours a day devoted to the activity, preferably on a regular basis).
4. Expectation that business assets will increase in value.
5. The success of the taxpayer in similar or related activities (e.g., past successes, even if prior to the relevant five-year period).
6. History of income or losses with respect to the activity (e.g., increases in receipts from year to year, unless losses vastly exceed receipts over a long period of time).
7. The amount of occasional profits, if any, that are earned.
8. Financial status of the taxpayer (wealth sufficient to support a hobby would weigh against the profit motive).
9. Elements of personal pleasure or recreation (if significant traveling is involved and little work accomplished, the court may be suspicious of profit motive).

No single factor will determine the results. The case of *Deering v. Blair* provides an example of how the factors are used. Deering was the executor of the estate of Reginald Vanderbilt, whose financial affairs and residence were in New York. Vanderbilt had purchased a farm near Portsmouth, Rhode Island, because he was interested in horses, and operated it as a business. The business produced little income, but Vanderbilt claimed business expenses of more than $25,000 in each of three years. The fact that Vanderbilt did not rely on the income from the farm for his livelihood was considered by the court in making its decision. The court held that despite the fact that he had several employees and advertised the farm's horse boarding and rental services, the purpose for operating the farm was not to produce a profit. Rather, the land was used for pleasure, entertaining, exhibition, and social diversion. Thus, the business deduction was disallowed.

While a new business is not presumed to be engaged for profit until it shows a profit three out of five years, deductions have been allowed in cases when this test is not met. In *Allen v. Commissioner*, the tax court decided to allow business deductions for the proprietors of a ski lodge that was rented out during the ski season. The deduction was allowed even though the lodge did not show a profit during the years in question and despite the fact that the proprietors did not depend on the income from the lodge for their livelihood. They did, however, keep accurate records and did not use the lodge for their personal pleasure. Consequently, they were able to show that the lodge was operated as a business.

In *Engdahl v. Commissioner*, the tax court found a profit motive on the part of the taxpayers who were considering retirement and wanted to supplement their incomes by operating a horse ranch. The court held that, despite a series of losses, the taxpayers had kept complete and accurate records reviewed by an accountant, had advertised the operation, had taken their horses to shows, and had worked up to fifty-five hours per week on the operation. Additionally, the assets of the ranch had appreciated in value. All these facts showed that the taxpayers had a profit motive, and therefore, the business expense deductions were allowed.

Once you have established yourself as engaged in a business, all your *ordinary and necessary* expenditures for that business are deductible business expenses. This would include supplies, workspace, kitchen equipment, research, professional books and magazines, travel for business purposes, certain conference fees, advertising and other promotional expenses, postage, legal and accounting fees, and employee wages.

SPECIAL RULES FOR PAYROLL TAXES ON TIPS

One of the more complex issues that arises in the restaurant industry is the tax treatment of tips. Tips received from customers by restaurant employees are generally subject to withholding taxes. The amount received by the employee must be reported to the employer by the 10th of the month following the month in which the tips were received. The employee's report should include the amount of cash tips received, as well as the amount of tips that the employer paid over to the employee from charge or debit card customers. No report is required for months when the tips are less than $20. The report form that is used is IRS Form 4070, *Employee's Report of Tips to Employer*, or a similar statement. The statement needs to be signed by the employee and also include the following:

- the employee's name, address, and Social Security number;
- the employer's name and address;
- the month or period that the report covers; and,
- the total of tips received during the month or period.

IN PLAIN ENGLISH

The employer must collect income taxes on the employee's tips, including employee Social Security and Medicare taxes. These taxes may be collected from the employee's wages or from other funds that the employee makes available for this purpose.

A couple of programs have been implemented by the IRS to help employers comply with the tip-reporting requirements. The first is the *Tip Rate Determination Agreement* (TRDA). In this program, the employer enters into an agreement with the IRS to report cash and charge tips to employees at a fixed percentage rate. Another is the *Tip Rate Alternative Commitment* (TRAC). In this program, the employer agrees to encourage employees to properly report all of the tips received. In addition, periodic education about tip-reporting requirements is provided. In return, the IRS will limit the circumstances under which it will later assess taxes to the employer for any unreported tips found.

In *Fior D'Italia, Inc.*, the U.S. Supreme Court considered the validity of the IRS's aggregate estimation of tips method. In this case, the IRS did a compliance check on a restaurant employer relating to tips reported by the employees and used an *aggregate estimation of tips method*. Under this method, the credit card slips were examined and the IRS determined the average percentage rate for tips paid by the charge customers. It was then assumed that cash-paying customers also paid at this same rate. The estimated total tips were then calculated by multiplying the tip rate by the employer's total gross receipts. This total was then compared to the actual amount of tips reported by the employees. Taxes were then assessed by the IRS on the amount they estimated was not reported. The Supreme Court held that the Internal Revenue Code authorized the IRS to use this aggregate estimate method.

FICA Tax Credit on Tips

Restaurants may claim a tax credit for FICA taxes—also known as Social Security taxes—that are paid on eligible tip income. A tax credit is a dollar-for-dollar reduction of tax liability. This tax credit is available regardless of whether the employee reported the tips. The amount of tips needed to bring the employee's hourly rate up to the minimum wage is not eligible for the FICA deduction, nor does it qualify for a tax credit. You should discuss this further with your tax advisor.

DEDUCTIONS FOR THE USE OF A HOME IN BUSINESS

In the past, one of the most significant problems of deductible expenses has been the home office deduction; however, the rules for home office deductions have relaxed in recent years. This is very important to some food-based business owners, as it is not uncommon for a small business to run its food-based business from home. Many food-based business owners, especially caterers, see no need for renting a separate office, given that maintaining a separate office can be costly and unnecessary. Others, of course, choose to maintain their business office at home for purposes of privacy and to maximize the use of the restaurant space.

Tax law changes have made taking a home office deduction much more attractive than it has been in the recent past. The benefits of taking a home office deduction should be looked at carefully. The home office deduction allows various home expenses to be deducted against the net business income. Expenses that fall into this category include, but are not limited to:

- mortgage interest;
- real estate taxes;
- home repairs and maintenance;
- rent;
- utilities;
- insurance;
- security system; and,
- depreciation.

Indirect expenses are those that benefit both the business and the personal use portions of the home. The business portion of the expense is taken as a percentage of the total spent. The business use percentage is determined by dividing the square footage of space used for business by the total square footage.

Direct expenses are those that were made to improve only the business use portion of the home. These amounts are allowed in full.

In order for an area of your home to be considered for business use, it must be used regularly and exclusively. *Regularly* means that the space is consistently used for business purposes only, meaning that occasional use does not qualify. *Exclusively* means that the area is used only for the business purpose. Note that there is an exception for the storage of inventory. Under this circumstance, the area does not have to be exclusive. Generally, an area is used for business if it meets the mentioned tests and is:

- the principal place of business (this includes administrative use—a home office will generally qualify as a business use for administrative work if the area is used exclusively and regularly and there is no other location available for the taxpayer to conduct these activities);

- a place to meet clients (such as catering customers); or,
- used for business purposes and is a separate structure from the taxpayer's personal residence.

When the office is in a structure separate from the principal residence, the requirements for tax deductibility are more relaxed. The structure must be used exclusively and on a regular basis, just as an office in the home. However, when the office is in a separate structure, it need only be used *in connection with* the business, not as the principal place of business.

When taxpayers use a portion of their homes for storage of business materials, the requirements for tax deductibility of the storage are also more relaxed. The dwelling must be the sole, fixed location of the business, and the storage area must be used on a regular basis for the storage of the business equipment or supplies. The room used for storage need not be used entirely or exclusively for business, but there must be a separately identifiable space suitable for storage of the business-related items.

The primary tax advantage of the home office deduction comes from a deduction for an allocable portion of repairs, utility bills, and depreciation. Otherwise, these would not be deductible at all. The allocable portion is the square footage of the space used for the business, divided by the total square footage of the house, and multiplied by the taxpayer's mortgage interest, property taxes, etc. Determining the amount of allowable depreciation is highly complex, and you should discuss it with your accountant or tax advisor.

The total amount that can be deducted for an office or storage place in the home is artificially limited. The amount that can be deducted is determined by taking the total amount of money earned in the business and subtracting the allocable portion of mortgage interest, property taxes, and other deductions allocable to the business. The remainder is the maximum amount that you can deduct for the allocable portion of repairs, utilities, and depreciation. In other words, your total business deductions in this situation cannot be greater than your total business income minus all other business expenses. The office-at-home deduction, therefore, cannot be used to create a net loss, but any disallowed home office expense can be carried forward indefinitely and deducted in future years against profits from the business.

If you sell the home, any business deductions taken for depreciation expense after May 6, 1997 will have to be recaptured and taken as income. This is essentially a timing wash of taking the expense in one year and taking the same amount back as income in the year you sell the home. It is no longer necessary to split out the gain between personal and business use.

OTHER PROFESSIONAL EXPENSES

As mentioned earlier, tax-deductible business expenses include not only the workspace, but also all the ordinary and necessary expenditures involved in your food-based business. Current expenses, including the cost of items with a useful life of less than one year, are fully deductible in the year incurred. Salaries and employee benefits, food ingredients, advertising, insurance premiums, utilities, legal and accounting expenses, and the like are all examples of current expenses.

Certain kinds of expenses, however, often cannot be fully deducted in the year in which made but can be extended over several tax years. For example, the purchase of equipment that has a useful life of more than one year, such as kitchen equipment and restaurant furniture, is a *capital expenditure*. These kinds of capital expenditures cannot be fully deducted in the year the equipment is purchased. Instead, the taxpayer must *depreciate* or allocate the cost of the item over the item's estimated useful life. Although the actual useful life of professional equipment will vary, fixed periods have been established in the tax code over which depreciation may be deducted.

In some cases, it may be difficult to decide whether an expense is a capital expenditure or a current expense. Repairs to equipment are one example. If you spend $200 repairing your dishwasher, this expense may or may not constitute a capital expenditure. The general test is determining whether the amount spent restoring the appliance adds to its value or substantially prolongs its useful life. Since the cost of replacing short-lived parts of an appliance to keep it in efficient working condition does not substantially add to its useful life, such a cost would be a current cost and would be deductible. The cost of rebuilding the dishwasher, on the other hand, significantly extends its useful life. Thus, such a cost is a capital expenditure and must be depreciated.

For most restaurant (and other) businesses with net income, however, an immediate deduction can be taken when equipment is purchased. For 2005, up to $100,000 of such purchases may be expensed for the year and need not be depreciated at all. This expense election may be used to wipe out the income of the business but not create a loss. Any additional amount not expensed in the first year will be carried forward to depreciate in future years.

As mentioned, in addition to fees paid to lawyers or accountants for business purposes, employee salaries and benefits are also deductible as a current expense.

TRAVEL EXPENSES

On a business trip, whether within the United States or abroad, your ordinary and necessary expenses, including travel and lodging, may be 100% deductible if your travel is solely for business purposes (except for luxury water travel). Business meals and meals consumed while on a business trip are deductible up to 50% of the actual cost. If the trip primarily involves a personal vacation, you can deduct business-related expenses at the destination, but you may not deduct the transportation costs.

If the trip is primarily for business but part of the time is given to a personal vacation, you must indicate which expenses are for business and which for pleasure. In such cases, a portion of the business-related expenses will be nondeductible. This is not true in the case of foreign trips if one of the following exceptions applies:

- you had no substantial control over arranging the trip;
- less than 25% of the time is spent in non-business activity;
- the trip outside the United States was for a week or less; or,
- a personal vacation was not a major consideration in making the trip.

If you are claiming one of these exceptions, you should be careful to have supporting documentation. If you cannot take advantage of one of the exceptions, you must allocate expenses for the trip abroad according to the percentage of the trip devoted to business as opposed to vacation.

The definition of what constitutes a *business stay* can be very helpful to the taxpayer in determining a trip's deductibility. Travel days, including the day of departure and the day of return, count as business days if travel outside the United States is for more than seven days and business activities occurred on such days. Any day that the taxpayer spends on business counts as a business day, even if only a part of the day is spent on business. A day in which business is canceled through no fault of the taxpayer counts as a business day. Saturdays, Sundays, and holidays count as business days, even though no business is conducted, provided that business is conducted on the Friday before and the Monday after the weekend, or on one day on either side of the holiday.

ENTERTAINMENT EXPENSES

Entertainment expenses incurred for the purpose of developing an existing business are also deductible in the amount of 50% of actual cost; however, you must be especially careful about recording entertainment expenses. You should record the amount, date, place, type of entertainment, business purpose, substance of the discussion, the participants in the discussion, and the business relationship of the parties who are being entertained. Keep receipts for any expenses over $75. You should also keep in mind the stipulation in the tax code that disallows deductibility for expenses that are lavish or extravagant under the circumstances.

No guidelines have yet been developed as to the definition of the term *lavish or extravagant*, but one should, nevertheless, be aware of the restriction. If tickets to a sporting, cultural, or other entertainment event are purchased, only the face value of the ticket is allowed as a deduction. If a skybox or other luxury box seat is purchased or leased and is used for business entertaining, the maximum deduction now allowed is 50% of the cost of a non-luxury box seat.

EXPENSES THE IRS SCRUTINIZES

The prior sections cover business travel and entertainment expenses both inside and outside the United States. The rules are more stringent for expenses incurred while attending conventions and conferences outside of the United States. The IRS tends to review very carefully any deductions for attendance at business seminars that also involve a family vacation, whether inside the United States or abroad. In order to deduct the business expense, the taxpayer must be able to show, with documentation, that the reason for attending the meeting was to promote production of income. Normally, for a spouse's expenses to be deductible, the spouse must be a co-owner or employee of the business.

IN PLAIN ENGLISH

Often, seminars will offer special activities for husbands and wives and will provide appropriate IRS documentation.

As a general rule, the business deductions are allowed for conventions and seminars held in North America. The IRS is taking a closer look at cruise ship seminars and is requiring two statements to be attached to the tax return. The first statement substantiates the number of days on the ship, the number of hours spent each day on business, and the activities in the program. The second statement must come from the sponsor of the convention to verify the initial information. In addition, the ship must be registered in the United States and all ports of call must be located in the United States or its possessions. The deduction is also limited to $2,000 per individual per year. Again, the key for the taxpayer taking this sort of deduction is careful documentation and substantiation.

RECORDKEEPING

Keeping a logbook or expense diary is probably the best line of defense for the restaurant owner with respect to business expenses incurred while traveling. If you are on the road, keep the following things in mind.

- With respect to travel expenses:
  - keep proof of the costs;
  - record the time of departure;
  - record the number of days spent on business; and,
  - list the places visited and the business purposes of your activities.
- With respect to transportation costs:
  - keep copies of all receipts in excess of $75, and if traveling by car, keep track of mileage and
  - log all other expenses in your diary.

Similarly, with meals, tips, and lodging, keep receipts for all expenditures over $75 and make sure to record all less-expensive items in your logbook.

IN PLAIN ENGLISH

Food-based business owners may also take tax deductions for their attendance at trade shows, seminars, retreats, and the like, provided they are careful to document the business nature of the trip. Accurate recordkeeping is critical for tax preparation.

CHARITABLE DEDUCTIONS

The law provides that an individual or business can donate either money or property to qualified charities and take a tax deduction for the donation. Individuals are afforded more favorable deductions for donations of money or property they own than are businesses that donate a product or service. Individuals, such as chefs, whose services are auctioned for a charity may not take a tax deduction for their time, even if they are otherwise highly compensated.

The tax law requires independent appraisals in a form prescribed in the IRC for donated property. In addition, if the taxpayer personally receives any benefit from the charity, the amount deducted must be reduced by the fair market value of the benefit received. Benefits could include, for example, attendance at museum openings or merchandise such as books, tapes, or CDs. Since this area can be quite technical, you should consult with your tax advisor before making any charitable donations.

There have been some abuses on the part of charities that resulted in misappropriations of donated funds. If you have any question about the validity of a particular charity, you should contact your state attorney general's office or the local governmental agency that polices charitable solicitations in your area.

HEALTH INSURANCE

Self-employed individuals may deduct the amount paid for medical insurance for themselves, their spouses, and their dependents.

IN PLAIN ENGLISH

If you do not know whether a particular activity is deductible, you should consult with a competent accountant or tax advisor before embarking on it. In any case, consultation with qualified tax professionals is always advisable, to ensure maximum benefits.

19

RENTING COMMERCIAL SPACE AND ZONING ISSUES

A restaurant, by definition, is a commercial enterprise and must, therefore, occupy a commercial space. As a result, unless you own the building your business occupies, you will probably find it necessary to evaluate the terms and conditions of a commercial lease. Commercial leases are much more subject to negotiation and pitfalls than residential leases, which are more tightly regulated in most states. You should consult an attorney with experience in negotiating commercial leases, preferably restaurant leases, before signing one.

Landlords typically employ the services of a broker when attempting to rent commercial space. In addition, many restaurateurs hire brokers to assist them with lease negotiations. This discussion is intended to alert you to some of the topics that should arise in your discussion with your lawyer or real estate broker.

To begin with, the exact space to be rented should be identified in detail in the lease. Determine whether there is a distinction between the space leased and the actual space that is usable. Often, tenants are required to pay rent on commercial space measured from *wall to wall* (commonly referred to as a "vanilla shell"), even though after the area is built out, the resulting usable space may be significantly smaller.

If your space is in a shopping center or office building and you share responsibility for common areas with other tenants, these responsibilities should be spelled out. The lease should address who is responsible for cleaning and maintaining common areas, when the common areas will be open or closed, and what other facilities (such as restrooms and storage) are available.

Another important item is the cost of the space. Determine if you will be paying a flat monthly rental or one that will change based on your earnings at the location, as is often the case in shopping centers and office buildings. In order to evaluate the cost of the space, you should compare it with other similar spaces in the same locale. Do not be afraid to negotiate for more favorable terms. Care should be taken not to sign a lease that will restrict you from opening another facility close to the one being rented.

It is also important for you to consider the period of the lease. If, for example, you are merely renting a booth at a food fair or event, then you are only concerned with a short term. On the other hand, if you intend to rent for the foreseeable future, it is a good idea to get an option to extend the lease because, when you advertise and promote your restaurant, your location is one of the things about which you will be telling people. Moving can cause a lot of problems with mail and telephone numbers. Besides, if you move every year or two, some customers may feel that you are unstable and occasional patrons may not know where to find you after you move. Worse still, they may find a competitor in your old space. In fact, a restaurant's goodwill is often defined as including a stable location.

Long-term leases are recordable in some states. Recording is generally accomplished by having the lease filed in the same office where a deed would be filed. Your real estate attorney or broker can assist you with this. If you are in a position to record your lease, it is probably a good idea to do so, since you will then be entitled to receive notices, legal and otherwise, which are related to the property.

It is essential for you to determine whether there are any restrictions on the particular restaurant activity you wish to perform on the leased premises. For example, the area may be zoned so as to prohibit you from having certain forms of entertainment. It is a good idea to insist on a provision that puts the burden of obtaining any permit or variances on the landlord, or, if you are responsible for them, the inability to obtain them should be grounds for terminating the lease without penalty.

Be sure the lease provides that you are permitted to use any sign or advertising on the premises, or that it spells out any restrictions. It is not uncommon, for example, for historic-landmark laws to regulate signs on old buildings.

You should also be aware that extensive remodeling may be necessary for certain spaces to become suitable for your use. If this is the case, then it is important for you to determine who will be responsible for the costs of remodeling, who will determine the contractors to be used, and who owns the tenant improvements. In addition, it is essential to find out whether it will be necessary for you to restore the premises to their original, pre-remodeled condition when the lease ends. This can be expensive and, in some instances, impossible.

The *Americans with Disabilities Act* (ADA) requires places of public accommodation to be reasonably accessible. The law is broadly interpreted and includes restaurants. The term *reasonable accommodation* is not precise, and thus it is important to determine what must be done in order to fulfill the requirements of this federal statute. Typically, approximately 25% of the cost of any covered remodel must be allocated to items that aid accessibility. These would include, among other things, levered door openers, Braille signs, larger bathroom stalls, wheelchair ramps, elevators, and approved disability-accessible doors. You should determine whether the cost of complying with the ADA will be imposed on the landlord, the tenant, or both.

Environmental laws may inhibit the use of your space for certain substances. It is essential for you to determine whether any of the materials used in your restaurant will violate federal, state, or local rules with respect to hazardous or other prohibited materials. In addition, there can be hazardous materials cleanup problems resulting from prior uses of the space to be occupied by you. For example, if the space was previously used by a drycleaner, chemical company, automotive repair business, or the like, there may be a requirement to conduct an expensive cleanup operation prior to any occupation. Likewise, if your building contains any asbestos or lead-based paint, there may be an increase in the costs of remodeling and occupation. It is essential for you to spell out in the lease who will bear the costs of any environmental compliance.

WHO PAYS FOR WHAT?

If you need special hookups, such as water or electrical lines, you should determine whether the landlord will provide them or whether you will have to bear the cost. Of course, if the leased premises already have the necessary facilities, you should question the landlord regarding the cost of these utilities. Determine if they are included in the rent, or are paid separately.

In some locations, garbage pickup is not a problem, since it is one of the services provided by the municipality. On the other hand, it is common for renters to be responsible for their own trash disposal. For restaurants, this can be quite expensive and should be addressed in the lease.

Customarily, the landlord will be responsible for the exterior of the building. It will be the landlord's obligation to make sure that it does not leak during rainstorms and that it is properly ventilated. Notwithstanding this fact, it is important for you to make sure the lease deals with the question of responsibility if, for example, the building is damaged and some of your property is damaged or destroyed.

IN PLAIN ENGLISH

If you have to take out insurance for the building, as well as its contents, your costs will greatly increase. Determine who will be responsible for insuring what.

Similarly, you should find out whether or not it will be your obligation to obtain liability insurance for injuries that are caused in portions of the building not under your control, such as common hallways and stairwells. It is imperative that you have your own liability policy for accidental injuries or accidents that occur on your leased premises.

SECURITY AND ZONING

A good lease will also contain a provision dealing with security. If you are renting indoor space in a shopping center or office building, it is likely that the landlord will be responsible for external security, although this is not universally the case. If you are renting an entire building, it is customarily your responsibility to provide whatever security you deem important. If installing locks or an alarm system is something in which you are interested, you should address the question in your lease negotiations.

Another issue, not often considered, is whether the space is free of unwanted ghosts. Recently, the landlords of a Florida entertainment complex sued two restaurant owners for refusing to move into a building they claim is haunted. Although the landlords offered to arrange for an exorcism, neither of the restaurateurs were of a religious faith that practices exorcism, and they chose to back out of their lease. As part of the suit, the judge is being asked to determine whether the building is haunted and, if so, whether the ghosts would interfere with the restaurants' business.

Does the lease have any restrictions on deliveries, their time, or location? Since most restaurants receive bulky deliveries, your lease should contain a provision that will give you the flexibility you desire.

If the place you wish to rent will be used as both your personal dwelling and for business, other problems may arise. It is quite common for zoning laws to prohibit certain activities, such as restaurants or catering, when the area is zoned residential. Conversely, most commercially zoned areas prohibit residential occupation. You should consult with your attorney before attempting to operate out of your home or to live in your commercial space.

It is essential for you to be sure that every item agreed upon between you and the landlord is stated in writing. This is particularly important when dealing with leases, since many state laws provide that a long-term lease is an interest in land and can be enforced only if in writing.

IN PLAIN ENGLISH

The relationship between landlord and tenant is an ancient one that is undergoing a good deal of change. Care should be taken when examining a potential business location to determine exactly what you can do on the premises and whether the landlord or municipal rules will allow you to use the location for its intended purpose.

HOME-BASED OPERATIONS

Many catering businesses are home based, and it is not uncommon to attempt to expand those businesses into boutique restaurants or coffee shops. The problems raised by the multiple use of a dwelling can be divided into two basic areas—whether local zoning regulations legally allow operating a commercial food business and living in the same place, and whether the income tax laws recognize the realities of home-based food businesses. For a full discussion of the income tax considerations of designating a part of your home as an office or food business, see Chapter 18.

Local Zoning Restrictions

In residential areas, regulations may require permits and restrict the size and use of the workspace. The state health department, for example, must approve all commercial kitchens.

For the person who wants to maintain a commercial food operation (such as catering or gourmet food packaging) from home, several types of restrictions may apply. The space devoted to the business activity may be limited to a certain number of square feet; outbuildings may or may not be allowed. The type of equipment used may also be restricted. Noise, smoke, and odor restrictions may apply, and approval may be required from all or some of the neighbors. If remodeling is contemplated, building codes must also be considered.

You also may have to obtain a home-occupation permit or, in most areas, a business license. The application fee for either of these will normally be a flat fee or a percentage of annual receipts from the business activity. Depending upon the success of the business, this could become a substantial expense. In addition, your homeowner's or renter's insurance policy may contain some restrictions relating to commercial activity. You should contact your insurance broker to find out whether or not your policy contains such limitations and what can be done to deal with them.

Since the zoning laws that prohibit the operation of home-based businesses were generally enacted for the purpose of preserving a residential quality in residential neighborhoods, including air quality, traffic flow, and noise, it is possible these laws could be violated by the operation of a home-based commercial food business. While a catering business would likely not be deemed a violation under these laws, a coffee shop or boutique restaurant may very well. There is a risk in establishing any home-based business without complying with the laws as they are written or obtaining a proper exemption from them.

20

PENSION PLANS

One of the methods by which a restaurant owner may attract and retain key personnel is to provide certain benefits. Today, one of the most important benefits for employees is the ability to participate in a retirement plan. In addition, any form of succession planning will necessitate the establishment of a method by which the senior generation can step down and hand off control of the business. In order to create an effective succession plan, it is necessary to implement an arrangement that provides an economic incentive for senior workers to retire. This is likely to be a retirement plan.

A retirement plan is a written savings program. If the plan meets specific rules and regulations, then it is called a *qualified plan*, which means contributions are tax deductible for the person or the business making the investments. Income taxes on the investment earnings are delayed until benefits are paid to participants. A qualified plan is one of the last remaining tax shelters available to highly compensated individuals. It may be used to set aside funds for retirement and to attract and retain key employees. If properly structured and invested on a prudent basis with a diversified portfolio of investments, the plan should provide financial security for the individual's retirement.

When choosing a plan, select the type that will most satisfactorily meet your needs and those of your employees. There are essentially two types of qualified plans—defined benefit and defined contribution.

DEFINED BENEFIT PLANS

Contributions to a *defined benefit plan* are determined by a relatively complex formula and are then monitored by an enrolled actuary. The promised benefit is not to exceed the lesser of 100% of the employee's annual average income for the three highest salaried consecutive years or a specified amount, which is adjusted annually and dependent on changes in the Consumer Price Index. For the current permissible amount, see the IRS website at **www.irs.gov**. *Excess earnings* (investment income greater than the assumptions made by the actuary) are used to reduce the cost of contributions to the plan by the employer.

Normally, defined benefit plans are appropriate when the business owner is *mature*, with less than ten to fifteen working years until retirement. Defined benefit plans are appropriate—and potentially beneficial—for restaurants that have enjoyed considerable financial success with limited fluctuations in cash flow. The defined benefit plan can be designed to drain excess funds and allocate them to retirement on behalf of the senior preferred participant (the principal owner). In many instances, this same advantage can be attained through the use of an age-weighted defined contribution plan, such as a profit-sharing or target-benefit plan.

DEFINED CONTRIBUTION PLANS

In a *defined contribution plan*, the contribution on behalf of the participant is defined and is usually either a discretionary amount or a percentage of the participant's annual compensation (ignoring compensation in excess of $210,000). The benefit that will be available to the participant at retirement is not defined. Investment earnings increase the retirement benefit for the plan participants, and the longer the period over which investments are accumulated and interest is earned, the greater the amount of benefits that will be available to the participants at retirement.

IN PLAIN ENGLISH

A major difference between a defined contribution plan and a defined benefit plan is who bears the risk of poor investment performance. The employer bears this risk in defined benefit plans, whereas participants bear this risk in defined contribution plans.

Profit-sharing plans, money-purchase plans, and salary savings or reduction plans, such as 401(k)s and SIMPLE plans, are all defined contribution plans, as are Simplified Employee Pension Plans (SEPs) and Employee Stock Ownership Plans (ESOPs).

Profit-Sharing Plans

If the income from your restaurant varies significantly from year to year, a profit-sharing plan may be the most appropriate type of plan to offer your employees. Contributions may be determined at or after the end of the tax year. Contributions to the plan can be determined by a vote of the restaurant management (i.e., managing partners or the board of directors) or by a formula previously designated in the plan's documents. It is no longer required that business entities, such as corporations or certain types of LLCs, actually have a profit in order to make a contribution. The maximum deductible contribution to a profit-sharing plan is now 25% of an employee's annual compensation, with each participant's total annual addition limited to $42,000 per year.

Salary Savings or Reduction Plans

These plans, which include 401(k)s, are a variant of profit-sharing plans. Under this type of plan, the employee elects to have a percentage of his or her gross salary diverted into a qualified plan. The employee's contributions are pretax dollars, so this type of plan provides the employee with significant tax savings.

Depending on the plan, the employer may elect to match all or a portion of the contributions made by the employee. Usually, the amount of the matching contribution has a percentage limit.

The main feature of salary savings or reduction plans is that a portion of the cost shifts from the employer to the employee. The business, therefore, makes a smaller cash contribution.

A major drawback is the limitation of contributions by highly compensated employees. The maximum contributions allowable continuously change and can be found on the IRS website. In addition, owners and highly compensated employees may not be allowed to save the maximum amount if the savings rate of the other employees is too low. They are generally allowed to save about 2% of compensation more than the average of the non-highly compensated employees. To avoid being limited by this restriction, you may consider a safe harbor 401(k) plan that requires advance notice to participants and a nonforfeitable employer contribution. In 2006, 401(k) plans will be allowed to accept Roth contributions.

Simplified Employee Pension Plans

These plans are often viewed incorrectly as an alternative to the more highly structured qualified plans. The maximum contribution that the employer may contribute per participant to a SEP continues to change and can be found on the IRS website. Contributions are based on an equal percentage of annual salary for all employees 21 years or older who have performed service for the employer during at least three out of five years and have received a minimum salary specified by the tax laws. Although its low maintenance cost is an initial attraction, its simplicity results in significant inflexibility that many employers are not willing to accept, since those whose employment has been terminated must share in any contribution and all contributions are 100% vested and nonforfeitable.

Salary Reduction Simplified Employee Pension Plans (SAR/SEPs) could no longer be created after December 31, 1996. Existing SAR/SEPs were grandfathered in and are allowed to exist until the employer terminates them. Another salary reduction plan, called the SIMPLE IRA, was introduced to replace the SAR/SEP. This plan is available to employers with a maximum of 100 employees. Employees are eligible if they earned at least $5,000 during either of the previous two years and are expected to earn at least $5,000 during the current year. These requirements can be reduced or eliminated if the employer waives them. The maximum employee contribution for 2005 is $10,000 for participants under the age of 50 and $12,000 for participants aged 50 or older. The employer is required to match up to 3% of the employee compensation. Vesting for the employer contributions is 100% and immediate.

Money-Purchase Plans

A money-purchase plan is a type of defined contribution plan that has a fixed funding requirement, such as 10% of compensation of all eligible participants. It also requires that participants be offered a qualified joint and survivor annuity as a form of benefit distribution. It has the same tax deduction and annual addition limits that apply to profit-sharing plans. Most new plan sponsors choose the profit-sharing plan instead, and since 2002, many money-purchase plans have been converted to profit-sharing plans.

Employee Stock Ownership Plans

In an ESOP plan, the majority of the assets are shares of stock in the corporate plan sponsor. Generally, ESOPs are not useful for owners of small restaurants.

Hybrid Plans

The target-benefit plan is receiving renewed interest as a result of changes in income tax law. This hybrid plan combines the contribution and benefit levels of a defined contribution plan with the recognition for mature employees found in defined benefit plans. Another hybrid, the age-weighted profit-sharing plan (AWPSP), is also available. As with the target-benefit plan, the contributions are weighted or skewed toward senior employees.

DESIGNING AND DOCUMENTING A PLAN

The creation of a qualified plan requires the creation and adoption of a written plan document and trust agreement before the end of the first plan year. A summary plan description must also be drafted to inform participants about the plan. Documentation is available in two forms—prototype documents and individually drafted documents. Each form has its own advantages and limitations. It is, therefore, essential to work with an experienced professional when selecting and establishing a plan.

IN PLAIN ENGLISH

Since 1982, federal tax laws have allowed unincorporated businesses the same status as corporations with regard to qualified retirement plans. Further, this same legislation eliminated the need for a corporate trustee (who was approved by the IRS), thus allowing the self-employed person to be the trustee of his or her own plan.

Many qualified plans of small businesses are top-heavy. This is a special status that results from key employees having more than 60% of the plan's benefits. As a result, minimum contribution rules and faster vesting rules apply. The minimum contribution is the lesser of 3% of compensation or the highest rate allocated to a key employee. The vesting schedule options are a three-year cliff or a graded schedule of 20% per year from the second to the sixth year of employment.

Plans may be combined, or *stacked*, in order to more specifically meet the needs of the business. However, this creates a need for separate sets of rules and limitations. Stacking also increases the amount of administrative paperwork and forms, thus driving up the cost of operating and maintaining the plan. Fortunately, the need to stack plans was significantly reduced in 2002, when the deduction limit of profit-sharing plans was raised from 15% to 25%.

The design features outlined below can be used to limit or reduce the cost of rank-and-file employees in the employer-sponsored plan.

Vesting

A key element of any qualified plan is rewarding long-term service by employees. One method used to limit benefits for employees who have been employed for a relatively short period of time is by a *vesting* schedule that forfeits all or some of the participant's employer-provided benefits. Vesting means having rights in, which is to say that the employee has the right to all or part of his or her benefits in the retirement plan.

Currently, there are two primary vesting schedule formulas.

1. *Five-year cliff vesting.* This schedule does not allow vesting for employees with fewer than five years of service. Upon completion of five years of service, the employee is 100% vested in all employer-provided benefits. When the plan is top-heavy, the longest permitted cliff vesting schedule is three years.

2. *Three-to-seven-year graded vesting.* This vesting schedule provides for 20% vesting after three years of employment and an additional 20% for each subsequent year. After completing seven years of employment, the employee is eligible to receive 100% of the employer-provided benefits upon termination of employment. When the plan is top heavy, the graded schedule must start with the second year of employment rather than the third year. A non-top-heavy plan's vesting schedule, as it applies to employer matching contributions, must also be as fast as two to six years.

Minimum Hours

The plan sponsor may limit the participation of employees by permanently excluding those who work fewer than 1,000 hours per year and then by limiting each year's contributions to those who have worked at least 500 hours during the year. This feature can be very important for restaurants that use temporary or part-time employees.

Minimum Age

The plan sponsor may also limit participation of employees through the use of a minimum-age requirement. Current law allows an employer to postpone participation by employees under 21 years of age. At the time the employee reaches age 21, he or she enters the plan and all of that employee's years of employment are counted in the vesting formula. This too can be very important for restaurants.

Unions

Employees that are a part of a collective bargaining unit may specifically be excluded from participation in a qualified plan established by an employer for its non-union employees, provided that retirement benefits were the subject of good faith bargaining.

Integration with Social Security

This feature allows the plan sponsor to recognize contributions made on behalf of the employee to Social Security. An integrated plan (also referred to as allowing *permitted disparity*) has an extra contribution for those whose compensation is greater than the Social Security wage base.

Investments in a Qualified Plan

The primary governing law regarding investments made by a qualified plan comes from the *Employee Retirement Income Security Act* (ERISA). That law imposes the use of the *Prudent Expert Investment Principle*, which means that investments should be made with primary consideration given to what an expert, rather than an amateur, investor would do.

There are a plethora of investment opportunities, including stocks, bonds, money market accounts, real estate, and partnership interests. It is, therefore, essential that you confer with a registered investment advisor or a certified financial planner to structure your plan investments based on the plan's goals, the economy, and other relevant factors.

21

ESTATE PLANNING

No matter how big your restaurant is and no matter how successful you are, the time that you will work with your business is limited by either retirement or death. Prudent restaurateurs will make appropriate plans for both, which is commonly known today as *succession planning*. One of the most important aspects of succession planning is estate planning. Another aspect of succession planning is retirement, which was discussed in Chapter 20.

Proper estate planning will require the assistance of a knowledgeable lawyer and perhaps also a life insurance agent, an accountant, a real estate agent, a business appraiser, and a bank trust officer. What help will be needed and from whom will depend on the nature and size of the estate. This chapter considers the basic principles of estate planning. This discussion is not a substitute for the aid of a lawyer experienced in estate planning; rather, it is intended to introduce you to the basic principles, alert you to potential problems, and aid you in preparing to work with your estate planners.

THE WILL

A *will* is a legal instrument by which a person directs the distribution of his or her property upon death. The maker of the will is called the *testator*. Recipients of gifts are known as *beneficiaries* or *legatees*. Gifts given by a will are referred to as *bequests* (personal property) or *devises* (real estate). Certain formalities are required by state law to create a valid will. About thirty states allow only formally witnessed wills, requiring that the instrument be in writing and signed by the testator in the presence of two or more witnesses. The other states allow either witnessed or unwitnessed wills. If a will is entirely handwritten and signed by the testator, it is known as a *holographic will.*

A will is a unique document in two respects. First, if properly drafted, it is *ambulatory*, meaning it can accommodate change, such as applying to property acquired after the will is made. Second, a will is *revocable*, meaning that the testator has the power to change or cancel it at any time. Even if a testator makes a valid agreement not to revoke the will, the power to revoke it remains (of course, under such circumstances, if the testator uses that power, he or she may be liable for breach of contract).

Generally, courts do not consider a will to have been revoked unless it can be established that the testator either (1) performed a physical act of revocation, such as burning or tearing up a will with intent to revoke it, or (2) later executed a valid will that revoked the previous will. Most state statutes also provide for automatic revocation of a will, in whole or in part, if the testator is subsequently divorced or married.

To change a will, the testator must either execute a supplement, known as a *codicil*, which has the same formal requirements as those for creating a will, or a new will. To the extent that the codicil contradicts the will, the contradicted parts of the will are revoked.

Payment of Testator's Debts

When the testator's estate is insufficient to satisfy all the bequests in the will after debts and taxes have been paid, some or all of the bequests in the will must be reduced or even eliminated entirely. The process of reducing or eliminating bequests is known as *abatement*, and the priorities for reduction are set by state law according to the category of each bequest. The legally significant categories of gifts are generally as follows:

- specific bequests or devises, meaning gifts of identifiable items ("I give to X all the furniture in my home");
- demonstrative bequests or devises, meaning gifts that are to be paid out of a specified source unless that source contains insufficient funds, in which case the gifts will be paid out of the general assets ("I give to Y $1,000 to be paid from my shares of stock in ABC Corporation");
- general bequests, meaning gifts to be paid out of the general assets of an estate ("I give Z $1,000"); and,
- residuary bequests or devises, or gifts of whatever is left in the estate after all other gifts and expenses are satisfied ("I give the rest, residue, and remainder of my estate to Z").

Intestate property, or property not governed by a will but part of the testator's estate, is usually the first to be taken to satisfy claims against the estate. (If the will contains a valid residuary clause, there will be no such property.) Next, residuary bequests will be taken. If more money is needed, general bequests will be taken, and lastly, specific and demonstrative bequests will be taken together in proportion to their value. Some states, however, provide that all gifts, regardless of type, abate proportionately.

DISPOSITION OF PROPERTY NOT WILLED

If the testator acquires more property during the time between signing the will and death, the disposition of such property will also be governed by the will. If such property falls within the description of an existing category in the will (e.g., "I give all my stock to X; I give all my real estate to Y"), it will pass along with all similar property. If it does not and the will contains a valid residuary clause, such after-acquired property will go to the residuary legatees. If there is no residuary clause, such property will pass outside the will to the persons specified in the state's law of intestate succession.

When a person dies without leaving a valid will, this is known as dying *intestate*. The estate of a person who dies intestate is distributed according to the state law of intestate succession, which specifies who is entitled to what parts of the estate. In general, intestate property passes to those persons having the nearest degree of kinship to the decedent. An intestate's surviving spouse will always receive a share, generally at least one-third of the estate. An intestate's surviving children generally get a share. If some of the children do not survive the intestate, the grandchildren of the intestate may be entitled to a share *by representation*. Representation is a legal principle meaning that if an heir does not survive the intestate but has a child who does survive, that child will represent the nonsurviving heir and receive that parent's share in the estate. In other words, the surviving child stands in the shoes of a dead parent in order to inherit from a grandparent who dies intestate.

If there are no direct descendants surviving, the intestate's surviving spouse will take the entire estate or share it with the intestate's parents. If there is neither a surviving spouse nor any surviving direct descendant of the intestate, the estate will be distributed to the intestate's parents or, if the parents are not surviving, to the intestate's siblings by representation. If there are no surviving persons in any of these categories, the estate will go to surviving grandparents and their direct descendants. In this way, the family tree is constantly expanded in search of surviving relatives. If none of the persons specified in the law of intestate succession survive the testator, the intestate's property ultimately goes to the state. This is known as *escheat*. It should be noted that the laws of intestate succession make no provision for friends, in-laws, or stepchildren. Children adopted by the testator are treated the same as natural children for all purposes.

State law will often provide a testator's surviving spouse with certain benefits from the estate even if the spouse is left out of the testator's will. Historically, these benefits were known as *dower* in the case of a surviving wife or *curtesy* in the case of a surviving husband. In place of the old dower and curtesy, modern statutes give the surviving spouse the right to *elect* against the will and, thereby, receive a share equal to at least one-fourth of the estate. Here again, state laws vary. In some states, the surviving spouse's elective share is one-third. The historical concepts of dower and curtesy are in large part a result of the law's traditional recognition of an absolute duty on the part of the husband to provide for the wife. Modern laws are perhaps better justified by the notion that most property in a marriage should be shared because the financial success of either partner is due to the efforts of both.

ADVANTAGES TO HAVING A WILL

A will affords the opportunity to direct distribution of one's property and to set out limitations by making gifts conditional. For example, if an individual wishes to donate certain property to a specific charity but only if certain conditions are adhered to, a will can make such conditions a prerequisite to the donation.

A will permits the testator to nominate an executor, called a *personal representative* in most states, to watch over and administer the estate in accordance with the testator's wishes and the law of the state where the will is being handled. If no executor is named in the will, the court will appoint one. A will permits the testator to give property to minors and to regulate the timing and uses of the property given (e.g., funds to be used exclusively for education). If the testator has unusual types of property, such as antiques, artworks, or secret recipes, it is a good idea to appoint joint executors, one with financial expertise and the other with expertise in valuation in the genre in question. If joint executors are used, some provision should be made in the will for resolving any deadlock between the two. For example, a neutral third party might be appointed as an arbitrator who is directed to resolve any impasses after hearing both sides. It is also advisable to define the scope of the executor's power by detailed instructions.

A lawyer's help will be necessary to set forth all of these important considerations in legally enforceable, unambiguous terms. It is essential in a will to avoid careless language that might be subject to attack by survivors unhappy with the will's provisions. A lawyer's assistance is also crucial to avoid making bequests that are not legally enforceable because they are contrary to public policy (e.g., if an individual gets married, the bequest will fail).

ESTATE TAXES

In addition to giving the testator significant posthumous control over division of property, a carefully drafted will can greatly reduce the overall amount of estate tax paid at death. The following information on taxing structures relates to federal estate taxation. State estate taxes often contain similar provisions, but state law must always be consulted for specifics.

The Gross Estate

The first step in evaluating an estate for tax purposes is to determine the *gross estate*. The gross estate will include not only the decedent's property but all property over which the deceased had significant control at the time of death. In addition to certain bank accounts, examples would include investments that have been structured to avoid probate, certain life insurance proceeds and annuities, jointly held interests, and revocable transfers.

Under current tax laws, the executor of an estate may elect to value the property in the estate either as of the date of death or as of a date six months after death. The estate property must be valued in its entirety at the time chosen. If the executor elects to value the estate six months after death and certain pieces of property are distributed or sold before then, that property will be valued as of the date of distribution or sale.

Fair market value is defined as the price at which property would change hands between a willing buyer and a willing seller when both buyer and seller have reasonable knowledge of all relevant facts. Such a determination is often very difficult to make, especially when items such as a nonpublicly traded business (such as a family-owned restaurant), antiques, artwork, and other collectibles are involved. Although the initial determination of fair market value is generally made by the executor when the estate tax return is filed, the Internal Revenue Service may disagree with the executor's valuation and assign assets a much higher fair market value.

When an executor and the Internal Revenue Service disagree with regard to valuation, the court will decide the matter. In most cases, the burden will be on the taxpayer to prove the value of the asset. Thus, expert testimony and evidence of the sale of the same or similar properties will be helpful, as in cases involving comparable property. In general, courts are reluctant to determine valuation by formula.

Generally, estate taxes must be paid when the estate tax return is filed (within nine months of the date of death), although arrangements may be made to spread payments out over a number of years, if necessary. It is not uncommon for executors to be forced to sell properties for less than full value in order to pay taxes. This can be avoided by obtaining insurance policies, the proceeds of which can be set up in a trust, for paying of the taxes.

The law allows a number of deductions from the gross estate in determining the amount of the taxable estate. The taxable estate is the basis upon which the tax owing is computed. The following section gives you a closer look at some of the key deductions used to arrive at the amount of the taxable estate.

The Taxable Estate

Figuring the taxable estate is the second major step in evaluating an estate for tax purposes. Typical deductions from the gross estate include funeral expenses, certain estate administration expenses, debts and enforceable claims against the estate, mortgages and liens, and, perhaps most significant, the marital deduction and the charitable deduction.

The *marital deduction* allows the total value of any interest in property that passes from the decedent to the surviving spouse to be subtracted from the value of the gross estate. The government will eventually get its tax on this property when the spouse dies but only to the extent such interest is included in the spouse's gross estate. The spouse, of course, may limit or eliminate the estate tax on his or her estate by implementing certain estate planning procedures. This deduction may occur even in the absence of a will making a gift to the surviving spouse, since state law generally provides that the spouse is entitled to at least one-fourth of the overall estate regardless of the provisions of the will.

The *charitable deduction* refers to the tax deduction allowed upon the transfer of property from an estate to a recognized charity. Since the definition of a charity for tax purposes is quite technical, it is advisable to insert a clause in the will providing that if the institution specified to receive the donation does not qualify for the charitable deduction, the bequest shall go to a substitute qualified institution at the choice of the executor.

Once deductions are figured, the taxable estate is taxed at the rate specified by the *Unified Estate and Gift Tax Schedule*. The unified tax imposes the same rate of tax on gifts made by will as on gifts made during life. It is a *progressive tax*, meaning the percent paid in taxes increases with the amount of property involved. The rates rise significantly for larger estates; for example, from 18%, when the cumulative total of taxable estate and taxable gifts is under $10,000, to 49%, when the cumulative total is over $2,000,000. Federal estate tax is also reduced by state death tax credit or actual state death tax, whichever is less. Note that since the estate tax laws have changed, many of the states that were *pick-up tax states* now actually have taxes higher than the state exemption amount.

Tax credits result in an exemption that is available to every estate. For tax years 2006, 2007, and 2008, the exclusion amount is $2,000,000; in tax year 2009, the exclusion amount is $3,500,000.

IN PLAIN ENGLISH

There are additional exemptions for families with qualifying businesses (which may include restaurants) or farms. These exemptions, combined with the unlimited marital deduction, allow most estates to escape estate taxes altogether.

DISTRIBUTING PROPERTY OUTSIDE THE WILL

Property can be distributed outside the will by making *inter vivos* gifts (given during the giver's lifetime), either outright or by placing the property in an irrevocable trust prior to death. A potential advantage to distributing property outside the will is that the property escapes the delays and expense of probate, the court procedure by which a will is validated and administered. It used to be that there were also significant tax advantages to making inter vivos gifts rather than making gifts by will, but since the estate and gift tax rates are now unified, there are few remaining tax advantages. One remaining advantage to making an inter vivos gift is that if the gift appreciates in value between the time the gift is made and death, the appreciated value will not be subject to estate tax. If the gift were made by will, the added value would be taxable, since the gift would be valued on the estate tax return as of date of death (or six months after). This value difference can represent significant tax savings for the heirs of someone whose restaurant business suddenly becomes successful and rapidly increases in value.

The other advantage to making an inter vivos gift involves the yearly exclusion. A yearly exclusion of $11,000 per recipient is available on inter vivos gifts. For example, if $15,000 worth of gifts were given to an individual in one year, only $4,000 worth of gifts will actually be taxable to the donor, who is responsible for the gift tax. A married couple can combine their gifts and claim a yearly exclusion of $22,000 per recipient, though each can gift only $11,000 tax free. Gifts made within three years of death used to be included in the gross estate on the theory that they were made in contemplation of death. Recent amendments to the tax laws, however, have done away with the three-year rule for most purposes. The three-year rule is still applicable to gifts of life insurance and to certain transfers involving stock redemption or tax liens. The rule also applies to certain valuation schemes, the details of which are too complex to discuss here.

The donor must file gift tax returns for any year in which gifts made to any one donee exceeded $11,000. It is not necessary to file returns when a gift to any one donee amounts to less than $11,000. If the valuation of the gift will become an issue with the IRS, it may be a good idea to file a return anyway. Filing the return starts the three-year statute of limitations running. Once the statute of limitations period has expired, the IRS will be barred from filing suit for unpaid taxes or for tax deficiencies due to higher government valuations of the gifts. However, if a taxpayer omits includable gifts amounting to more than 25% of the total amount of gifts stated in the return, the statute of limitations is extended to six years, and there is no statute of limitations for fraudulent returns filed with the intent to evade tax.

In order to qualify as an inter vivos gift for tax purposes, a gift must be complete and final. Control is an important issue. If a giver retains the right to revoke a gift, the gift may be found to be testamentary in nature, even if the right to revoke was never exercised (unless the gift was made in trust). The gift must also be delivered. An actual, physical delivery is best, but a symbolic delivery may suffice if there is strong evidence of intent to make an irrevocable gift. An example of symbolic delivery is when the donor puts something in a safe and gives the intended recipient the only key.

Another common way to transfer property outside the will is to place the property in a trust that is created prior to death. A *trust* is simply a legal arrangement by which one person holds certain property for the benefit of another. The person holding the property is the *trustee*. Those for whose benefit it is held are the *beneficiaries*. To create a valid trust, the giver must identify the trust property, make a declaration of intent to create the trust, transfer property to the trust, and name identifiable beneficiaries. If no trustee is named, a court will appoint one. The *settlor*, or creator of the trust, may also be designated as trustee, in which case segregation of the trust property satisfies the delivery requirement. Trusts can be created by will, in which case they are termed *testamentary trusts*, but these trust properties will be probated along with the rest of the will. To avoid probate, the settlor must create a valid *inter vivos trust*.

Generally, in order to qualify as an inter vivos trust, a valid interest in property must be transferred before the death of the creator of the trust. If the settlor fails to name a beneficiary for the trust or to make delivery of the property to the trustee before death, the trust will likely be termed testamentary. Such a trust will be deemed invalid unless the formalities required for creating a will were complied with.

A trust will not be termed testamentary simply because the settlor retained significant control over the trust, such as the power to revoke or modify the trust. For example, when a person makes a deposit in a savings account in his or her own name as trustee for another and reserves the power to withdraw the money or to revoke the trust, the trust will be enforceable by the beneficiary upon the death of the depositor, providing the depositor has not, in fact, revoked the trust. Many states allow the same type of arrangement in authorizing joint bank accounts with rights of survivorship as valid will substitutes. Property transferred under one of these arrangements is thus passed outside the will and need not go through probate. Even though such an arrangement escapes probate, the trust property will probably be counted as part of the gross estate for tax purposes, because the settlor retained significant control. In addition, if the deceased settlor created a revocable trust for the purpose of decreasing the share of a surviving spouse, in some states the trust will be declared *illusory*—in effect, invalid. The surviving spouse is then granted the legal share not only from the probated estate but also from the revocable trust.

Life insurance trusts can be used for paying estate taxes. The proceeds will not be taxed if the life insurance trust is irrevocable and the beneficiary is someone other than the estate, such as a friend or relative in an individual capacity or a business. This is especially important for restaurant owners, since, without a life insurance trust, their survivors might be forced to sell estate assets for less than their real value in order to pay estate taxes.

PROBATE

Briefly described, *probate* is the legal process by which a decedent's estate is administered in a systematic and orderly manner and with finality. The laws that govern the probate process vary among the states. One of the principal functions of probate administration is to provide a means to transfer ownership of a decedent's probate property. Accordingly, probate administration occurs without regard to whether the decedent died testate or intestate. In the course of probate administration, the following occurs.

- A decedent's will is admitted to probate as the decedent's last will.
- Someone (referred to as the personal representative, executor, or administrator) is appointed by the court to take charge of the decedent's property and financial affairs.
- Interested persons are notified of the commencement of probate administration.
- Information concerning the decedent's estate is gathered.
- Probate property is assembled and preserved.
- Debts and taxes are determined, paid, or challenged.
- Claims against the decedent's estate are paid or challenged.
- Conflicting claims of entitlement to the decedent's property are disposed of.
- At the conclusion of the process, the remaining estate property is distributed to the appropriate persons or entities.

While probate administration is pending, distributions of the decedent's property are suspended to allow creditors, claimants, devisees, and heirs the opportunity to protect their respective rights.

Probate property consists of the decedent's solely owned property as of the date of death. Property jointly held by the decedent and another person with the right of survivorship (e.g., a residence or stock certificates owned jointly with right of survivorship) passes to the survivor and is not a part of the decedent's probate estate. Likewise, the proceeds of life insurance on the decedent's life are not part of the probate estate (unless the estate is the designated beneficiary). It is possible, therefore, for a wealthy individual to die leaving little or no probate property.

CONCLUSION

All businesspeople, including those in the restaurant industry, should give some thought to estate planning and take the time to execute a proper will. Without a will, there is simply no way to control the disposition of one's property. Sound estate planning may include transfers outside of the will, since these types of arrangements typically escape the delays and expenses of probate. Certain types of trusts can be valuable will substitutes, but they may be subject to challenge by a surviving spouse. Since successful estate planning is complex, it is essential to work with a lawyer skilled in this field.

22

HOW TO FIND A LAWYER AND AN ACCOUNTANT

Most people engaged in commercial food-based businesses expect to seek the advice of a lawyer only occasionally, for counseling on important matters such as the decision to incorporate or the purchase of a building. If this is your concept of the attorney's role in your business, you should reevaluate it. Most restaurant and catering businesses would operate more efficiently and more profitably in the long run if they had an ongoing relationship with a business attorney that allows the attorney to get to know the business well enough to engage in preventive legal counseling and to assist in planning, thus making possible the solution of many problems before they occur.

If your food-based business is small or undercapitalized, you are doubtless anxious to keep operating costs down. You probably do not relish the idea of paying an attorney to get to know your business if you are not involved in an immediate crisis. It is a good bet, however, that a visit with a competent business lawyer right now will result in the raising of issues vital to the future of your business. There is good reason why larger, successful, commercial food-based businesses employ one or more attorneys full time as in-house counsel. Ready access to legal advice is something you should not deny your business at any time for any reason.

An attorney experienced in business law can give you important information regarding the risks unique to your food-based business. Furthermore, a lawyer can advise you regarding your rights and obligations in your relationship with present and future employees, the rules that apply in your state regarding the hiring and firing of employees, real estate issues, and so forth. Ignorance of these issues and violation of the rules can result in financially devastating lawsuits and even criminal penalties. Since each state has its own laws covering commercial food-based business practices, state laws must be consulted on many areas covered in this book. A competent local business attorney is, therefore, your best source of information on many issues that will arise in the running of your business.

IN PLAIN ENGLISH

Most legal problems cost more to solve or defend after they arise than it would have cost to prevent their occurrence in the first place.

Litigation is notoriously inefficient and expensive. You do not want to sue or be sued if you can help it. The expense is shocking. The cost of defending a case filed against you or your business is something you have no choice but to incur, unless you choose to default, which is almost never advisable.

The lawyer who will be most valuable to a young business will likely not be a Perry Mason or Johnnie Cochran but, rather, a meticulous person who does most of his or her work in an office, going over your business forms, your employee contracts, or your corporate bylaws. This person should have a good reputation in the legal community, as well as in the business community. You might pay over $200 per hour for the attorney, but if the firm has a good reputation, it likely employs a well-trained professional staff that can reduce the amount of attorney time required.

One of the first items you should discuss with your lawyer is the fee structure for her or his services. You are entitled to an estimate, though unless you enter into an agreement to the contrary with the attorney, the estimate is just that. Business lawyers generally charge by the hour, though you may be quoted a flat rate for a specific service, such as incorporation or drafting a simple will.

FINDING A LAWYER

If you do not know any attorneys, ask other restaurant businesspeople if they know any good ones. You want either a lawyer who specializes in the restaurant business or a general practitioner who has many satisfied food-based business clients. Finding the lawyer who is right for you is like finding the right doctor—you may have to shop around a bit. Most local and state bar associations have referral services. A good tip is to find out who is in the business law section of the state or local bar association, or who has served on special bar committees dealing with law reform. It may also be useful to find out if any articles covering the area of law with which you are concerned have been published in either scholarly journals or continuing-legal-education publications, and if the author is available to assist you. It may be a good idea to hire a specialist or law firm with a number of specialists, rather than a general practitioner. While it is true that you may pay more per hour for the expert, you will not have to pay for the attorney's learning time, and experience is valuable. In this regard, you may wish to keep in mind that it is uncommon for a lawyer to specialize in business practice and also handle criminal matters. Thus, if you are faced with a criminal prosecution, then you should be searching for an experienced criminal defense lawyer.

One method by which you can attempt to evaluate an attorney in regard to representing business clients is by consulting the Martindale-Hubbell Law Directory in your local county law library or online at **www.martindale.com**. While this may be useful, the mere fact that an attorney's name does not appear in the book should not be given too much weight, since there is a charge for being included and some lawyers may simply have chosen not to pay for the listing. You may also wish to search the World Wide Web. Many law firms have established websites, and the larger firms usually include extensive information about the firm, its practice areas, and its attorneys; for example, my firm's site is **www.dubofflaw.com**. There are also numerous attorney directories on the Web. Here too the fact that a lawyer is not listed may be meaningless, since they are virtually all subscription services.

After you have obtained several recommendations for attorneys, it is appropriate for you to talk with the attorneys for a short period of time to determine whether you would be comfortable working with them. Do not be afraid to ask about their background, experience, and whether they feel they can help you.

Once you have completed the interview process, select the person who appears to best satisfy your needs. The rest is up to you. Contact your lawyer whenever you believe a legal question has arisen. Your attorney should aid you in identifying which questions require legal action or advice and which require business decisions. Generally, lawyers will deal only with legal issues, though they may help you to evaluate business problems.

The attorney-client relationship is such that you should feel comfortable when confiding in your attorney. This person will not disclose your confidential communications and a violation of this rule can be considered an ethical breach that could subject the attorney to professional sanctions.

If you take the time to develop a good working relationship with your attorney, it may well prove to be one of your more valuable business assets.

FINDING AN ACCOUNTANT

In addition to an attorney, most food-based businesses will need the services of a competent accountant to aid with tax planning, the filing of periodic reports, and annual tax returns. Finding an accountant with whom your business is compatible is similar to finding an attorney. You should ask around and learn which accountants are servicing businesses similar to yours. State professional accounting associations and licensing boards may also provide a referral service or point you to a directory of accountants in your area. You should interview prospective accountants to determine whether you feel you can work with them and whether you feel their skills will be compatible with your business needs.

Like your attorney, your accountant can provide valuable assistance in planning for the future of your business. It is important to work with professionals you trust and with whom you are able to relate on a professional level.

GLOSSARY

401(k). A type of plan provided by an employer for its employees that requires periodic payments during employment so that the employee can obtain post-retirement income benefits. Its name is derived from the initial section of the Internal Revenue Code, which created it.

A

acceptance. A term used in contract law to describe an element of a contract, which occurs after an offer has been made.

accountant. A trained professional who provides accounting services such as setting up and maintaining a company's books and tax preparation. *See certified public accountant.*

accounts payable. An accounting term used to define monetary obligations owed by one to another.

accounts receivable. An accounting term used to define monetary obligations that one is entitled to from another.

accumulated earnings tax. A tax imposed by the federal government on earnings that have been accumulated over time and which are deemed to be excessive.

action. Sometimes referred to as cause of action, this is the legal claim or right that one has against another. It is frequently written in the form of a legal document known as a complaint, which is filed in court and used to begin a lawsuit.

addendum. A document attached at the end of another document, customarily intended to supplement the terms of the document to which it is attached.

adjusted basis. The basis of an item is its cost or fair market value that is adjusted for tax purposes by deducting depreciation and other offsets allowable under the Internal Revenue Code. This concept is frequently used when valuing property for tax or related purposes.

affidavit. A statement sworn to or affirmed by the party making the statement, who is known as an affiant. Affidavits are written and the signature is notarized. Because of this, affidavits carry a great deal of weight and may be used in legal proceedings or other official purposes, such as in real estate transactions or in legal proceedings when a sworn oath is required.

agency. The relationship between one person, known as the principal, and another, known as the agent. Customarily, the agent works for or on behalf of the principal and is subject to the principal's control or right of control. Typically, the agent owes a duty to the principal.

agent. *See agency, principal.*

agreement. An arrangement, written or oral, whereby two or more parties reach an understanding. When conforming to the requirements of contract law, it is known as a contract. If one or more of the requirements for a legal contract are missing, the agreement may be subject to certain legal defenses and, thus, not enforceable.

amendment. A term used when an agreement is modified, as when a contract is changed.

Americans with Disabilities Act of 1990 (ADA). A federal statute enacted by Congress for the purpose of providing individuals with defined disabilities the opportunity to obtain fair treatment in employment, housing, transportation, and the like. The courts have been wrestling with the definition of disability for purposes of interpreting the statute and with the amount of reasonable accommodation required to be provided under the Act.

antidilution. A term used in trademark law to describe one of the forms of protection available to trademark owners under the law. It prohibits another from weakening, tarnishing, disparaging, or otherwise undermining the strength and credibility of the protected trademark.

antitrust laws. The laws used to prevent monopolies and unlawful arrangements that are intended to manipulate or control a particular market and unlawfully affect pricing, as well as other key market factors. The antitrust laws are enforced by both government regulation (federal and state) and by litigation.

apparent authority. A legal term used to define the authority an agent appears to have when dealing with third persons. This is intended to protect the third person's reasonable expectations when dealing with the agent, and is available for third-person protection even when contrary to the express instructions of the principal.

appreciation. Financial and accounting term used to define the increase in value of property, whether tangible or intangible, that occurs over time. Thus, a house frequently appreciates in value as real estate prices increase. Similarly, a copyright, which is intangible, may increase in value when the protected work has received positive critical acclaim or popularity.

apprentice. An individual who assists another in a particular trade or profession in order to learn the trade or profession.

articles of incorporation. Legal document filed with the state in which a company desires to do business as a corporation. It is the charter or creating instrument for the corporation. It defines the authority granted by the state for the company to be conducted in the corporate form, and is analogous to a constitution. All business corporations are created under the law of the state in which they are incorporated, and may do business in other states by filing the appropriate document(s) in those states as a foreign (chartered in another state) corporation doing business in that state.

articles of organization. A legal document filed with the state in which a business desires to do business as a limited liability company (LLC). It is the charter or creating instrument for the LLC. It defines the authority granted by the state for the company to be conducted as an LLC, and is analogous to a constitution. All LLCs are created under the law of the state in which they are created, and may do business in other states by filing the appropriate document(s) in those states as a foreign (chartered in another state) LLC doing business in that state.

asset. Financial or accounting term used to describe cash or property. The property can be tangible, such as real estate and office equipment, or intangible, such as intellectual property and goodwill.

assignment for the benefit of creditors. A legal term used in bankruptcy and collections law to define an arrangement whereby assets of a debtor are assigned to another (the creditor, trustee, or receiver) for the benefit of one or more creditors. This can take the form of a formal court-administered plan or an informal arrangement worked out between the parties.

attorney. A professional who has been licensed to practice law in the state or other jurisdiction by which the license has been issued and whose conduct is regulated by state bar associations and the highest court of the state or jurisdiction. Attorneys must be licensed to practice in every court in which they appear. Customarily, attorneys are graduates of post-graduate law schools and have passed one or more bar examinations.

attorney-client privilege. A legal doctrine established for the purpose of enabling a client to communicate freely with his or her attorney. All communications between the client and attorney (or attorney's staff) that are not in the presence of any other person are privileged and may not be disclosed by the attorney without the client's permission.

attorney-in-fact. A person who is not actually a lawyer but is a person authorized to perform a specific act or combination of acts described in a document known as a power of attorney on behalf of the person granting the power. The person granting the power must sign this document and that person's signature must be notarized. The power may be general or specific, as defined in the document. In some jurisdictions and for some purposes, a power of attorney may be recorded; that is, filed with the appropriate governmental agency.

audit. An accounting term used to describe a review, typically of financial statements or tax returns. The audit is intended to verify the accuracy of the document and is conducted by an auditor, who is typically a skilled professional.

B

bankruptcy. The legal term defining the consequences of insolvency. In other words, when liabilities are greater than assets or when bills cannot be paid in the ordinary course of one's business, one is technically insolvent or bankrupt. Laws have been enacted that provide relief for those who are insolvent, as well as for their creditors.

blue sky law. A common term used to define state securities laws enacted for protection of those who invest in businesses. The term comes from a statement in Congress referring to the victims of the 1929 depression who bought securities whose values were artificially inflated as people who obtained nothing more than chunks of "blue sky."

board of directors. The governing board of a business entity charged by statute with responsibility for administering the business and affairs of that entity. It is frequently used in the context of corporate boards of directors, though it can refer to the administrative board of other types of entities, such as nonprofit corporations, limited liability companies, or the like.

bona fide occupational qualifications (BFOQs). Qualifications reasonably necessary to the safe and efficient performance of the job where, but for this exception, the employment practice might be in violation of antidiscrimination laws.

branding. The term used to describe the identification and reputation of a product or service. This concept has been used by businesses to describe the process of identifying the qualities, unique characteristics, reputation, market awareness, and the like of specific products or services. One of the most famous brands in the world today is Coca-Cola.

business plan. A document used to describe the process of developing a new or existing business.

buy-sell agreement. A document customarily used by business organizations for the purpose of establishing a formal arrangement whereby the ownership interest in the business may be sold or transferred only in accordance with the terms of the agreement. These agreements typically impose restrictions on sale or transfer to outsiders and establish methods for valuing the interest when the owner desires to transfer the interest, dies, or becomes incapacitated. These agreements are frequently used in closely held businesses, as distinguished from those that are publicly traded.

bylaws. Formal documents adopted by corporations for administering the internal affairs of the company. They typically cover the rules and regulations for calling meetings, defining key positions, and the like. Bylaws may not be broader in scope than the company's articles of incorporation. Articles of incorporation are analogous to a constitution, and define the boundaries of a company's power and authority. The bylaws are analogous to laws and statutes, and are the rules and regulations for implementing the powers and authority. Bylaws are not filed with any governmental agency, but are kept in the corporation's minute book.

C

cannibalizing. The act of a franchisor permitting or establishing a new location of the franchise in close proximity to an existing franchise operation.

capital expenditures. Payments made to acquire long-term (capital) assets, such as real property or equipment.

cash discount. A reduction granted a customer for paying cash on delivery, rather than obtaining credit and delaying payment.

cashier's check. A check purchased from a bank and issued by the bank.

caterer. A person or entity who prepares and provides food, drink, and service, customarily for a particular event. Thus, a wedding would be serviced by a caterer who would prepare the food and drink, and assist with serving these items to the invited guests.

certificate of incorporation. The document issued by many states evidencing the formation of a corporation in that state. It is used to establish that a corporation is in good standing in that state. It may be required when a corporation desires to do business in another state.

certified check. A check that has been certified by the issuing bank, which means that the bank segregates adequate funds from the depositor's account to pay the check, and the certification means that the bank is guaranteeing payment of the check.

certified public accountant (CPA). A professional who has passed the examinations required by the appropriate state agency to provide kinds of accounting services. These services include, for example, setting up and maintaining a company's books and tax preparation. One of the services unique to CPAs is providing audited financial statements.

Chapter 7. A type of federal bankruptcy for individuals and businesses whereby all nonexempt assets are made available to creditors, who are paid in a prescribed order according to an approved schedule, and the debtor is discharged from all further outstanding obligations to the listed creditors.

Chapter 11. A type of federal bankruptcy for businesses, which permits the debtor to propose a plan to pay creditors according to a specific schedule and discharge all outstanding debts.

Chapter 13. A type of federal bankruptcy for individuals, which permits the debtor to propose a plan to pay creditors according to a specific schedule and discharge all outstanding debts.

check. A financial instrument whereby the payor (person writing the check) instructs the bank to pay the defined amount to the order of the designated payee (person or entity to whom the check is written).

civil law. The body of law adopted in some jurisdictions, including Louisiana, based on the Napoleonic Code and following prescribed rules or statutes, rather than adhering to past practices or precedent, as in the common law.

civil liability. The legal process for recovery of money or property or compelling the doing of things for the benefit of individuals and businesses, rather than imposing penalties or extracting obligations to the governmental jurisdiction. It is administered by private attorneys and individuals, rather than through a district or prosecuting attorney on behalf of the government.

closely held business. A business owned by a small number of people or other businesses, rather than one that is publicly held or traded on the stock market. It is frequently a business arrangement between one or more families or groups of friends, though the term could describe a larger group of owners, so long as the group is small enough to avoid the necessity of complying with the technical requirements set forth in the state and federal securities laws for publicly held businesses.

collateral. The term used to define assets of a borrower that may be available to a lender as a means of repaying a loan. For example, when a bank is asked to lend money, it will usually require the prospective borrower to provide a list of the borrower's available assets in order to determine whether the borrower has sufficient assets, if liquidated, to repay the loan. The bank may or may not require the assets to be secured or encumbered for the purpose of guaranteeing repayment.

collective works. Works defined by the federal copyright statute as including periodicals, anthologies or encyclopedias, in which contributions consisting of separate and independent works themselves are assembled into a collective whole.

collusion. A legal term defining an unsavory arrangement between two or more entities for an improper purpose.

commingling. Combining assets from two or more sources. The commingling could be legitimate where, for example, a husband and wife have a joint checking account. It could also be improper, as in situations where a mom and pop corporation pays the personal obligations of the owners from corporate funds or corporate obligations from the owners' individual funds.

common law. The legal system based on English Common Law that follows past practice or legal precedent, known as *stare decisis*. In this process, rules established in court cases become binding and are followed until modified, extended, or reversed. This should be distinguished from civil law, which is based upon the Napoleonic Code and is limited to statutory pronouncements.

common stock. The form of stock issued by a corporation that has unrestricted voting rights, dividend rights, and ownership in the corporation. It is the kind of stock every corporation must have, and is distinguished from preferred stock, which must, by definition, must have some form of preference in either dividends or distribution on dissolution, or both.

complaint. The legal document filed in a court that begins a lawsuit. This document, along with the summons, must be properly served on behalf of the complainant (plaintiff) on the other party (defendant) in order to continue the lawsuit.

confirming memorandum. A written document sent by one party to another for the purpose of confirming the terms of an oral arrangement.

conflict of interest. An ethical concept whereby a party has divided loyalties. For example, when a partner in a partnership is given a cash payment of $10 for a service rendered and belatedly realizes that, instead of one crisp $10 bill, there were two stuck together, the partner is forced to decide whether he should disclose to his partner the fact that the client overpaid. A lawyer who represents two parties who have opposing interests is in a conflict of interest and may, under the rules of many bar associations, be required to suspend representation of both parties. Alternatively, if the conflict is merely theoretical, then most bar associations permit the lawyer to continue representing both parties, provided the facts are disclosed to both parties in writing and there is an appropriate written waiver of the theoretical conflict by all.

consideration. A contract element, which requires the giving or receiving of something of value by one party in exchange for something of comparable value from the other party. Consideration can be in the form of money, property, services or an agreement to refrain from some action. The law tends to require the parties to give or receive things of comparable potential value in order for the consideration to be deemed valid.

consignment. A legal arrangement whereby the property of one party is entrusted to another for purposes of sale. The person who entrusts the property, who must be the owner or lawful possessor, is known as the consignor, and the person receiving the property is known as the consignee. The consignment agreement may be oral or written and, if in writing, it may be recorded with the appropriate government office. Many states have enacted special legislation dealing with unique forms of consignment, such as fine art, crafts, and collectibles.

Consumer Price Index (CPI). A financial tool used to define the increase or decrease in a defined list of consumer products and services in a particular geographic area during a specified period of time.

contract. A legal concept whereby one offers consideration to another in exchange for the other providing comparable consideration. To be legally valid, all contracts require an offer, acceptance, and consideration. They may oral or written. There are other legal requirements for certain types of contracts; for example, contracts for the sale of real property (land) and personal property worth $500 or more must be in writing. *See acceptance, consideration, offer.*

cooling-off period. Concept whereby a consumer is given a specified period of time to reflect on an otherwise valid contract and, if desired, rescind it before it is performed by either party. For example, many states permit a three-day period within which a consumer may cancel contracts obtained by door-to-door salespeople.

copyright. The right whereby any original work of authorship that is put in a tangible form is protected by law. In the United States, the copyright laws have been enacted pursuant to the enabling provision set forth in Article I of the United States Constitution. The most recent copyright statute was enacted in 1976 and became effective January 1, 1978. This law continues to evolve and has been amended a number of times. It is known as the Copyright Revision Act of 1976, as amended. There are numerous treaties throughout the world dealing with copyright on a multinational level.

corporate shield and **corporate veil.** The terms used to define the limited liability available for those who conduct business through corporate or other business entities. It is said that shareholders in corporations and owners of limited liability companies are shielded by the limitation of liability available to them when they properly conduct business through these entities. Creditors cannot pierce the corporate veil or penetrate the corporate shield without establishing a valid legal reason to do so, and the reasons available are very limited.

corporation. A business entity created by one or more persons pursuant to the corporate code of the state in which the business is to be formed.

counteroffer. An offer presented by an offeree, or recipient of an offer, from another, which rejects the original offer and provides a new offer. It converts the original offeror into an offeree. Once the give and take is completed and an agreement is reached, there is a contract.

creditor. One who is owed an obligation by another, known as a debtor. In business, the term is more commonly used to define one who is owed money.

D

damages. The compensation sought or awarded for legal injury sustained.

debt. An obligation owed by one (debtor) to another (creditor).

debtor. One who is owes an obligation to another, known as a creditor. In business, the term is more commonly used to define one who owes money.

debentures and bonds. Legal debt instruments frequently used by corporations to evidence debt. When the debt is secured by one or more identified assets, such as a mile of railroad track, the instruments are bonds. When the debt is secured by all of the debtor's assets, the instruments are known as debentures. Bonds are also issued by governmental entities for specific designated purposes, such as building libraries, schools, and the like, or funding a particular project.

defined benefit plan. A retirement plan that pays a specific amount after the employee retires. This payment stream is used to determine the method and amount necessary to fund the plan.

defined contribution plan. A retirement plan that establishes the amount to be paid into the plan, and the benefits then flow from the pre-retirement contribution.

depreciation. Financial and accounting term whereby the useful life of an item is estimated and the value of the item is reduced on a yearly basis according to a prescribed schedule. For tax purposes, the Internal Revenue Service has established prescribed periods of depreciation for various items.

derivative work. A copyright concept whereby a work is taken from, or based on, a prior work.

design defect. A defect in the design of a product that results in the product being defective and may result in liability for the designer of the product. This should be distinguished from a manufacturing defect, where liability would fall to the manufacturer of the product.

discharge. The legal concept whereby a debtor in bankruptcy is permitted to extinguish all prebankruptcy debts when the legal requirements of the bankruptcy law are followed.

disclaimer. A legal device whereby a party may avoid responsibility for warranties that have either been expressly given or are implied by law. In order for a disclaimer to be valid, it must comply with the legal requirements set forth in the statute governing warranties and disclaimers.

dissolution. The formal process by which the existence of an entity, such as a corporation, limited liability company, limited partnership, or the like, is terminated. This can either be mandatory, by court order, or voluntary. It can also be involuntary, as when the annual report required by state law and the accompanying annual fees are not tendered.

dividend preference. A payment defined by a preferred stock instrument setting forth the amount (in either dollars or percentage) that must be paid to the holders of the preferred stock before any dividends are paid to the holders of common stock.

E

e-commerce. Shorthand for electronic commerce, which is the practice of engaging in commercial activities using the computer network known as the Internet or World Wide Web.

electronic signature. The electronic communication adopted by a party for purposes of taking advantage of the E-SIGN statute and consummating contracts through e-commerce.

Electronic Signature in Global and National Commerce Act (E-SIGN). A federal statute that prescribes a method whereby an electronic signature may be used for purposes of validating contracts in cyberspace, which contracts are binding in the same manner as they would be if entered into through traditional means.

employee stock option plan (ESOP). A plan established by a business entity using the company's stock for purposes of funding an employee retirement plan.

express warranty. A statement of fact or representation by a seller with the respect to quality or other attributes of particular goods to be sold. *See also implied warranty.*

F

fair use. A copyright concept developed by case law and codified in the Copyright Revision Act of 1976, as amended, to provide a defense for one who copies the protected work of another when the copying satisfies the guidelines set forth in the statute.

Federal Trade Commission (FTC). The federal agency charged by Congress with responsibility for policing interstate commerce and trade within the United States and at its borders. It has also assumed responsibility for policing activities on the World Wide Web when those activities affect commerce in the United States.

fiduciary. The term used to define one who owes a duty to another. The scope of that duty varies from relationship to relationship, and has been more carefully defined in the myriad of cases dealing with individuals who owe or are owed the duty. Classic examples of fiduciary relationships are the agency relationship (where both parties owe a fiduciary duty to each other) and the trust relationship (where the trustee is held to owe a fiduciary duty to beneficiaries).

first sale doctrine. A copyright concept whereby the copyright owner may control the first sale of a copyrighted work. Resales of that work, absent an agreement to the contrary, may be made without involving the copyright owner. For example, a book publisher may, by virtue of the copyright in the book, control the first sale of that book, but absent some agreement to the contrary, a purchaser may resell the book without involving the publisher in the resale.

foreign corporation. A corporation doing business in a state other than the state by which it is incorporated.

franchise. A legal term used to define a process whereby trademarks, know-how, and other business assets are combined, described, and licensed to another for the purpose of that other attempting to replicate the original business. It is also used to describe a restaurant using such franchised assets. A classic example of a franchise is McDonald's.

franchising. A process whereby a successful business pattern is licensed by the originator (franchisor) so that a licensee (franchisee) can create comparable businesses. In order for a franchising arrangement to be legal, the franchisor must comply with federal and state requirements and provide potential franchisees with the disclosures required by those laws.

full disclosure. The concept of providing all relevant and pertinent information when securities are offered for sale or sold. The securities laws require full and fair disclosure of all material facts relevant to the transactions involved.

G

general partner. The person or entity who has full personal liability in a partnership. A general partner can be one of the parties involved in a general partnership, which is defined as two or more persons who are co-owners engaged in a business for profit, or the person or entity who runs a limited partnership and has full personal liability for the acts, contracts, or omissions of that business entity.

goodwill. An intangible, which has been defined in cases as the propensity of customers to return to a business. It has also been defined as including the business's reputation, marketability, and success.

gray market. The market that develops when a legally licensed product is introduced into a market other than the one in which it is licensed. For example, a trademark owner in the United States may license the use of its mark in Canada, since the owner has captured the U.S. market. If the Canadian licensee begins selling the Canadian-licensed products in the United States, those sales of otherwise legally licensed merchandise in the restricted market of the United States would be gray market sales.

H

holographic will. A handwritten will, signed by the person writing it.

hostile environment. Used in employment law, a situation whereby comments of a sexual nature, offensive sexual materials, or unwelcome physical conduct are so frequent and serious as to be deemed sexual harassment.

I

implied contract. A contract created by the law for the purpose of preventing injustice. It is a contract that the parties may or may not have expressly agreed to. For example, when a restaurant owner calls a supplier to order a shipment of vegetables without discussing payment, there is an implied agreement to pay for that shipment.

implied warranty. A warranty implied by law that exists whether or not the parties have negotiated for it. Classic implied warranties are the implied warranty of merchantability, the implied warranty of fitness for a particular purpose, the implied warranty of title, and the implied warranty that the item is not infringing the intellectual property rights of another. Implied warranties may, if the party against whom they are enforceable comply with the statute, be disclaimed.

independent contractor. A person who engages in his or her own independent business and provides goods or services to another. An independent contract is distinguished from an employee, who is employed by another for purpose of providing goods or services. The legal distinction between these two categories is that an employer has the right of control over the conduct of an employee's activities, whereas the employer does not have a right of control over the conduct of an independent contractor's activities; rather, the employer contracts for the results.

inherently dangerous goods. Items which, by virtue of their design or manufacturing defects, may expose the seller to liability in the event an injury is sustained from the defect. An example of an inherently dangerous item is a vehicle tire with a design defect such that it blows out when the vehicle on which it is mounted exceeds 40 mph.

insurable interest. An interest that a party must have in the continued existence of property or person such that damage to the property or person would cause the insured a financial loss or other tangible deprivation. An insurable interest is required in order to prevent one from using an insurance contract as a means of gambling or to prevent one from procuring insurance and having an incentive to destroy that which is insured.

intellectual property. The body of law that deals with products of the mind. It includes patent law, copyright law, trademark law, trade secret law, and other forms of protection for creative works.

Internet Service Provider (ISP). A business that provides access to the Internet, usually for a fee. Examples of ISPs include MSN and AOL.

Internet surf days. Days specified by the Federal Trade Commission (FTC) on which law enforcement officials, consumer protection agencies, and trade groups surf the Internet with regard to a specific type of false advertising or illegal scheme.

intestate. The legal term defining a person who dies without a will.

inter vivos trust. A trust created by a person during his or her lifetime.

individual retirement account (IRA). This is a form of pension account created by Congress for individuals.

J

joint and several. The term used to define the liability of two or more individuals who are each liable for the entire amount of any damages awarded, or a pro rata share of those damages, depending on the wishes of the person in whose favor the damages are awarded.

joint venture. An arrangement between two or more persons to accomplish a specific task. It is distinguishable from a partnership, in that a partnership is established for the purpose of conducting an ongoing business, whereas a joint venture is created for the purpose of achieving a specific goal. Thus, if two or more persons get together for the purpose of building an apartment complex, it would be a joint venture; if the agreement goes on to say that they will continue to manage it on an ongoing basis, it would be a partnership. A joint venture can be expressed, when the parties work out their terms, or implied, when the parties merely perform the identified task.

joint work. The term defined by Section 101 of the Copyright Revision Act of 1976, as amended, as a work created by two or more persons contributing their creative elements and intending that those elements be combined into a unitary whole. Cases have established that the contributions of each must be independently copyrightable. A classic example of a joint work is an illustrated text, where one creates the illustrations and the other prepares the text.

judgment creditor. A person or entity in whose favor a court has rendered a money judgment.

judgment debtor. A person or entity against whom a court has awarded a money judgment.

jurisdiction. The word used to define a place where a lawsuit may be properly filed, a corporation may be created, a building may erected, or the like. It is a geographic area that has been defined by statute or case law for specific purposes. In the context of litigation, jurisdiction refers to the court system within which a case may be filed; for example, the United States District Court will accept jurisdiction of only those cases that deal with federal questions or involve citizens of different states or foreign countries, and amounts in excess of $75,000. Local courts, on the other hand, have different jurisdictional requirements.

K

key-person insurance. A type of insurance procured on the life of a person key (important) to a business. It is typically obtained by the business entity to compensate it for the loss it will sustain when the key person dies.

L

lawyer. *See attorney, attorney-in-fact.*

license. A permitted use. In business, licensing is typically used to permit one to use the intellectual property of another. For example, a copyright owner may license the use of a copyrighted design. Licensing may also refer to other permitted uses; for example, states issue driver's licenses and municipalities issue business licenses.

life insurance trust. A form of trust created for the purpose of owning a life insurance policy and distributing the proceeds of that policy when the insured party dies.

limited liability company (LLC). A business form that allows those who conduct business through it to enjoy the benefits of limited personal liability while electing the method by which the entity is to be treated for tax purposes. It was created to overcome the restrictions imposed on small business that could qualify for S corporation status.

limited liability partnership (LLP). Similar to a limited liability company, except that it was created for the purpose of allowing partners in partnerships to have a personal liability shield similar to those who conduct business through corporations.

limited partner. A person or entity who owns an interest in a limited partnership but who is a passive investor and who enjoys limited liability.

limited partnership. A partnership having one or more general partners with full personal liability and one or more limited partners who may enjoy limited liability but may not play an active role in conducting the business of the limited partnership. It is created by statute and the partnership must comply with the limited partnership statute of the jurisdiction in which it is created.

liquidation. The process of converting assets to cash and distributing the cash. It should be distinguished from dissolution, which refers merely to the legal relationship between those who are conducting the business. For example, when a general partner in a general partnership dies, there is a dissolution by virtue of the death of a partner. The remaining partners may, if their agreement permits, continue the partnership or, if the agreement does not or they do not wish to, they may then liquidate the partnership by converting its assets to cash and properly distributing the cash.

litigation. The term used to describe filing and prosecuting or defending a lawsuit.

M

Magnuson-Moss Warranty Act. A federal statute that imposes requirements for warranties when products are sold in interstate commerce.

material safety data sheets (MSDSs). Documents that contain important information about specific hazardous substances, including common and chemical names, physical and health hazards, directions for safe handling, and recommendations for protective equipment and emergency first aid procedures.

merger and acquisition. The terms used to define corporate and other business entity arrangements whereby two or more entities are formally combined, or one entity is acquired by another. A merger is a situation where two or more business entities are combined together and the combined entity emerges as a single entity. Acquisitions are when one business entity acquires another business entity or only the assets of another entity. Both mergers and acquisitions are regulated by statute. That is, the business organization statutes regulate the process and the federal, as well as state, securities laws also impose requirements on entities covered by them.

minutes. Written records of meetings of corporations, LLCs, and other business entities. Minutes are customarily kept in the organization's minute book.

money order. A financial instrument purchased from an authorized seller, which includes banks, post offices, and many retailers. *See also cashier's check, certified check.*

multi-level marketing (MLM). A form of doing business whereby a product or service is distributed through a multitiered structure. The structure is referred to as a down line and, customarily, each person in the line receives some compensation for down line sales. It is referred to as multi-level marketing, since each person is able to both sell product or service and enlist down line distributors, who can establish their own sales and distribution networks as well. The consumer who pays for the product or service is actually providing a revenue stream that flows up through all distribution levels. Classic examples of successful multi-level marketing are Amway and Mary Kay Cosmetics.

O

offer. An element of contract whereby one party, known as the offeror, presents an opportunity, known as the offer, to another party, known as the offeree. If the offer is accepted, a contract is made.

operating agreement. The document that defines the internal workings of a limited liability company. By statute, the agreement can be extremely flexible, and the law provides the parties creating the agreement the ability to determine whether the organization will be run by its owners, a panel of owners, or a single manager, as well as whether the organization will be taxed as an entity or not. This document is not filed with any governmental agency, but is kept in the organization's minute book.

P

partner. *See general partner, limited partnership, limited liability partnership.*

partnership. *See general partnership, limited partnership, limited liability partnership.*

partnership agreement. The agreement between two or more persons who desire to conduct business in a partnership form. A partnership agreement can be expressed, when the parties work out the arrangements between themselves; implied, when they merely conduct their business as a partnership; oral; or, written. When the parties do not work out the details of a formal partnership agreement, the law imposes certain terms on the relationship.

patent or letters patent. Legal document issued by the government to those who comply with the strict and technical requirements of the patent law. It is a form of intellectual property.

pension plan. A plan adopted for the purpose of providing a pension for individuals who retire so they can augment the Social Security payments obtained from the government.

preferred stock. A form of stock that contains some form of preference. The preference can be in the payment of a dividend; that is, the holders of this type of stock must receive a dividend payment before any dividends may be paid to holders of common stock. The preference may also be in the form of a liquidation payment; that is, when the entity is dissolved and liquidated, holders of preferred stock with liquidation preferences must be paid the preference before holders of common stock will receive any payment on account of their interest in the liquidated company. Preferred stock can have either or both of these forms of preference.

principal. The term used to define the person on whose behalf an agent acts and who controls or has the right to control the conduct of the agent. This term also refers, in a financial context, to the amount upon which interest is calculated.

pro forma. A Latin legal term meaning as a matter of form, referring to court rulings that have the purpose of moving proceedings ahead. This term may also be used with regard to financial documents.

product liability. The legal doctrine that applies to situations where a defective product results in injury to person or property. The defect can be a design defect or a manufacturing defect.

profit-sharing plans. Plans whereby business owners agree to share business profits with participants in the plan. These plans are very technical and require specialists to assist in their formation and administration.

progressive discipline. A term of art used in employment situations to define the process whereby an individual is subjected to some form of discipline in varying degrees of intensity, often from polite reprimands to loss of employment.

Q

qualified plan. Refers to a pension or other plan that qualifies for special tax treatment under the Internal Revenue Code and state taxing statutes.

R

reasonable accommodation. An adjustment or modification to a job or workplace to enable an employee to perform the essential functions of the job as required by the Americans With Disabilities Act (ADA). Each situation must be evaluated in order to determine whether the desired modification is reasonable. Reasonable accommodation is also a modification of a building or area to allow access by disabled persons, including wheelchair ramps and Braille markings on elevators.

receiver. A person who is appointed on an interim basis to administer a business for the benefit of creditors or others. A receiver is typically appointed by court order and reports to the court.

reorganization. The process whereby a business may be restructured for the purpose of satisfying its creditors when it is unable to pay them in the regular course of business. Reorganizations can involve use of the business entity's stock or ownership interest as vehicles for payment. Non-insolvency reorganizations can occur when businesses are restructured for the purpose of accomplishing other goals; for example, a business may reorganize in order to change its business form, add or delete new product lines, or the like.

royalties. Periodic distributions paid pursuant to a licensing agreement.

S

S corporations. Corporations that comply with the requirements set forth in the Internal Revenue Code and elect to be treated, for tax purposes, as if they were still run as sole proprietorships or partnerships.

scheduled property. Property specifically identified and listed on a schedule appended to an insurance policy for the purpose of insuring the scheduled property set forth on the list.

Securities and Exchange Commission (SEC). A federal agency charged by Congress with responsibility for policing the securities market.

securities exemption. The term used to define specific and technical requirements necessary to avoid having to register securities with either the federal Securities and Exchange Commission or the state securities agency (in every state in which the security is to be sold). The two most common federal exemptions are the intrastate offering exception, for securities that are offered for sale and sold only within the boundaries of one state, and the exemption available for those potential purchasers of the security who are deemed sophisticated or wealthy enough not to need the protection of the securities laws.

security interest. The interest created by statute in favor of a party, known as the secured party, in the assets of another for the purpose of protecting an obligation owed the secured party by the other party. A security interest may be perfected by having the proper document filed with the appropriate governmental agency.

service mark. A trademark used to identify a particular service with its provider. Service marks may be registered with the federal Trademark Office and appropriate state offices, as well. Classic examples of service marks for airlines providing travel services are Western Airlines' slogan "The only way to fly" and Braniff's "We move our tail for you."

shareholder. The person or entity owning stock in a corporation.

shareholders' agreement. The agreement between a corporation's shareholders and the corporation governing certain rights and restrictions of the owners with respect to their stock.

shareholder's derivative action. A cause of action provided the owner of stock in a corporation to vindicate a right or redress a wrong to the corporation. A shareholder's derivative action may be brought by the holder of even one share of stock in a corporation, though certain procedural restrictions are imposed when the ownership interest is small.

shareholder or annual meeting. The meeting required by the state corporation code for every corporation. It must be held at least once a year for the purpose, among other things, of electing the corporation's board of directors.

Simplified Employee Pension Plan (SEPP). A type of pension plan permitted by statute for employees.

sole proprietorship. The term used to define a business owned by a single individual.

Statute of Frauds. A law that was first enacted in England for the purpose of preventing fraud and perjury. It recognized the fact that certain transactions are so touched with the public interest that they should not be permitted enforcement over the objection of a party unless they were evidenced by a writing signed by that party, though parties could voluntarily perform the transactions if they wished. Since the English feudal system was a governmental process based on land ownership, one of the first transactions covered by the law was real estate transfers. The law was later extended to cover transactions in goods in excess of a certain value. The law also prohibited oral wills, since it would be too easy for unscrupulous individuals to misstate the wishes of a dead person. These laws have been refined and adopted in the United States.

stock. Refers to the ownership interest in a corporation and, traditionally, was evidenced by a stock or share certificate. The stock can be common or preferred. In addition, both common and preferred stock may be issued in different classes, typically identified by alphabetical designations (e.g., "class A stock").

stock or share certificate. The document used to evidence stock ownership in a corporation. Historically, it was a steel-engraved form, though some companies created unique and distinctive versions of their certificates. Today, many stock transactions are electronic, and no physical certificates are issued.

stock option. A method by which an individual or business may acquire the right to obtain corporate stock at a defined price for a limited period. Options themselves are tradable and, in fact, there is an option exchange. Those who deal in options are said to trade on equity, since their exchanges are for the appreciation in the value of the underlying stock, rather than trading in the stock itself.

stockholder or **shareholder.** The individual or entity owning stock in a corporation.

T

tax. The term used to define a government's right to extract payment from its citizens.

tip pooling. An arrangement whereby those restaurant employees who receive gratuities contribute them to a pool, which is then distributed in accordance with a prearranged plan. The pool may be distributed based on criteria such as job duties, tenure, and the like.

Tip Rate Alternative Commitment (TRAC). A program in which the employer enters into an agreement with the IRS to report tips to employees at a fixed percentage rate.

Tip Rate Determination Agreement (TRDA). A program in which the employer agrees to encourage employees to properly report all tips received and to provide periodic education about tip-reporting requirements.

trade dress. A form of intellectual property law that was initially developed through cases for the purpose of protected the unique and non-functional characteristics of product packaging. It was later extended by case law to cover everything from product design to the look and feel of restaurants. It has even been used to protect the distinctive characteristics or look and feel of an artist's distinctive style.

trade secrets. Those items (including processes, plans, formulas, and recipes) that have commercial advantage and are kept confidential.

trademark. Any words, phrases, names, symbols, logos, or combination of them, when used to identify a product or service. *See service mark.*

trust. A legal arrangement whereby a person, referred to as the settlor, trustor, or creator, conveys property to another, referred to as the trustee, for the benefit of one or more persons or entities, known as beneficiaries. The trustee is a fiduciary, owing a duty to the beneficiaries.

trustee. *See trust.*

Truth-in-Lending Act. A federal statute requiring certain lenders (usually institutional lenders) to comply with its requirements when loans are made.

Truth-in-Menu laws. Laws that require certain disclosures, which must be provided to customers on request, to back up claims regarding nutrition or health.

U

Uniform Commercial Code (UCC). A body of commercial law adopted in every state of the United States. Its periodic modifications may not have been universally accepted.

Uniform Offering Circular. The document required by statute to be used when franchises are offered for sale.

unincorporated association. An association of two or more persons who have not adopted a legal business form. Since the individuals are conducting business without having the benefit of a liability shield, such as through corporations, LLCs, or the like, they are legally partners and, thus, have full personal liability for the debts and other obligations of the business.

unscheduled property. Property not specifically identified on an insurance schedule; that is, property that is not scheduled property. *See scheduled property.*

utility patent. A patent on a novel invention (process, machine, manufactured product, compound, and mixture), which patent is issued by the United States government for twenty years from the date the application is filed. Distinguished from *design patents* and *plant patents*. Also referred to as a *mechanical patent*.

V

venture capital. Funding obtained from business speculators who provide money in exchange for ownership interest, control, and other defined benefits of the business. Since venture capitalists frequently provide large sums of money in a single block, they are customarily in a position to extract more rewards than individuals or businesses that invest modest amounts. Many venture capitalists were burned by the so-called technology meltdown and, thus, the availability of venture capital today is limited.

venue. The legal requirement imposed in litigation defining the specific court where a case must be filed and tried.

vesting. The process whereby an individual's interest in a retirement or pension plan is secured. For example, many pension plans provide that plan participants are vested 20% per year for five years; thus, an employee who leaves the company after three years will be 60% vested and entitled to receive only 60% of the amount that would otherwise have been available to a fully vested participant.

vicarious liability. A common law term that means that liability is being imposed on one who has not committed a wrongful act. It is liability without fault, generally resulting from the relationship between parties involved; thus, an innocent employer may be liable for the wrongful acts of a negligent employee.

voting trust. An arrangement whereby shareholders or owners of interests in other business entities pool those interests and agree to have them voted in a particular way. These are typically formal arrangements embodied in technical documents that comply with the business code of the state in which the entity is created.

W

warranty. A form of guarantee that is either expressed or implied by law and provides protection to the purchaser when the characteristics warranted are not present.

wholesome food. Food that is free from foreign materials and dangerous substances.

winding up. The process whereby a business completes its activities and prepares to end its operations. This can be a technical dissolution and liquidation.

works made for hire. The copyright term used to define works created by employees within the scope of their employment, or by independent contractors whose work is specially ordered or commissioned and the arrangement is embodied through a written contract, which arrangement falls into one or more of the categories enumerated in the statute.

World Intellectual Property Organization (WIPO). A multinational organization created for the purpose of administering the interface of copyright laws between its member nations.

Z

zoning. The government's designation of limitations on the use of land and structures. Classic examples of zoning laws are those that prohibit commercial activities in residential areas and those that prohibit individuals from living in commercial structures.

APPENDIX: RESTAURANT ASSOCIATIONS

This appendix provides contact information for a variety of restaurant-related associations. It includes national organizations, and state-specific organizations, as well as contact information for a few international organizations.

NATIONAL

National Restaurant Association
1200 17th Street, NW
Washington, DC 20036-3097
Phone: 800-424-5156
Fax: 202-331-5946
www.restaurant.org

The Green Restaurant Association
38 Harold Street
Sharon, Massachusetts 02067-2544
Phone: 858-452-7378
www.dinegreen.com

National Association of Catering Executives
9881 Broken Land Parkway
Suite 101
Columbia, Maryland 21046
Phone: 410-290-5410
Fax: 410-290-5460
www.nace.net

Zagat Survey, LLC
4 Columbus Circle
3rd Floor
New York, New York 10019-1100
Phone: 800-333-3421
Fax: 212-977-9760
www.zagat.com

STATE

Alabama
Alabama Restaurant Association
61 Market Place
Suite B
Montgomery, Alabama 36117-4910
Phone: 334-244-1320
Fax: 334-244-9800
www.alabamarestaurants.com

Alaska

Alaska Cabaret, Hotel, Restaurant
   and Retailer's Association
1111 East 80th Avenue
Suite 3
Anchorage, Alaska 99518-3312
Phone: 800-478-2427
Fax: 907-274-8640
www.alaskacharr.com

Arizona

Arizona Restaurant and Hospitality
   Association
2400 North Central Avenue
Suite 109
Phoenix, Arizona 85004-1300
Phone: 800-888-0701
Fax: 602-307-9139
www.azrestaurant.org

Arkansas

Arkansas Hospitality Association
603 South Pulaski Street
Little Rock, Arkansas 72201-2921
Phone: 501-376-2323
Fax: 501-376-6517
www.arhospitality.org

California

California Restaurant Association
1011 10th Street
Sacramento, California 95814-3501
Phone: 800-765-4842
Fax: 916-447-6182
www.calrest.org

Colorado

Colorado Restaurant Association
430 East 7th Avenue
Denver, Colorado 80203-3605
Phone: 800-522-2972
Fax: 303-830-2973
www.coloradorestaurant.com

Connecticut

Connecticut Restaurant Association
100 Roscommon Drive
Suite 320
Middletown, Connecticut 06457-1591
Phone: 800-382-5619
Fax: 860-635-6400
www.ctrestaurantassoc.org

Delaware

Delaware Restaurant Association
P.O. Box 8004
Newark, Delaware 19714-8004
Phone: 866-372-2545
Fax: 410-838-4885
www.dineoutdelaware.com

District of Columbia

Restaurant Association of Metropolitan
   Washington
7926 Jones Branch Drive
Suite 530
McLean, Virginia 22102-3371
Phone: 703-356-1315
Fax: 703-893-4926
www.ramw.org

Florida

Florida Restaurant and Lodging Association
230 South Adams Street
Tallahassee, Florida 32301
Phone: 888-372-9119
Fax: 850-224-9213
www.flra.com

Georgia

Georgia Restaurant Association
480 East Paces Ferry Road
Suite 7
Atlanta, Georgia 30305-3324
Phone: 404-467-9000
Fax: 404-467-2206
www.garestaurants.org

Hawaii

Hawaii Restaurant Association
1451 South King Street
Suite 503
Honolulu, Hawaii 96814-2509
Phone: 808-944-9105
Fax: 808-944-9109
www.hawaiirestaurants.org

Idaho

Idaho Lodging and Restaurant Association
134 South 5th Street
Boise, Idaho 83702-5949
Phone: 208-342-0777

Illinois

Illinois Restaurant Association
200 North LaSalle Street
Suite 880
Chicago, Illinois 60601-1030
Phone: 800-572-1086
Fax: 312-787-4792
www.illinoisrestaurants.org

Indiana

Restaurant and Hospitality Association of Indiana
200 South Meridian Street
Suite 350
Indianapolis, Indiana 46225-1076
Phone: 800-678-1957
Fax: 317-673-4210
www.indianarestaurants.org

Iowa

Iowa Restaurant Association
8525 Douglas Avenue
Suite 47
Des Moines, Iowa 50322-2929
Phone: 800-747-1453
Fax: 515-276-3660
www.iowahospitality.com

Kansas

Kansas Restaurant and Hospitality Association
3500 North Rock Road
Building 1300
Wichita, Kansas 67226-1335
Phone: 316-267-8383
Fax: 316-267-8400
www.krha.org

Kentucky

The Kentucky Restaurant Association
133 Evergreen Road
Suite 201
Louisville, Kentucky 40243-1484
Phone: 800-896-0414
Fax: 502-896-0465
www.kyra.org

Louisiana

Louisiana Restaurant Association
2700 North Arnoult Road
Metairie, Louisiana 70002-5916
Phone: 800-256-4572
Fax: 504-454-2299
www.lra.org

Maine

Maine Restaurant Association
5 Wade Street
Augusta, Maine 04330-6318
Phone: 207-623-2178
Fax: 207-623-8377
www.mainerestaurant.com

Maryland

The Restaurant Association of Maryland
6301 Hillside Court
Columbia, Maryland 21046-1048
Phone: 410-290-6800
Fax: 410-290-6882
www.marylandrestaurants.com

Massachusetts

Massachusetts Restaurant Association
333 Turnpike Road
Suite 102
Southborough, Massachusetts 01772-1775
Phone: 508-303-9905
Fax: 508-303-9985
www.marestaurantassoc.org

Michigan

Michigan Restaurant Association
225 West Washtenaw
Lansing, Michigan 48933
Phone: 800-968-9668
Fax: 517-482-7663
www.michiganrestaurant.org

Minnesota

Hospitality Minnesota
305 East Roselawn Avenue
Saint Paul, Minnesota 55117-2031
Phone: 651-778-2400
Fax: 651-778-2424
www.hospitalitymn.com

Mississippi

Mississippi Hospitality and Restaurant
    Association
5 Riverbend Place
Flowood, Mississippi 39232-7618
Phone: 800-898-0343
www.msra.org

Missouri

Missouri Restaurant Association
1810 Craig Road
Suite 225
St. Louis, Missouri 63146-4761
Phone: 877-413-7029
Fax: 314-576-2999
www.morestaurants.org

Montana

Montana Restaurant Association
1645 Parkhill Drive
Suite 6
Billings, Montana 59102-3067
Phone: 800-388-0236
Fax: 406-256-0785
www.mtretail.com/rest.htm

Nebraska

Nebraska Restaurant Association
1610 South 70th Street
Suite 101
Lincoln, Nebraska 68506-1565
Phone: 800 770-8006
Fax: 402-488-4014
www.nebraska-dining.org

Nevada

Nevada Restaurant Association
1500 East Tropicana Avenue
Suite 114-A
Las Vegas, Nevada 89119-6516
Phone: 702-878-2313
Fax: 702-740-8606
www.nvrestaurants.com

New Hampshire

New Hampshire Lodging and Restaurant
    Association
14 Dixon Avenue
Suite 208
Concord, New Hampshire 03301-4957
Phone: 603-228-9585
Fax: 603-226-1829
www.nhlra.com

New Jersey

New Jersey Restaurant Association
126 West State Street
Trenton, New Jersey 08608-1102
Phone: 800-848-6368
Fax: 609-599-3340
www.njra.org

New Mexico

New Mexico Restaurant Association
9201 Montgomery, NE
Suite 602
Albuquerque, New Mexico 87111-2470
Phone: 800-432-0740
Fax: 505-343-9891
www.nmrestaurants.org

New York

New York State Restaurant Association
455 New Karner Road
Albany, New York 12205-3821
Phone: 518-452-4222
www.nysra.org

North Carolina

North Carolina Restaurant Association
6036 Six Forks Road
Raleigh, North Carolina 27609-3899
Phone: 919-844-0098
Fax: 919-844-0190
www.ncra.org

North Dakota

North Dakota Hospitality Association
1025 North 3rd Street
Bismarck, North Dakota 58501
Phone: 701-223-3313
Fax: 701-223-0215
www.ndhospitality.com

Ohio

Ohio Restaurant Association
1525 Bethel Road
Suite 301
Columbus, Ohio 43220-2054
Phone: 800-282-9049
Fax: 614-442-3550
www.ohiorestaurant.org

Oklahoma

The Oklahoma Restaurant Association
3800 North Portland Avenue
Oklahoma City, Oklahoma 73112
Phone: 800-375-8181
Fax: 405-942-0541
www.okrestaurants.com

Oregon

Oregon Restaurant Association
8565 SW Salish Lane
Suite 120
Wilsonville, Oregon 97070-9633
Phone: 800-462-0619
Fax: 503-682-4455
www.ora.org

Pennsylvania

Pennsylvania Restaurant Association
100 State Street
Harrisburg, Pennsylvania 17101-1024
Phone: 800-345-5353
Fax: 717-236-1202
www.parestaurant.org

Rhode Island

Rhode Island Hospitality and
    Tourism Association
832 Dyer Avenue
Cranston, Rhode Island 02920-6714
Phone: 401-223-1120
Fax: 401-223-1123
www.rihospitality.org

South Carolina

The Hospitality Association of
    South Carolina
3612 Landmark Drive
Suite B
Columbia, South Carolina 29204-4039
Phone: 803-765-9000
Fax: 803-252-7136
www.schospitality.org

South Dakota

South Dakota Retailers Association
Hospitality Division
320 East Capitol Avenue
Pierre, South Dakota 57501-2519
Phone: 800-658-5545
Fax: 605-224-2059
www.sdra.org/restaura.htm

Tennessee

The Tennessee Restaurant Association
P.O. Box 681207
Franklin, Tennessee 37068-1207
Phone: 866-798-9191
Fax: 615-771-2370
www.thetra.com

Texas

Texas Restaurant Association
1400 Lavaca Street
Austin, Texas 78701
Phone: 800-395-2872
Fax: 512-457-4100
www.restaurantville.com

Utah

Utah Restaurant Association
420 East South Temple
Suite 355
Salt Lake City, Utah 84111-1317
Phone: 801-322-0123
www.utahdineout.com

Vermont

Vermont Lodging and Restaurant Association
13 Kilburn Street
Burlington, Vermont 05401-4750
Phone: 802-660-9001
Fax: 802-660-8987
www.vlra.com

Virginia

Virginia Hospitality and Travel Association
2101 Libbie Avenue
Richmond, Virginia 23230-2621
Phone: 804-288-3065
Fax: 800-828-7781
www.vhta.org

Washington

Washington Restaurant Association
510 Plum Street, SE
Suite 200
Olympia, Washington 98501-1587
Phone: 800-225-7166
Fax: 360-357-9232
www.wrahome.com

West Virginia

West Virginia Hospitality and Travel
   Associaion
P.O. Box 2391
Charleston, West Virginia 25328-2391
Phone: 304-342-6511
www.wvhta.com

Wisconsin

Wisconsin Restaurant Association
2801 Fish Hatchery Road
Fitchburg, Wisconsin 53713-3120
Phone: 800-589-3211
Fax: 608-270-9960
www.wirestaurant.org

Wyoming

Wyoming Lodging and Restaurant
   Association
211 West 19th Street
Cheyenne, Wyoming 82001
Phone: 307-634-8816
www.wlra.org

INTERNATIONAL

Canadian Restaurant and Foodservices Association

316 Bloor Street West
Toronto, Ontario M5S 1W5
Canada
Phone: 800-387-5649
Fax: 416-923-14350
www.crfa.ca

International Hotel and Restaurant Association

48, Boulevard de Sébastopol
75003 Paris
France
Phone: [011 +] 33-1-44-88 92 20
Fax: [011 +] 33-1-44-88 92 20
www.ih-ra.com

INDEX

401(k)s, 219, 220

A

abatement, 227
accountants, 3, 17, 24, 32, 40, 48, 53, 54, 55, 57, 77, 169, 173, 174, 189, 195, 198, 202, 204, 208, 225, 239, 242, 243
    finding, 242
accumulated earnings, 195
advertising, 73, 74, 76, 77, 91, 103, 104, 119–125, 128, 137–140, 169, 198, 203, 211
Age Discrimination in Employment Act, 176
alcoholic beverages, 158, 159
Americans with Disabilities Act (ADA), 176, 179, 180, 211
annual appraisal, 23
antidilution, 92, 99
antidiscrimination laws, 176, 179
arbitration, 20, 23, 136, 229
articles of incorporation, 9, 10, 23
assets, 2, 4, 7, 13, 21, 24, 36–39, 43, 46, 47, 49, 50, 129, 190, 197, 198, 221, 227, 231, 236, 242
assigning a lease, 38
at will, 5, 171, 173, 181, 187
attorneys, 2, 14, 17, 18, 22–25, 45, 52, 53, 55, 57, 66, 77, 82, 83, 98, 100, 101, 113, 115, 119–122, 125, 129, 131, 138, 139, 152, 153, 168, 173, 176, 178, 180, 181, 183, 188, 208, 209, 210, 214, 239–243
    fees, 53, 66, 98, 113, 115, 153, 176, 194, 198, 204
    finding, 241

B

balance sheet, 40
bankruptcy, 3, 11, 49, 130
banks, 25, 27, 33–52, 122, 143, 168, 225, 230, 235
basis of the bargain, 146
beneficiaries, 226, 234
benefits, 11, 25, 54, 66, 76, 96, 97, 100, 171, 174, 176, 179, 183, 194, 201, 203, 204, 208, 217, 219, 222, 223, 224, 229
bequests, 226, 227, 230
Berne Convention, 104
best efforts underwriting, 56
blue sky laws, 54
bona fide occupational qualifications, 180
bonds, 11, 39, 46, 51, 224
bookings, 42
borrower, 34, 35, 37, 38, 39, 40, 42, 43, 47, 49, 50
branding, 87
broker, 89, 159, 160, 167, 209, 210, 215
business expense, 160, 192, 198, 206

business market, 28, 29, 54, 130, 167
business name, 18, 136
business outlook, 40
business plan, 27, 28, 29, 30, 31, 32, 41, 44, 48
business stay, 205
buy-sell agreements, 23
bylaws, 1, 10, 22, 240

C

C corporation, 12, 14, 25, 195
capital, 4, 5, 7, 9, 10, 11, 19, 21, 27, 29, 32, 33, 36, 37, 51, 52, 53, 190, 193, 203, 204
capital expenditure, 203, 204
capitalization, 17, 24
cash flow, 36, 37, 40, 41, 48, 218
catering, 4, 28, 42, 61, 65, 196, 202, 214, 215, 239
certificates of ownership, 22, 51
character, 5, 35, 115, 128, 130
charitable deduction, 231, 232
children, 161, 174, 182, 191, 192, 228
Civil Rights Act, 176, 177, 178
co-op insurance fund, 168
codicil, 226
coinsurance clause, 165
collapsible corporation, 196
collateral, 35, 37, 39, 42, 43, 44, 46, 47, 48, 49
commercial space, 209–215
    wall to wall rent, 209
common law, 90, 91, 92, 93, 104, 107, 159
comparative advertising, 121, 139
competition, 29, 30, 76, 98, 135
conditional offer, 62
confidential information, 82, 83, 134, 141, 242
confirming memorandum, 66, 67, 68
consignment, 129, 130, 131
consumer price index (CPI), 218
Consumer Product Safety Act, 158
contracts, 8, 9, 20, 22, 47, 51, 55, 59–71, 105, 106, 108, 109, 129, 131, 144, 146, 148, 149, 151, 161–165, 171–176, 181, 186, 187, 191, 196, 226, 240
    breach of, 9, 59, 60, 134, 148, 149, 153, 226, 242
    express, 60
    implied, 60, 61
    oral, 60, 63–69, 129
    written, 63, 66–69, 108, 109, 151, 171
Copyright Act of 1909, 110, 111, 113
copyright law, 79, 103, 104, 106, 110, 113
    publication, 104, 111, 113, 114, 123

Copyright Revision Act of 1976, 104, 111, 112
corporations, 1, 6, 8–14, 17, 18, 21–25, 28, 53, 65, 114, 136, 193–196, 219, 222, 227
cosign, 8, 37
credit card, 64, 144, 185, 200
creditors, 2, 7, 8, 11, 130, 236
creditworthiness, 34, 35, 38, 48
cruise ship, 206
customers, 30, 61, 64, 70, 75, 120, 142, 144, 146, 147, 151, 155, 158, 160, 169, 172, 177, 199, 200, 202, 210
cyberspace, 70, 133-134, 136, 137, 138, 139, 140, 142, 144
cyberterrorism, 143

D

damages, 54, 98, 112, 113, 114, 152, 153, 159, 160, 171, 173, 176, 186, 187
debt-to-equity ratio, 44, 48, 52
debts, 2, 3, 4, 8, 36–52, 191, 227, 231, 236
decedent, 228, 230, 232, 236, 237
deductions, 6, 11, 168, 189, 190, 196, 198, 200, 202–208, 217, 219, 231, 232
defective, 87, 150, 152, 155, 156, 157, 160
defined benefit plans, 218, 219, 221
defined contribution plans, 218, 219, 221
Department of Labor, 184, 185
depreciation, 38, 190, 201, 202, 203, 204
derivative work, 105, 109
devises, 226, 227
direct expenses, 201
disclaimers, 150, 151, 152, 153
disclosures, 54, 55, 74, 81, 83, 84, 138, 175-176
dissolution, 5, 9, 20, 21
distress sale, 44, 49
distribution of profits, 4, 5, 12, 19, 104, 105, 156, 193, 194, 221, 226, 229, 230
dividends, 10, 11, 196
domain names, 76, 135, 136, 137
double taxation, 11, 194, 195
dower, 229
dram shop, 159

E

Electronic Signatures in Global and National Commerce Act (E-SIGN), 70
email, 70, 141, 142
Employee Retirement Income Security Act (ERISA), 224

Employee Stock Ownership Plans (ESOPs), 219, 221
employees, 3, 8, 11, 14, 24, 25, 83, 84, 85, 108,
116, 122, 142, 159, 163, 169, 171–193, 197,
198, 199, 200, 203, 204, 206, 217–224, 240
eligibility, 174, 182
handbooks, 142, 176, 181, 187
hiring, 8, 169, 170, 173, 174, 176, 179, 187,
191, 240
termination, 23, 171, 173, 174, 176, 178, 185,
186, 187, 188, 223
entertainment expenses, 205, 206
entrepreneurs, 1, 7, 13, 35, 44, 73
Equal Employment Opportunity Commission
(EEOC), 176, 178, 179, 180
Equal Pay Act, 176, 177, 178
escheat, 228
estate planning, 22, 225, 227–235, 237
European Patent Office, 80
excess earnings, 218
exclusive copyright rights, 105, 107
executive summary, 28
executors, 197, 229, 230, 231, 232, 236
exempted use, 105, 115
exemption, 52, 116, 192, 215, 232
express warranties, 145, 146, 147, 151

F

Fair Credit Reporting Act, 174
Fair Labor Standards Act (FLSA), 183, 184
fair use, 115, 116, 117
Family and Medical Leave Act (FMLA), 182
famous marks, 99
Federal Trade Commission (FTC), 74, 119, 120,
138, 158
FICA. *See Social Security*
financial statements, 47, 48, 75
firewalls, 141
firm underwriting, 56
first sale doctrine, 105
food poisoning, 22, 122, 148, 157, 180
food-based, 80, 196, 200, 203, 207, 239, 240, 241,
242
foreclosing, 44, 49
franchise, 38, 73, 74, 75, 76, 77
cannibalizing, 76
franchisee, 38, 74, 75, 76, 89
fraudulent, 162, 234

G

geographic locations, 123
goods, 42, 60, 63–69, 74, 75, 87, 88, 89, 91,
94–100, 130, 135, 145–151, 164, 167
governing board, 24, 25
gross estate, 230, 231, 232, 233, 235

H

hazards, 175
heirs, 9, 228, 233, 236
home office, 200–203, 214, 215
hostile environment, 178

I

illusory, 235
implied warranties, 147, 149, 150, 151, 152
income, 3, 6, 7, 11–14, 21, 25, 69, 170, 185,
189–206, 214–219, 221, 224
independent contractor, 8, 108, 109, 169, 170, 173,
185, 186
indirect expenses, 201
Individual Retirement Account (IRA), 3, 221
infringement, 18, 91, 92, 95, 97, 98, 103, 109, 112,
114, 115, 116, 125, 134, 136, 137, 139, 142,
150
inherently dangerous, 156, 170
initial public offering (IPO), 54
injury, 8, 119, 121, 155, 156, 157, 160, 170, 173,
178, 182, 183
innocent infringer, 111
installments, 190, 191
insurance, 2, 11, 23, 25, 38, 39, 42, 47, 69, 139,
153, 158–171, 173, 174, 201, 203, 208, 213,
215, 225, 230, 231, 234, 235, 236, 237
key-person, 23
intellectual property, 39, 46, 73, 82, 83, 84, 85, 101,
127, 128, 129, 133, 134, 136, 137, 139, 140,
144, 150, 172
inter vivos, 233, 234, 235
Internal Revenue Code, 14, 190, 200
Internal Revenue Service (IRS), 3, 6, 193, 195, 196,
199, 200, 206, 218, 220, 222, 234
Form 4070, 199
internet advertising, 138, 139
Internet Corporation for Assigned Names and
Numbers (ICANN), 136
Internet Service Providers (ISPs), 134, 142
intestate, 227, 228, 236
inventory, 36, 39, 42, 44, 46, 55, 167, 201
investors, 6, 7, 10, 23, 29, 31, 51, 52, 53, 56, 224

J

job descriptions, 31, 180
Jobs and Growth Tax Relief Reconciliation Act, 190
joint ventures, 3, 4
joint work, 107, 108, 109, 110
just cause, 187

K

kitchen equipment, 36, 163, 166, 198, 203

L

Lanham Act, 92, 95, 97, 98, 100, 124
lavish or extravagant, 205, 206
lawyers. *See attorneys*
lease, 38, 66, 104, 105, 209, 210, 211, 212, 213, 214
legal persons, 22
lender, 34–50
liabilities, 1–9, 12–18, 21, 22, 38, 41, 49, 54, 55, 103, 106, 113, 122, 125, 134, 136, 137, 139, 140, 142, 150, 153, 155–163, 170, 171, 173, 176, 178, 188, 190, 192, 193, 194, 196, 200, 213, 226
licenses, 2, 73, 105, 106, 127, 128, 129, 137, 159, 215
lien, 38, 150
likelihood of confusion, 99, 137
limited liability company (LLC), 6, 13, 14, 21, 22, 23, 24, 25, 28, 193, 194, 195, 196
limited partnerships, 6, 7, 15, 51
limited warranty, 153
lines of credit, 36, 55
liquidation, 7, 11, 21
loans, 7, 11, 24, 27, 33–50, 52, 55, 104, 105
   amount, 37
   limitations, 45
   proposal, 34
   repayment, 40
look and feel, 124

M

Madrid Accord, 99, 100
Magnuson-Moss Warranty Act, 152
management, 4, 5, 6, 10, 20, 22, 28, 30, 31, 35, 41, 44, 45, 50, 52, 53, 74, 75, 174, 176, 177, 178, 181, 182, 219
marital deduction, 231, 232, 233
market value, 38, 39, 43, 44, 49, 61, 190, 208, 230, 231

material safety data sheets (MSDSs), 175
materiality, 165
mechanical patent. *See utility patent*
merchandising, 28, 30, 129, 130, 131, 208
merchant, 67, 87, 88, 147, 148, 150
minimum hours, 223
minority owners, 14
model, 147
money-purchase plan, 221
mortgage, 38, 201, 202

N

naked license, 127
nature of your business, 28
negligence, 3, 156, 170, 173
negotiable note, 190
noncompetition agreements, 172
nondelegable, 170

O

Occupational Safety and Health Administration (OSHA), 175
Official Gazette, 93
operating agreement, 22, 23
originality, 105, 109, 110
overtime, 174, 181, 183, 184

P

package design, 124
particular purpose, 149, 151
partnerships, 1–15, 17–21, 25, 28, 51, 192–195, 224
passive investment income, 195, 196
past practices, 68
Patent and Trademark Office (PTO), 81, 89, 93, 94, 95, 97, 99, 100, 136
patent laws, 79, 80, 81
patent or padlock dilemma, 81
payroll, 174, 175, 191, 194, 199
pension, 3, 25, 194, 217, 219, 220, 221, 223
perfect, 46, 148
permitted disparity, 224
perpetual existence, 9
personal representative. *See executor*
pick-up tax states, 232
premium, 161, 162, 163, 165, 168
preponderance of evidence, 64
prima facie, 96
Principal Register, 92, 95, 96, 97

privacy, 122, 181, 187, 200
privatizing, 56
pro forma, 188
pro rata, 13, 168
probate, 230, 233, 235, 236, 237
products, 28–31, 42, 53, 54, 76, 80, 87–92, 98, 100,
    108, 119, 121, 123, 124, 127, 128, 142, 145,
    148, 149, 150, 152, 153, 155–160, 208
professionals, 29, 32, 40, 50, 54, 77, 116, 135, 160,
    169, 172, 175, 180, 183, 197, 198, 203, 208,
    222, 240, 242, 243
profit-and-loss statement, 40
profit-sharing, 25, 218, 219, 221, 222
profits, 3–7, 11, 12, 13, 19, 25, 30, 40, 42, 44, 48,
    51, 53, 98, 107, 114, 130, 162, 168, 194–198,
    203, 218, 219, 221, 222
progressive discipline, 188
progressive tax, 232
property, 2, 11, 19, 21, 38, 39, 46, 51, 73, 82–85,
    96, 101, 127–130, 133, 134, 136, 137, 139, 140,
    144, 150, 161, 162, 164–167, 172, 190, 202,
    207, 208, 210, 212, 226–237
    scheduling, 166
Prudent Expert Investment Principle, 224

Q
qualified plan, 217, 219, 222, 223, 224
quality, 75, 88, 100, 127, 128, 129, 145, 147, 148,
    181, 184, 215
quid pro quo, 178

R
reasonable accommodations, 179, 211
recipes, 73, 81, 82, 83, 84, 128, 129, 134, 163, 172,
    229
recordkeeping, 41, 167, 169, 196, 198, 207
Register of Copyrights, 112, 113
registered agent, 25
repairs, 62, 201, 202, 203
representation, 228
retirement plan, 194, 217, 223
revenues, 3, 14, 36, 39–42, 45, 49, 129, 190, 191,
    200, 231
revocable, 226, 230, 235
risks, 2, 3, 6, 7, 13, 29, 35, 43, 45, 76, 77, 108, 140,
    141, 148, 153, 156–162, 166, 167, 168, 175,
    176, 191, 215, 219, 240

S
S corporations, 12, 13, 14, 25, 195
salaries, 11, 19, 25, 31, 36, 41, 171, 183, 184, 185,
    191, 192, 193, 203, 204, 219, 220, 221
salary basis, 183
sample, 147
Schedule K-1, 6
scope of employment, 108
Secretary of State, 18, 130
securities, 3, 27, 36, 37, 38, 39, 43, 44, 45, 46, 51,
    52, 54, 55, 56, 57, 76, 83, 112, 141–144, 150,
    170, 171, 174, 181, 185, 192, 195, 199, 200,
    201, 213, 217, 224
Securities and Exchange Commission (SEC), 54, 55,
    57
security interest, 46, 150
self-employed, 194, 208, 222
serious health condition, 182
server protection, 141
service marks. *See trademarks*
services, 3, 5, 8, 11, 18, 24, 28, 30, 31, 54, 61, 63,
    69, 74, 75, 87, 88, 89, 91, 94, 95, 98, 99, 100,
    119, 121, 135, 137, 147, 159, 169, 180, 193,
    197, 208, 209, 212, 241, 242
sexual harassment, 177, 178, 179, 181
shareholders, 8–13, 22, 23, 25, 53, 55
shares. *See stocks*
signature dishes, 30, 128, 134, 146, 157
signature loans, 35
simple majority vote, 5
Simplified Employee Pension Plans (SEPs), 219, 220,
    221
Small Business Administration (SBA), 29, 34
Social Security, 170, 174, 185, 192, 195, 199, 200,
    224
software, 27, 70, 103, 105, 113, 140–144, 181
sole proprietorships, 1–5, 11–14, 17, 28, 194, 195
Sonny Bono Term Extension Act, 114
spam, 142
spouse, 182, 206, 228, 229, 232, 235, 237
stacked retirement plans, 222
standard deduction, 192
standby underwriting, 56
Statute of Frauds, 64, 65, 67, 69
stockholders. *See shareholders*
stocks, 6, 9, 10, 11, 13, 22, 23, 39, 46, 51, 52, 55,
    56, 172, 196, 219, 221, 224, 227, 234, 237
    common, 10
    preferred, 10, 11, 218
substantial performance, 60
succession planning, 217, 225

supervisor, 178, 181
Supplemental Register, 92, 95, 97
supplies, 2, 30, 36, 39, 42, 175, 198, 202
sureties, 37, 38

T

taxes, 1, 3, 5, 11, 12, 13, 14, 19, 21, 25, 41, 42, 48, 160, 168, 170, 172, 173, 174, 185–208, 214, 215, 217, 219, 220, 221, 222, 227, 230–236, 242
tender offers, 56-57
testator, 226–230
Tip Rate Alternative Commitment (TRAC), 199
Tip Rate Determination Agreement (TRDA), 199
tips, 184, 185, 199, 200, 207
    aggregate estimation, 200
    tip-pooling, 184, 185
trade dress, 123, 124, 150
trade secrets, 79–85, 128, 129, 133, 134, 141, 172, 181
trade usage, 148
Trademark Law Revision Act of 1988 (TLRA), 92, 93
trademarks, 18, 39, 73, 74, 76, 87–101, 119, 123, 124, 127, 128, 129, 135, 136, 137, 142, 150
    abandonment, 98
    intent-to-use, 89, 93–96, 98
    notice of allowance, 94
    prohibited, 96
    secondary meaning, 90
    used in commerce, 88, 89, 90, 93, 97
transferability of ownership, 9, 23
transportation, 159, 160, 174, 179, 204, 207
travel expenses, 204, 207
Treasury Regulations, 197
trust, 234, 235
Truth-in-Menu laws, 120

U

UCC-1, 130, 131
ultrahazardous. See inherently dangerous
Unified Estate and Gift Tax Schedule, 232
Uniform Commercial Code (UCC), 63, 66, 130, 145, 147
Uniform Offering Circular, 74
Uniform Resource Locator (URL), 135, 136
unintended partnership, 7
unions, 116, 143, 174, 179, 224
unique, 28, 84, 88, 90, 123, 124, 128, 130, 163, 226, 240
unitary whole, 107, 110

utilities, 201, 202, 203, 212
utility patent, 80

V

valuable consideration, 74
venture capital, 27, 32, 33
vesting, 221–224
vicarious liability, 178
viruses, 142, 143
voting deadlock, 22, 24

W

wage, 171, 174, 177, 183, 184, 185, 200, 224
waitstaff, 151, 184
warranty of title, 149, 151
whistleblowing, 187
wholesaler, 65, 150, 151
wholesome, 148
wills, 226, 227, 229, 230, 232, 233, 235, 237
work time, 185
workers' compensation, 170, 173, 175, 176, 185, 186, 194
works made for hire, 108, 111, 114
World Intellectual Property Organization (WIPO), 140
World Wide Web, 34, 91, 120, 133–136, 141, 242
wrongful act, 9, 22, 171

Z

zero tolerance, 181
zoning, 209, 211, 213, 214, 215

ABOUT THE AUTHORS

Leonard D. DuBoff is an internationally recognized expert who has lectured on legal issues throughout the world. He began his legal career in New York, then relocated to Palo Alto, California, where he started teaching at the Stanford Law School. Subsequently, he moved to Portland, Oregon, where he taught law at Lewis & Clark Law School. DuBoff spent almost a quarter of a century teaching business and intellectual property law.

While a full time law professor, DuBoff was also Of Counsel to law firms and maintained that relationship until 1994, when he left full-time teaching to found his own law firm that specializes in business and intellectual property law. DuBoff has received academic awards from President Lyndon Johnson and New York Governor Nelson Rockefeller. In 1990, he received the Governor's Arts Award from Oregon Governor Neil Goldschmidt.

In addition to practicing law, DuBoff has also been involved in assisting with legislation. In the late 1980s, he testified in support of the *Visual Artist's Rights Act of 1990,* at the request of Senator Edward Kennedy of Massachusetts. He has also provided Congress with testimony related to several cultural and intellectual property treaties and he has worked with state legislatures on their legislation as well.

A prolific author, DuBoff has written numerous articles for scholarly journals, practical articles for lawyers' bar publications, and articles for nonlawyers as well. He has regular columns in several publications. He is coauthor of the law school text *Art Law Cases and Materials*.

He has also written a host of other books including:
Art Law: Domestic and International
Deskbook of Art Law, two volume set
The Book Publishers Legal Guide
The Antique and Art Collector's Legal Guide
Art Law in a Nutshell

His business encyclopedia series includes:
The Crafts Business Encyclopedia
The Art Business Encyclopedia
The Entertainment Business Encyclopedia

His (In Plain English)® series includes:
The Law (In Plain English)® for Small Business
The Law (In Plain English)® for Crafts
Business And Legal Forms (In Plain English)® for Craftspeople
The Law (In Plain English)® for Galleries
The Law (In Plain English)® for Healthcare Professionals
The Law (In Plain English)® for Writers
The Law (In Plain English)® for Photographers
Hi Tech Law (In Plain English)®

Christy O. King is an attorney in Portland, Oregon, where she practices with The DuBoff Law Group, LLC. She is coauthor of the *Deskbook of Art Law* and *Art Law in a Nutshell*, and editor-in-chief of the *Critical Issues* newsletter published by the DuBoff Law Group. She is the author of numerous articles in the field of intellectual property and art law, and has an active practice representing clients in intellectual property, business, and corporate law matters.